i

B. Jay Wilson

BARACK

"HUSSEIN"

OBAMA

THE MAN

BEHIND

THE

IMAGE

WHAT THE MEDIA HASN'T TOLD US

B. JAY WILSON

About the Author

B. Jay Wilson is a natural-born citizen of the United States who believes that America's dream of becoming a country free of dictatorship came at a high price over two hundred years ago when our forefathers dared to leave a country of oppression to step foot on the unchartered American soil. Most of those who were searching for a new life died before realizing their dream. But the few who survived lived on giving thanks to God for the Country and the freedom of religion and speech that He had provided for them.

America was separated for a while by the Civil War, but the North and the South overcame and once again became united.

In 2001 terrorists attacked our Country and brought down the Twin Towers in New York. Our Country rallied together, determined to fight against the oppressors. Our American flag flew as *one spirit* ready to fight the terrorist who were trying to break our spirit and take away that freedom that we as a nation fought for.

B. Jay has taken the task of writing a book giving tribute to a Country who will, once again, stand against another oppressor who is seeking to destroy these United States as we know it.

* * * * * * * * * *

iv

ACKNOWLEDGEMENT

THANK YOU, MIKE, FOR YOUR WILLINGNESS AND PATIENCE IN GUIDING ME THROUGH THE PROCESS OF PREPARING THIS BOOK FOR PUBLICATION. WITHOUT YOU THIS GOAL COULD NOT HAVE BEEN ACHIEVED.

First printing, July 2009
© November, 2008 B. Jay Wilson

ISBN: 978-0-615-30452-6

Cover Photo by: Public Domain

Publisher & CompanyB, LLC

publishercompb@yahoo.com

PROLOGUE

Promised Changes!

For America
or
Islam

People have written books, made films and used television media to warn the United States of Obama's inadequacy to lead our country....all political. The possibility that President Obama could have an agenda to lead our country into the hands of the Muslim world has been completely ignored. Thus far our eyes are still closed to the fact that Muslims declare that they will fight against America, in America to bring us into Islam.

The documentary DVD, *Obsession,* exposes Islam's plan to overtake the United States.[1] It was filmed undercover exposing the grotesque bloodshed by Muslims who vow to bring the world into Dar al-Islam, the land of those who have submitted to Allah, the Muslim community. The documentary is very graphic, and should not be watched by young children. The film confirms that Islam calls the United States *the devil* and teaches jihad to children as young as six years old. The film shows explicit footage of how they plan to infiltrate the United States with Muslims to take over our country and turn it into a land of Dar al-Islam (Muslim domain).

---

[1] *Obsession* CD – Circulated by: *The Clarion Fund* – New York, NY

Among those with a liberal slant, it is common practice that when they cannot refute solid evidence or counter reasonable, rational thought, they attack the messenger personally and label them *Right-Wing Conspiracy Extremists.* I'm not a racist; I am not prejudice, nor a *Right-Wing Extremist,* and I really feel no compulsion to defend myself for simply pointing out the obvious. What I am pointing out are well-documented observations, and I am asking Americans to make up their own minds. Very much like recent attacks on talk radio stations, and Rush Limbaugh in particular for speaking out for the voices of concerned Americans, these individuals (talk radio show hosts) are offering and pointing out the very obvious situations occurring in our society today, and for this they are being labeled *Right-Wing Conspiracy Extremists.*

A well coordinated effort has begun by President Obama and the left-leaning media to stifle conservative talk radio. The effort has been documented by the Media Research Center. The following news letter, written by L. Brent Bozell III, Founder and President of Media Research Center, appeared in the March 2009 issue of MRC's Monthly Members' Report www.MRC.org:

"The Media Research Center has been warning since 2006 that if liberals got enough power in Congress and the White House – backed by round-the-clock support from their allies in the media – they would try to shut down conservative talk radio. That time has come: The White House and the liberal media have declared war on Rush Limbaugh in particular and conservative talk radio in general. President Obama himself gave the signal to attack when he scolded GOP leaders in a White House meeting in January, declaring, "You can't just listen to Rush Limbaugh and get things done." The goal is to marginalize conservative opposition – and to be rid of it completely if possible. This can be accomplished by reinstating the so-called Fairness Doctrine, which liberal Democrats say

they intend to do. Or it can be done by regulating the ownership and broadcast licenses of radio stations, which the Obama team has hinted at. Or do both.

In either case, to stifle conservative opinion is the goal – and it is the single greatest threat in the history of our Republic to our sacred freedom of speech."

There is much more to the letter, but Mr. Bozell III ends his letter with a plea for help in fighting this potential disaster for our country's privilege to hear the truth. He ends his letter with this plea:

"The war on conservative talk radio has officially begun. The MRC is sounding the alarm every day. You can help us in this battle by telling your friends – give them this newsletter! – and by calling on lawmakers and public leaders to fight against the "Fairness Doctrine" or any attempt to limit free speech on the radio. You can also help by supporting the MRC in its mission. Onward we march!"

Mr. Bozell's plea is significant! To regulate or stifle our conservative talk shows will not only keep our country from getting the "real" story of what is happening in our country, but Christian radio talk shows will be scrutinized and limited to what they can say about Jesus Christ and the Plan of Salvation. With President Obama's blasphemies of God's Word and lack of respect for the Holy Bible, would it be presumptuous to say that President Obama will put restrictions on Christian radio talk shows? If so, then would it be logical to suspect that he and his liberal, non-believing ilk will try to put the same restrictions on pastors who are spreading the truth in America's church pulpits? I believe it is coming! President Obama enlightened the Muslim world while in Ankara, Turkey that the United States will never be at war with Islam. What is Islam? It's a Muslim world that wants to take over America. It's a Muslim world that is terrorizing and killing people who won't conform to the Islamic religion. It's a Muslim world against Christianity and America!

MyFox Orlando.com April 6, 2009 picked up President Obama's speech to the Muslim world while in the 99.6% Muslim country. This is what President Obama told the Muslims:

"We will convey our deep appreciation for the Islamic faith, which has done so much over the centuries to shape the world, including in my own country," he said.

In *his own* country! He was evasive again! Is he talking about Islam shaping Indonesia or the United States? It can't be the United States; Islam *has not* "shaped" America....yet! So there we have another question! Is Obama a Muslim? If so, is he from Indonesia or Africa? He goes on to say that America is not a Christian nation:

"We do not consider ourselves a Christian nation or a Jewish nation or a Muslim nation," he said at the news conference. *"We consider ourselves a nation of citizens who are bound by ideals and a set of values."*

My question is, "Why does President Obama think he has the right to include *all* of *America* in *his* ideology that America does not consider ourselves a Christian nation! *We* have been a Christian nation since day one of setting our feet on this soil. And I truly believe that our country will eventually stand up and fight for our rights to speak for ourselves as individuals, making our own decisions rather than have a president traveling the world telling other countries "who we are" "what we believe" "where *he* is going to lead us in religion." It's nonsensical for him to think that he can control the personal lives of American citizens. The president's job is to take care of America's economy and protect our country from the enemy, not try and dictate to us in a round-about way from a foreign soil through speeches whose religion we are going to accept. For over two hundred years we have had the privilege, as free individuals, to voice *our own* opinion and make *our* decisions about *our* religious beliefs. We don't need a president to travel about the world trying to convey to other countries that we are no longer the beacon of light for other nations to follow. Doesn't his ideology sound as though he is trying to discretely Islamize our country? Let's get back to what Mr. Bozell said about Obama planning to silence radio talk shows. How long will it take President Obama to stifle the Christian radio talk shows and T.V. news stations, and ultimately Christian pastors and evangelists.....how long did it take him to return to the United States?

Yes, I most certainly do get upset and lose my cool when I see and hear the President of the United States demean America. (He also made a slip of the tongue during his campaign tour when asked how many states he has been in. His answer was "fifty-seven states." Any American should have caught that slipup. *Islam* has fifty-seven states, not the United States.)

My heart is in this book, not to condemn a black man because he is black, but to defend our God's Holy name from false claims that He is Islam's god; to allow people to see where Obama has openly defamed Holy Scripture, *our* God and America with his offensive rhetoric and practice; to allow people to evaluate for themselves after reading this book his motive for change, and his definition of change in our government. (Keep in mind that the banner of *Change* that Obama and the Democrats so self-righteously waved over their heads, and in the face of a gullible electorate, all along the campaign trail did not necessarily mean change for the better.)

There is sufficient evidence to lead rational, intelligent people to suspect that President Obama has firm, *unspoken* changes in mind for the United States. That evidence suggests that Obama intends to use the presidency to force us from a democracy to socialism and, subsequently, right into Islam. And yes, Islam's fight for the implementation of Shari'a Law is finally coming to the United States courts.

A Viable Answer From the Past for Today's Problems!

For those of you who do not know the history of Marcus Tullius Cicero of Rome, Italy; Cicero lived from 106 BC to 43 B.C., and was a Roman philosopher, statesman, lawyer,

political theorist, and Roman constitutionalist. Cicero is widely considered one of Rome's greatest orators and prose stylists. He was elected Consul for the year 63 B.C. We as Americans should hold fast to what Cicero suggested for Rome's survival.

"The budget should be balanced, the treasury should be refilled, and the public debt should be reduced. The arrogance ofofficialdom should be tempered and controlled. And the assistance to foreign lands should be curtailed lest we become bankrupt." (Cicero, 63 B.C.)

During the *chaotic* latter half of the first century B.C., marked by civil wars and the *dictatorship* of Gaius Julius Caesar, Cicero championed a return to the *traditional republican government.* [2]

---

[2] Cicero – Wikipedia, the free encyclopedia

CHAPTER ONE

Barack *"Hussein"* Obama
Who Is He?
Who Is The Enemy?

Barack Obama - *Dreams from My Father* page 118 – Obama's Pakistani roommate in New York: *"...a well-built Pakistani who had come to New York from London two years earlier and found his caustic wit and unabashed desire to make money perfectly pitched to the city's mood. He had overstayed his tourist visa and now made a living in New York's high-turnover, illegal immigrant workforce."* [1]

Barack Obama - *Dreams from My Father* page 37: *"Like many Indonesians, Lolo (Lolo is Obama's stepfather) followed a brand of Islam that could make room for the remnants of more ancient animist and Hindu faiths. He explained that a man took on the powers of whatever he ate: One day soon, he promised, he would bring home a piece of tiger meat for us to share."* [2]

By: Aaron Klein – *WorldNetDaily* September 07, 2008: *"Obama, speaking to ABC's George Stephanopoulos on 'This Week.' Obama stated. 'What I was suggesting – you're absolutely right that John McCain has not talked about my*

---

[1] Pakistani underscore for emphasis
[2] Added (Lolo is Obama's stepfather) for clarity

Muslim faith.' Stephanopoulos immediately interrupted Obama, stating, 'Christian faith.' 'My Christian faith,' Obama quickly said."

How can President Obama be involved in plans for an Islamic takeover and rule of the United States? President Obama has been in the Oval Office less than three months and already we are seeing Muslims making the news. During his presidential campaign the cat was let out of the bag when news media learned that President Obama's middle name was "Hussein." The news that his father was a Muslim from Kenya Africa, and that he had lived in Indonesia with his mother and Muslim stepfather spread like wildfire. The news media in the United States provides us with details of interest [and] warnings when something is not right with our country.

Even though Obama managed to keep his Muslim family low-key, the media pounced on the idea that he is a Muslim and began bringing forth reports of Obama's background. It quickly came to light that Obama had been involved with Muslims throughout his life, and our country became a little nervous about the prospect of putting a man in the White House who had the same name as Saddam "Hussein." Obama tried to keep his identity low-key, but that just aroused more suspicion about his background. He managed to skirt the issue of his middle name by making jokes of it, claiming that people would reject him because he had a *"funny name."*

Whether people were curious or felt sorry for him, the strategy worked because it made people stand up and listen to what he had to say. Could that have been a mistake? He had the people's attention, so he used another tactic. He quickly mesmerized the country with a rumor that he was the coming Messiah (Jesus Christ) by telling Dartmouth students that a light would shine through a window, and a beam of light would come down on them and they would experience an "epiphany."[3]

For those of you who are not familiar with the word "epiphany," it means "an appearance of a god to its worshippers." Of course that speech made the news and people,

---

[3] Epiphany – St. Louis Post Dispatch Monday June 9, 2008

especially the youth, rallied to him. Did Obama ever deny that rumor?

His promise for *"Change"* in our country skyrocketed and the rumor that he was a Muslim was basically put to rest by most people, and was replaced by a barrage of questions about his [supposed] divinity.

President Obama, after finally managing to keep his middle name quiet during his presidential campaign, decided to use his Muslim middle name "Hussein" at his inauguration. That decision prompted the Muslim nations to speak out more blatantly about their beliefs that Obama is one of their own. And more than any other time in the history of the United States, the Muslims have openly revealed to America their religious beliefs and openness to help us in our financial crisis. It's as if they know that their presence, with their cultic religious beliefs, no longer needs to be suppressed in the United States.

One necessary step the Muslims need to take before they can control the United States and implement their religious beliefs into our society is to get their Shari'a Law incorporated into our judicial system. Their laws pertain more to religion as a means to control a county, rather than a democracy. Being under Muslim regime will be much worse than in the era when Christians had to hide or be killed. *All* people will either submit to Islam or be killed.

I suspect the reason that Islam is now more confident than ever that their goal can be achieved is because of President Obama's beliefs and willingness to establish dialog with the Muslim world, although that dialog may be thinly veiled as diplomacy designed to bridge cultural gaps in the name of world peace and to promote a more prosperous economy. It is widely suspected that Obama's desire to talk with Muslims is to more effectively help them make operational their long-held plans for America.

Our financial system is in crisis, and Islam knows it. What better time to move forward in their endeavor to globalize religion than in a time when the United States needs financial help! It is a widely-held opinion that President Obama has put us into this crisis to justify allowing the Islamic nations to step in with financial aid for our country. And you know what that will mean! Strings! Control!

Now, it can be argued that Obama inherited the current economic crisis from Bush, but Obama's economic policies are vastly different than those of Bush, and his track record so far in the first four months of his administration has certainly done nothing but to put an already-declining economy into an uncorrectable tail-spin.

Is Islam hoping to capitalize on our economic collapse? The following article was posted on Michelle Malkin, Syndicated Columnist and a *Fox News* contributor's website on November 6, 2008. Robert Kimmitt was Deputy Secretary of the Treasury from August 16, 2005 until January 20, 2009:

"The U.S. Treasury Department is submitting to Shari'a – the seditious religio-political-legal code authoritative Islam seeks to impose worldwide under a global theocracy. As reported in this space last week, Deputy Secretary of the Treasury Robert Kimmitt set the stage with his recent visit to Saudi Arabia and oil-rich Persian Gulf states. His stated purpose was to promote the recycling of petrodollars in the form of foreign investment here. Evidently, the price demanded by his hosts is that the U.S. government get with the Islamist financial program. While in Riyadh, Mr. Kimmitt announced: 'The U.S. government is currently studying the salient features of Islamic banking to ascertain how far it could be useful in fighting the ongoing world economic crisis.'" The writer went on to say, *"Islamic banking is a euphemism for a practice better known as "Shari'a-Compliant Finance (SFC)."*

Convincing the U.S. government to *"get with the Islamist financial program - SFC"* will be one step ahead in Islam's manipulative plan. Doesn't money talk? How many years has Islam planned to infiltrate the United States? Comparing their infiltration into our country to other countries they have conquered, one might say that it has been in the planning stages for years, but has just made a strong public appearance in America this past year.

A logical strategy to gain recognition in this country would be to introduce one of their own into the political arena. For the United States, because of our situation in the Middle East and terrorism in our country by these extremist, he will be one who claims that he can bring the enemy to live in peace with the world. What did Obama promise in his campaign speeches? His promise was to bring peace between America and the Middle East. Who is the enemy? From Obama's rhetoric in his two books, and other research revealed in this book, it appears from Obama's perspective that the United States is the enemy and Islam is the world.

Obama denies being a Muslim, but the rhetoric in his autobiography *Dreams from My Father* gives every indication that he is Muslim with a Muslim agenda. Watch his body language, listen closely to his speeches and read between the lines. With a slip of the tongue he said *"My Muslim faith."*[4] To this observer, almost every speech, with a style of Malcolm X and Louis Farrakhan, gives the impression of a militant attitude toward America and Christianity.

Obama is a clever man. He likely knew the *Islamic history* of the name *Hussein*, and he probably realized that using the name *Hussein* during the presidential campaign would mean a backward slide for his campaign to reach the Oval Office. So why, after his win, did he suddenly decide to use his middle name on the day he was sworn in as president of the United States? Was it because he knew the presidency would provide a safety net for him, that he could admit his true relationship with the Muslim world now without repercussions?

Soon after his win he made a statement to the world that he wanted our country to prosper with the Muslim world. That could be interpreted in a number of ways, but considering his long and personal relationship with Islam, was he telling the Muslim world, *"This is who I really am, I'm with you?"* Does he have an agenda to let Muslims know where he stands on Islam? Before he took the Office, Obama voiced his sentiment

[4] George Stephanopoulos – Aaron Klein – *WorldNetDaily* – September 7, 2008

about Muslims in his interview with *Chicago Tribune*: Aaron Klein – *WorldNetDaily* December 10, 2008:

"JERUSALEM – President-elect Barak Obama declared in an interview that he plans to deliver a major address in an Islamic capital as part of his global outreach, which he said would target the Muslim world. Obama speaking, 'I think we've got a unique opportunity to reboot America's image around the world and also in the Muslim world in particular,' Obama said in a free-engaging interview yesterday with the Chicago Tribune, promising an 'unrelenting' desire to 'create a relationship of mutual respect and partnership in countries and with peoples of good will who want their citizens and ours to prosper together.'"

Considering Islam's narrow interpretation of the concept of *partnership* and their complete intolerance and murderous hatred of any religion other than Islam, of which Obama is fully aware, what concessions is Obama willing to force down our throats in order to reboot America's image in the eyes of the Muslim world?

Did you notice that Obama said, *"...in the Muslim world in particular."* How big is the *Muslim world*? I can tell you that Indonesia, where President Obama was raised, has the world's largest Muslim population. I found the following article in the book *"Islam at the Crossroads"* page 73 written by Paul Marshall, Roberta Green and Lela Gilbert. It gives us a good insight into just how powerful this cult is:

"Christianity. It has almost 1.2 billion followers, with Muslims found in virtually every country in the world. The countries possessing the world's biggest Muslim populations are in Asia. The world's largest Muslim country, in terms of population, is Indonesia – a set of islands stretching from west of Thailand to the east of the Philippines. It has a population of about 210 million people, of whom some 85 percent are Muslim, meaning that it may have more followers of Islam than the entire Middle East."

Obama's first book gives the reader a look into his life of instability, low-self esteem, hatred of his own mixed blood and his search for his identity. That search led him to read Malcolm X's autobiography and other works written about him. Malcolm X was a radical Black Muslim who also had a problem dealing with his mixed blood.

Obama's entire book is cause for concern, but one statement in particular that he made about Malcolm X caught my attention, and I couldn't shake what he said. Because of that statement I will bring to light everything that I believe is crucial to keeping our country free from the power of someone who appears to be a *silent* radical activist.

In his book *Dreams from My Father* Obama admits to his own white mother's hatred of America and love for Indonesia. I will bring to light where his resolve seemed to be to follow the call of the radical Malcolm X (Head of Islam Nation whose goal was to bring the entire world to Islam). I will bring to light his admiration and positive acknowledgment of his relationship with an illegal Pakistani immigrant; his Muslim friends throughout his life; his own desire to return to Indonesia [85% Muslim] with his wife and children to share that part of his life with them. I will also present the history behind Obama's middle name *Hussein* and why Hamas terrorist endorse him as the President of the United States.

Obama's Political Agenda vs the Muslim's Political Agenda

The article below comes from a book written in 1999. You will easily see how the slow process of Islam can slip into our society virtually unnoticed. As you will see in the following article, Muslims have long been concerned about their lack of representation in the political process in the United State. It has taken them over ten years to get to a point where they feel free to pressure us into a financial agreement that will give them power and influence in the political arena. The next move after we accept their financial help.... the Shari'a Law will be instituted. Money does talk, you know! We know where the Muslims stand in our society today. Let's take a look at what they envisioned ten years ago. John L. Esposito - *The Oxford History of Islam* page 635:

"Regardless of their growing numbers in Europe and North America, and their increasing wealth in the United States and Canada, Muslims are aware that they have little political power to influence the government, the media, or the elites in the West. They have very few channels of communication to policy makers in the societies in which they live."

The Oxford History of Islam continues on page 635:

"The issue of participation in the political process is now being debated within the Muslim community. Can a Muslim participate in the running of a kuffar (unbelievers) society? Should they vote for representatives who are accountable to various interests? Would such participation lead to defending the freedom to engage in things Islamically prohibited? Ali Kettani, a North African consultant to the Saudi government on Muslim minority affairs, has called for Islamic political representation: 'Otherwise, Muslim politicians would be put in office by non-Muslim forces and would consequently be used to subjugate the Muslim community.'"

Ten years ago they were looking for a politically sound government in the United States that would adhere to their own laws. Considering the endorsements that Muslims gave Obama during his presidential campaign and congratulatory messages after he was elected, one would probably agree that the Muslims are on their way to achieving their goal. This following article is one of many stories about Muslims endorsing Obama during his campaign and after he had won the presidential election. Aaron Klein – *World Net Daily* posted May 15, 2008.

"Hamas isn't the only terrorist organization that endorsed Sen. Barack Obama in the 2008 race for the presidency of the U.S. WND's Jerusalem bureau chief Aaron Klein made world headlines last month after a top Hamas official, Ahmed Yousef, told him he 'hopes' Obama becomes president and compared the Illinois senator to President John F. Kennedy. 'We like Mr. Obama, and we hope that he will win the elections,' said

Yousef. 'I hope Mr. Obama and the democrats will change the political discourse...'"

What is left unsaid is: **Change the political discourse in whose favor?**

We must remember that when Obama wrote his first book, *Dreams from My Father,* he had no idea that his life would some day be scrutinized, or that he would be facing America with untold truth. He gave leave to the world of his inner-most feelings. The book, itself, convicts him of his denial that he has nothing to do with Islam, and gives every indication that he is a Muslim with a Muslim agenda. The first book reveals his life living in Indonesia with a Muslim stepfather and a mother who shouted, referring to Americans, *"They are not my people!"*[5]

Before we get deep into the book and Obama's link with Muslims, please let me take you to the reason behind the Muslim (Islam) hostility against nations who will not conform to their religion. It may help the reader to better understand Christianity in America, and Obama's misguided rhetoric in his political speeches.

Please keep in mind that the Muslim's god, Allah, is not the God of Christianity. Let's go there now:

The false Islamic teachings go back to the Old Testament of the Holy Bible and a promise that God made to Abraham. God promised Abraham that he would have a son, and through that son the world would be blessed. Muslims are taught in their Qur'an religious book that God told Abraham that Ishmael [son of Abraham through his wife's Egyptian servant, Hagar] was the promised son through whom all peoples on earth would be blessed.

The Muslims not only twisted God's Word around about *which* son God chose, they also misrepresented the fact that the blessing the earth would receive through Abraham's son's descendants would be the birth of Jesus Christ, coming as the Savior of the world. The *Jewish* nation would be blessed because Salvation would come through their lineage. No where

---

[5] They are not my people – *Dreams from My Father* page 47

in the Bible does it say that a member of the Arab nation would receive such a blessing. The blessing was to come through a Jew, and that was Isaac, Abraham's second son through his wife, Sarah, not Sarah's Egyptian maid-servant, Hagar.

Because of this fabrication, Muslims believe that Ishmael, Egyptian son of Hagar, was the rightful son through which the blessings of God would flow and that their people, descendants of Ishmael, are the chosen race and the chosen religion of the world.

Therefore, they follow the command from a man-made god to proselyte the entire world to Islam....feeling free to kill those who will not submit to their false god and practices. It is painfully clear by their fanaticism that they sincerely believe that they are right, but it is possible to be sincere, yet be sincerely wrong.

A comparison of the closed-minded, intolerant, hateful and murderous foundational tenants of Islam with the biblical illustrations of God's treatment of non-believers and saved sinners would reveal to any reasonable person that even if they discount the lineage of God's blessing and deny that Jesus is the Messiah, that the God of the universe would never condone the attitudes of hate, arrogance, pride and entitlement that Muslims display within and outside their culture. Reverence for God and their espoused intolerance of anything that remotely brings shame to God is a thinly and transparently veiled attempt to mask their own evil nature and predisposition for violence, self-indulgence and hatred for anyone who remotely suggests that they should change their sinful ways and hold themselves accountable to the true God.

We will see how God plans to deal with the Muslims (Modern-day Edomites - Arabs) for blaspheming His Holy name by promoting the teachings of a false god they call Allah and a false prophet called Mohammad. Here is the true story of God's plan:

Genesis 12:1-2 Now the LORD had said to Abram: "Get out of your country, from your family and from your father's house, to a land that I will show you. I will make you a great nation; I will bless you and make your name great; and you shall be a blessing. I will bless those who bless you, and I will curse him who curses you; and in you all the families of the earth shall be blessed." NKJV

As you can see below, there was a promise, but that promise was not meant for Ishmael and his Arab descendants:

Genesis 16:7-13 Now the angel of the LORD found her by a spring of water in the wilderness by the spring on the way to Shur. And He said, "Hagar, Sarai's maid, where have you come from, and where are you going?" She said, "I am fleeing from the presence of my mistress Sarai." The Angel of the LORD said to her, "Return to your mistress, and submit yourself under her hand." Then the Angel of the LORD said to her, I will multiply your descendants exceedingly, so that they shall not be counted for multitude." And the Angel of the LORD said to her: "Behold, you are with child, and you shall bear a son. You shall call his name Ishmael, because the LORD has heard your affliction. He shall be a wild man; his hand shall be against every man's hand and every man's hand against him. And he shall dwell in the presence of all his brethren." Then she called the name of the LORD who spoke to her, You-Are-the-God-Who-Sees; for she said, "Have I also here seen Him who sees me?" NKJV

The Holy Bible Genesis 17:17-21 – "Then Abraham fell on his face and laughed, and said in his heart, "Shall a child be born to a man who is one hundred years old? And shall Sarah, who is ninety years old, bear a child?" And Abraham said to God, "Oh that Ishmael might live before You!" Then God said: "No Sarah your wife shall bear you a son, and you shall call his name Isaac; I will establish My covenant with him for an everlasting covenant, and with his descendants after him. "And as for Ishmael, I have heard you. Behold, I have blessed him, and will make him fruitful, and will multiply him exceedingly. He shall beget twelve princes, and I will make him a great nation. But My covenant I will establish with Isaac, whom Sarah shall bear to you at this set time next year." Then He finished talking with him, and God went up from Abraham." NKJV

God did bless Ishmael, and Ishmael did exactly what God said he would do. He rebelled against God and his hand was against everyone. Ishmael's descendants became the Arab nations and they fought against (Israel) Isaac's descendants. They got away from God altogether and worshiped false gods.

Keep in mind as you read the following Scripture that God gave this land (Seir) to Esau, son-in-law of Ishmael, whose descendants became the Edomites (Arabs).

Ezekiel 35:1-15 – Moreover the word of the LORD came to me, saying, "Son of man, set your face against Mount Seir and prophesy against it," and say to it. Thus says the Lord GOD: "Behold, O Mount Seir, I am against you; I will stretch out My hand against you, and make you most desolate; I shall lay your cities waste, and you shall be desolate, then you shall know that I *am* the LORD. "Because you have had an ancient hatred, and have shed the blood of the children of Israel by the power of the sword at the time of their calamity, when their iniquity *came* to an end, "therefore, as I live," says the Lord God, "I will prepare you for blood, and blood shall pursue you; since you have not hated blood, therefore blood shall pursue you. "Thus I will make Mount Seir most desolate, and cut off from it the one who leaves and the one who returns.

"And I will fill its mountains with the slain; on your hills and in your hills and in your valleys and in all your ravines those who are slain by the sword shall fall. "I will make you perpetually desolate, and your cities shall be uninhabited; then you shall know that I *am* the LORD. "Because you have said, 'These two nations and these two countries shall be mine, and we will possess them,' although the LORD was there, "therefore, as I live," says the Lord God, I will do according to your anger and according to the envy which you showed in your hatred against them; and I will make Myself known among the when I judge you. "Then you shall know that I *am* the LORD. I have heard all your blasphemies which you have spoken against the mountains of Israel, saying, 'They are desolate; they are given to us to consume. "Thus with your mouth you have boasted against Me and multiplied your words against Me; I have heard *them.*" "Thus says the Lord God: "The whole earth will rejoice when I make you desolate. "As you rejoiced because the inheritance of the house of Israel was desolate, so I will do to you; you shall be desolate, O Mount Seir, as well as all of Edom –all of it! Then they shall know that I *am* the LORD."'" NKJV

The *two nations* mentioned in the Old Testament Scripture above in verse ten are Israel (North) and Judah (South). It is modern day Israel.

We have covered the history of God's promise to Abraham, the Jews. Now let's go to the beginning of the Muslim, Mohammad's, reign as a murderer and slaughterer of the human race: Hal Lindsey - *Everlasting Hatred – The Roots of Jihad* page 116-121:

*"**Enter Muhammad** - It was into this historical context that Mohammad launched his ministry. As cited in the last chapter, Mohammad's zealous crusade against polytheism made him increasingly unpopular in his hometown of Mecca. When they tried to kill him, he and his disciples fled to Yathrib. Not surprisingly, the Jews of Yathrib did not accept Mohammad's claim of being a Prophet. Mohammad's tried to win the Jews over by representing himself as simply a teacher of the creed of Abraham. He even adopted the Jewish Sabbath, some dietary laws and initially required prayer toward Jerusalem rather than Mecca."*

*"**Believe or be Beheaded** – The Jews, however, were not deceived and refused to acknowledge him as anything but a false prophet. This infuriated Mohammad. He turned to what would become his standard pattern – the sword. He marched against this Jewish tribe and besieged their village. When they surrendered and came out one by one, they were beheaded. The first Muslim massacre was executed on the Jews."*

*"**A Heritage of Brutality** - An example of their brutality and barbarity, after one Jewish town surrendered to the Muslims, approximately 1000 men were beheaded in one day. The women and children were sold into slavery. Else where, as the attacks on Jews continued, some managed to survive. Under a new Islamic policy, non-Muslims or 'infidels' were permitted to maintain their land so long as they paid a 50 percent tribute for 'protection.'"*

We saw how the Muslim religion started and spread like wildfire. It actually started with the Jewish people who were adamant about their faith in Almighty God, the true God of this world. But later on, *all* non-Muslims were considered infidels." The descendants of those radical Muslims have jumped the boundaries of an ocean that once protected the United States. Did they leave their bizarre religious practices behind? No! The news in America is picking up bizarre stories about Muslims right here in the United States committing honor killings and beheading people who try to escape the Islamic brutality.

My friends, the Muslims are here and if we do not stop the movement, we are going to pay the consequences. We have a man in the Oval Office right now who has a Muslim background; whose friends are Muslims and who has made it clear that he wants a friendly relationship with the Muslim world. (But at what cost to America?)

To get a better image of where Obama is coming from, perhaps the reader needs to know the history of Indonesia where President Obama spent the formative years of his life, attended a Muslim school in a country that his mother refused to leave; its population of Muslims and it's sentiment towards Americans.

Indonesia is made up of a group of islands in the Indian Ocean. Jakarta is the island Obama speaks of. Obama, himself, in his second book makes a statement about Indonesia's negative sentiment towards the United States. Barack Obama - *The Audacity of Hope* page 278:

"In a 2003 poll, most Indonesians had a higher opinion of Osama bin Laden than they did of George W. Bush."

When Obama wrote about the Indonesian poll, he didn't condemn the Indonesian country for their hatred of Bush and our country. Nor did he mention that he, in some subtle measure, tried to enlighten his Muslim friends or defend America, but rather he criticized *our* country and allowed the hatred to fester.

In the interest of fairness, it has to be stated that there is a degree of risk involved in defending America in a Muslim country, especially when you are very young and greatly outnumbered, but at some point, when the risk is diminished, say perhaps during his political campaigns, wouldn't one expect him to project to the Muslim world a more spirited defense of America, the America that he so adamantly claims he loves and cherishes?

It should also be noted that one of the mandates that God gives Christians is to proclaim the truth throughout the world. He does not hold us accountable for the decisions that others make to either accept of reject him once they hear the true Gospel, but we are mandated to tell the truth. God will take care of the harvest (number of souls saved), but he expects us to sow the seeds (spread the true Gospel according to Jesus Christ).

Now, it is debatable if Obama even knows the truth, since he has so eloquently misquoted scripture on numerous occasions (then claimed that *"Christians have not been reading their Bibles"* in an attempt to shift the ignorance and deception from his own shoulders). But if he is indeed a Christian, as he quickly acknowledged once corrected in his interview with George Stephanopoulos, then he has to realize the great disservice that he is doing to the entire Muslim word by failing to tell them the truth. What a horrible tragedy is inflicted on a people when they are allowed to believe a false doctrine that will ultimately cause them to be cast into Hell on judgment day! Mr. Obama, if you are a Christian as you claim, then you owe it to non-believers to tell them the Gospel truth, if you even know the truth yourself.

How do the Indonesians really feel about Christians in the country where Obama was raised? Let's see what is happening to Christians in Indonesia. Hal Lindsey's writes in *The Everlasting Hatred - The Roots of Jihad,* page 142:

"Indonesia, which has the largest Muslim population of any country in the world, is systematically killing and terrorizing Christians. More than 500 Churches have been burned and hundreds of Christians killed. Others have fled in fear for their lives."

The world's largest Muslim country, in terms of population, is Indonesia.[6] It was in this culture that Obama spent the formative years of his life living with his mother and Muslim stepfather and attended a Muslim school.

It is easy to see why Obama was so hesitant to defend America during his formative years. That kind of intimidation would frighten any child, and most adults. But wouldn't any God-loving American be equally outraged by the atrocities being committed around the world by Muslims, and would he speak so affectionately of them, and would he not wave the American flag more vigorously and more fervently proclaim the truth of the Gospel of Jesus Christ?

---

[6] Indonesia's population taken from the book *Islam At The Crossroads*

CHAPTER TWO

Obama reflects back to Indonesia throughout his books; yet, he has managed to keep our country totally in the dark about that part of his life, with the exception of a few bits and pieces that he brings out in his autobiography. He did tell us, however, that it took him less than six months to learn the Indonesian language, customs and legends.[7] (It is then necessarily true that he had to learn of Islam's hatred for infidels, Americans, and their plans to convert us or kill us, through any means possible, even political.)

One of the things he writes about in his book is the political coup that happened in Indonesia in 1965. After reading his description of what he thinks happened, one wonders if he resents the fact that the United States intervened and helped remove the communist President Sukarno from Indonesia. The coup had only been resolved months before he and his mother had moved to Jakarta to be with his Muslim stepfather, Lolo.[8]

How long did Obama say it took him to learn the Indonesian language, culture and legends? Evidently he made it a point to remember the history of Indonesia as well. He gives us a good description of Indonesia's geographical location, political history and the fact that it is the *largest Muslim nation* in the world. He also gives us his take on what happened during the 1965 coup in Indonesia and the United States involvement. This is what he writes in his books about the coup. Barack Obama - *The Audacity of Hope* page 271:

---

[7] *Dreams from My Father* page 36
[8] *Dreams from My Father* page 31-32

"With more than 240 million people, Indonesia's population ranks fourth in the world, behind China, India, and the United States. More than seven hundred ethnic groups reside within the country's borders, and more than 742 languages are spoken there. Almost 90 percent of Indonesia's population practice Islam, making it the world's largest Muslim nation."

Barack Obama - *The Audacity of Hope* page 273:

"With U.S. forces knee-deep in Vietnam and the domino theory still a central tenet of U. S. foreign policy, the CIA began providing covert support to various insurgencies inside Indonesia, and cultivated close links with Indonesia's military officers, many of whom had been trained in the United States. In 1965, under the leadership of General Suharto, the military moved against Sukarno, and under emergency powers began a massive purge of communists and their sympathizers. According to estimates, between 500,000 and one million people were slaughtered during the purge, with 750,000 others imprisoned or forced into exile."

What Obama failed to mention in his account of the conflict was that the majority of the thousands killed or forced into exile were with the Indonesian Communist Party (PKI) led by Sukarno.[9] Indonesia has a population of 237 *million* people.[10] Killing isn't pretty, but Obama made it sound like, with the help of the United States, over a million people were expunged from Indonesia.

President Sukarno was a communist whose regime terrorized Indonesia. And thirty-four years later Obama expounds on the killing of Indonesians who were terrorizing that country, calling it a *"slaughter"* rather than applauding Suharto, along with the United States help, for eliminating the terrorist and communist activity in that country and possibly saving tens of thousands of lives. It is this sort of anti-American

[9] History of 1965 coup in Indonesia – From: *Wikipedia, the free encyclopedia.org*

[10] Statistics on Indonesia population – From: *Wikipedia, the free encyclopedia.org*

slant to his reporting that leads one to wonder where his loyalties lie.

The two excerpts above were taken from Obama's second book *The Audacity of Hope* written in 2006. He covered the same incident in his first book, *Dreams from My Father* written in 1995, leaving out the incident about Suharto and the righteous killing of the communist terrorists. He reflected more on how his stepfather was affected by the Indonesian coup. His stepfather, Lolo, had been yanked from his (Obama's) young life and was pulled from college in Hawaii and brought back to Indonesia during the 1965 coup. The story in his second book appeared to be more political, while in the first book he showed anger because of how his stepfather's life was affected by the coup.

Obama had not seen his stepfather since he left Hawaii. Now he and his mother were joining Lolo in Indonesia. He was very young and impressionable when he first got to Indonesia.

Obama elaborates in his book about Lolo and the soldiers at the airport when he and his mother first arrived in Indonesia. *Dreams from My Father* page 32:

"People swirled around us, speaking rapidly in a language I didn't know, smelling unfamiliar. For a long time we watched Lolo talk to a group of brown-uniformed soldiers. The soldiers had guns in their holsters, but they appeared to be in a jovial mood, laughing at something that Lolo had said."

Obama writes in detail what happened to his stepfather, Lolo, after the coup. *Dreams from My Father* page 42:

"It was as if he had pulled into some dark hidden place, out of reach, taking with him the brightest part of himself. On some nights, she[11] would hear him up after everyone else had gone to bed, wandering through the house with a bottle of imported whiskey, nursing his secrets. Other nights he would tuck a pistol under his pillow before falling off to sleep."

Dreams from My Father page 45 – *"Power had taken Lolo and yanked him back into line just when he thought he'd*

---

[11] She – Obama's mother

escaped, making him feel its weight, letting him know that his life wasn't his own."

Obama was writing this in 1995. Was he showing bitterness because he felt that the United States was somehow responsible for his stepfather's defeat? If not, why was he expounding on the Indonesian coup again in his second book, only this time being more explicit about the United State's involvement in the conflict and giving the death toll of the Indonesia Muslims.

According to his book his stepfather's passport had been revoked and he was conscripted from Hawaii and into the Indonesian Army.[12] When he stepped off the plane in Indonesia, army officers met him and questioned him.[13] He ended up in the jungles of New Guinea for a year. It was after that time that Lolo sent for Obama and his mother.

Obama writes that some of the events in his book were taken from stories told by his family; however, Obama seems to remember very vividly this time in his life. Seeing the armed soldiers and hearing the stories about the coup must have made an indelible impression on a young boy who saw his stepfather change from a man full of life to a defeated man. He shows marked admiration and love for the Muslim stepfather whose life was dramatically changed from the man he knew in Hawaii. (Remember that Obama was in his mid-thirties when he was reflecting back to his childhood living with Lolo, and in his mid-forties when he was reflecting back again for the writing of his second book.)

There is no doubt that Obama had a close relationship with his stepfather and felt secure under his stepfather's care. Was this close relationship with his Muslim stepfather a compelling factor in his desire to seek out Muslims when he came to the United States? After all, his stepfather had taken him under his wing. He had taught him to box and had introduced him to the

---

[12] Lolo Conscripted into the Indonesian Army – *The Audacity of Hope* page 273

[13] Army officers - *Dreams from My Father* – page 45

Indonesian people as his son Barry (Barack) Soetoro[14] and taught him the religions of Indonesia. Obama writes in detail about life with this stepfather. Is Obama a Muslim? Judge for yourself. Barack Obama - *The Audacity of Hope* page 204:

"When my mother remarried, it was to an Indonesian with and equally skeptical bent, a man who saw religion as not particularly useful in the practical business of making one's way in the world, and who had grown up in a country that easily blended its Islamic faith with remnants of Hinduism, Buddhism, and ancient Animist tradition. [15] *During the [five years] that we would live with my [stepfather in Indonesia], I was sent first to a neighborhood Catholic school and then to a predominantly Muslim school; in both cases, my mother was less concerned with me learning the catechism or puzzling out the meaning of the [muezzin's] call to evening prayer than she was with whether I was properly learning my multiplication tables."* [16]

Barack Obama - *Dreams from My Father* page 30-31:

"We had lived in Indonesia for over three years by that time, the result of my mother's marriage to an Indonesian named Lolo, another student she had met at the University of Hawaii. His name meant "crazy" in Hawaiian, which tickled Gramps to no end, but the meaning didn't suit the man, for Lolo possessed the good manners and easy grace of his people. He was short and brown, handsome, with thick black hair and features that could have as easily been Mexican or Samoan as Indonesian; his tennis game was good, his smile uncommonly even, and his temperament imperturbable. For [two years,] from the time I was four until I was six, he endured endless hours of chess with Gramps and long wrestling sessions with me."

(Obama's gramps lived in Hawaii, not Indonesia. Note that Obama expounds on his admiration for Lolo, *"Lolo possessed*

---

[14] Jerome R. Corsi - *The Obama Nation* page 56
[15] Animist is beliefs in the existence of spirits separable from bodies
[16] Brackets added for emphasis

the good manners and easy grace of his people." Lolo was a Muslim…his people Muslim.)

Add the years up. Obama was under his Muslim stepfather's tutelage for seven years, two in Hawaii and five in Indonesia. He was a young boy at the time and in the formative years of his life. He clearly remembers the importance of his training for the *muezzin's call* to evening prayer. Muslims are commanded to pray to Allah [false god] five times a day. A muezzin [*Muslim*] initiates the beginning of the daily prayers.

Obama's mother was not the only one concerned about his education. Lolo, his stepfather, took every opportunity to educate the young man about the Muslim faith. Obama was in the car with his mother and Lolo on their way to his new home in Indonesia when he saw a giant monkey statue. Barack Obama - *Dreams from My Father* page 33:

"Who's Sukarno?" I shouted from the backseat, but Lolo appeared not to hear me. Instead, he touched my arm and motioned ahead of us. "Look," he said, pointing upward. There, standing astride the road, was a towering giant at least ten stories tall, with the body of a man and the face of an ape. "That's Hanuman," Lolo said as we circled the statue, "the monkey god." I turned around in my seat, <u>mesmerized</u> by the solitary figure, so dark against the sun, poised to leap into the sky as puny traffic swirled around its feet. "He's a great warrior," Lolo <u>said firmly</u>. "Strong as a hundred men. When he fights the demons, he's never defeated." [17]

Lolo <u>said firmly</u>! Lolo wasn't joking with Obama; he was dead serious about the statue being a monkey god. Obama was six years old when he saw the monkey god. Twenty seven years later he calls his experience with the god mesmerizing. In the eyes of Indonesians Hanuman he is one of the most popular gods of Hindus. The story of the Hanuman monkey god can be found on the *Wikipedia, free encyclopedia* website:

"Hanuman is one of the most popular <u>gods</u> of <u>Hindus.</u> He is also known by other names like *Hanumat.* His mother's name

---

[17] Emphasis added. Lolo "said firmly" – belief in the monkey and tiger

was *Anjana*. Based on her mother's name, *Hanuman* is sometimes called as *Anjaneya*, that is, one born of *Anjana*. His father's name was *Vayu*. According to Hindu mythology, *Vayu* is the god of winds. *Hanuma's* image shows him as a strong man with the face of a <u>monkey</u>. He also has a tail. *Hanuman* was awarded boon of Immortality by Mother Sita (Wife of Lord rama) and is still alive. *Hanuman is* a very powerful and strong god. He finds an important place in the <u>*Ramayana*</u>. He was a devotee of <u>*Rama,*</u> a form <u>(avatar)</u> of <u>*Vishnu,*</u> a god of Hindus."

These are the kinds of religions that Obama was taught while living in Indonesia. How much of his stepfather's teaching do you think stayed with Obama? In some of President Obama's campaign speeches he used the word *"myth,"* and he called God a *"sky god."* Is Obama comparing God with this mythical god, Hanuman? The Hanuman monkey god was a Hindus god, but Obama's stepfather not only practiced the Islamic religion, he practiced Hinduism as well; and more than likely taught Obama the religion, too. Barack Obama - *Dreams from My Father* page 37:

"Like many Indonesians, Lolo followed a brand of Islam that could make room for the remnants of more ancient animist and Hindu faiths. He explained that a man took on the powers of whatever he ate: One day soon, he promised, he would bring home a piece of tiger meat for us to share."

There are other false gods that Obama was introduced to. We need to understand that Obama's stepfather, Lolo's, teachings were not some "kidding" thing that father's in the United States might do. Obama was at a very impressionable age and Lolo was very adamant about the *monkey* god and the *tiger*.

How seriously did Obama take his stepfather's teaching that a man takes on the powers of what he eats? Was it a religious teaching? Your guess is as good as mine. Whether he is making up such stores or whether he is telling the truth, he will not divulge anything about his life in Indonesia other than what he wrote in his books.....and that isn't a whole lot! We do know, however, that the monkey god is very real to the Indonesians.

We have learned from several people who have investigated Obama's life that his stepfather enrolled him in school as a Muslim and as his son, Barry Soetoro. This excerpt taken from Jerome Corsi's book is a statement from one of Obama's closest childhood Muslim friends in Indonesia, Zulfan Adi. *Jerome Corsi - The Obama Nation* page 56 writes:

"Adi said neighborhood Muslims worshipped in a nearby house. When the muezzin sounded the call to prayer, Adi remembered seeing Lolo and Barry walk together to the makeshift mosque. "His mother often went to the church," Adi told the Times, "but Barry was a Muslim. I remember him wearing a sarong." (Obama was also known as Barry Soetoro.)

Jerome Corsi goes on to say on page 58 – *"Sometime in 1971, Obama was enrolled in Sekolah Dasar Negeri Besuki, a public school in the Mentenge District. Here the evidence is that Obama did receive the Islamic instruction in the Koran that he refers to in his autobiography."*

Can we speculate, by reading the Muslim's Qur'an, what Obama may have been taught in Muslim school? The following teachings are quoted directly from the Muslim's religious book The Holy Qur'an:

The Holy Qur'an C. 51 274 – 274 - *"We now return to the subject of Jihad, which we left at 2:214-216. We are to be under no illusion about it. If we are not prepared to fight for our faith, with our lives and all our <u>resources</u>, both our lives and our <u>resources</u> will be wiped out by our enemies."* [18] Jihad is "Holy War" against the infidel - anyone who is not a Muslim.

The Holy Qur'an 5:33 - *"The punishment of those who wage war against Allah and His Messenger, and strive with might and main for mischief through the land is: execution, or crucifixion, or the cutting off of hands and feet from opposite side, or exile from the land."*

We know that Obama attended a Muslim school in Indonesia, but did we know that he was also a member of

---

[18] Underscore for emphasis

Indonesian Boy Scout troop? Barack Obama - *Dreams from My Father* page 50 – Speaking of his mother:

"If I told her about the goose-stepping demonstrations my Indonesian Boy Scout troop performed in front of the president, she might mention a different kind of march, a march of children no older than me, a march for freedom."

Yes, the Indonesian Boy Scouts march as an army. The *"goose-step"* is a step in which the legs are raised high and knees kept unbent [like Hitler's army].

What are The Boy Scouts of America taught? They are taught honor for America and its Christian heritage. What would Boy Scouts of Indonesia be taught? Remember that Indonesia is 85% Muslim. What would your supposition be about Obama's belonging to an Indonesian Boy Scott troop, and his goose-stepping marching [before the president of Indonesia]? Would an Indonesian Boy Scott troop be trained to think kindly of Christians or Jews, or the infidel [non-Muslims]? Not according to the Muslim's Qur'an. Remember, these quotes are word-for-word coming directly from the Muslim's Qur'an:

The Holy Qur'an 5:51 - *DO NOT TAKE JEWS OR CHRISTIANS AS FRIENDS* – *"O ye who believe! Take not the Jews and the Christians for your friends and protectors; they are but friends and protectors to each other. And he amongst you that turns to them (for friendship) is of them. Verily Allah guideth not a people unjust."*

We have to remember that when the Muslims use the term *Christian*, they are grouping together all people who are not Muslim (with the exception of Jews). They believe that anyone who does not follow the teaching of Allah, or is a Jew, follows the Christian belief. The Qur'an does not acknowledge Jesus as the Messiah; therefore, they are not taught that there is a difference between Christians and non-Christians.

The Holy Qur'an Sura 5:72 – *"They do blaspheme who say: Allah is Christ the son of Mary."*

Christian Answer: The Holy Bible – Matthew 5:43-44 – "You have heard that it was said, 'you shall love your neighbor and hate your enemy.' 'But I say to you love your enemies, bless those who curse you, do good to those who hate you, and pray for those who spitefully use you and persecute you.'" NKJV

Our Holy God (the God of Christianity) is very adamant about His creation worshiping false gods.

Christian answer: The Holy Bible – Exodus 20:4-5 "You shall not make for yourself a carved image – any likeness of anything that is in Heaven above, or that is in the earth beneath, or that is in the water under the earth; you shall not bow down to them nor serve them. For I, the LORD your God, *am* a jealous God, visiting the iniquity of the fathers of the children to the third and fourth generations of those who hate Me." NKJV

Later in the book you will see where Obama's admiration for his stepfather, Lolo, and his powerful influence on Obama's life far outweighs other influential people in his life. But first let's see what his mother's sentiment was about the Muslim's religious holiday *Ramadan*.

Barack Obama - *Dreams from My Father* page 49:

"'If you want to grow up to be a human being," she would say to me, "you're going to need some values." Honestly – Lolo should not have hidden the refrigerator in the storage room when the tax officials came, even if everyone else, including the tax officials, expected such things. Fairness- the parents of wealthier students should not give television sets to the teachers during Ramadan."

Did Obama's mother recognize Ramadan (the most religious day of the Muslim year) as a holy day? Why did she caution Obama that it was wrong to give gifts on that particular religious holiday, Ramadan, if she was not practicing their religion? Can we assume from her strong ties with Indonesia that she esteemed the Indonesian culture?

It was interesting to read what Obama told the world in his book about his mother's position against the United States. Lolo, Obama's stepfather, was trying to convince Obama's mother to go to a company dinner party because Americans would be attending. Barack Obama - *Dreams from My Father* page 47:

> "*He would ask her how it would look for him to go alone, and remind her that these were her own people, and my mother's voice would raise to almost a shout. They are not my people*"

Barack Obama - *The Audacity of Hope* page 274 – "*My mother might scowl at the attitude she heard from other Americans in Jakarta, their condescension toward Indonesians, their unwillingness to learn anything about the country that was hosting them – but given the exchange rate, she was glad to be getting paid in dollars rather than the rupiahs her Indonesian colleagues at the embassy were paid.*"

Barack Obama - *The Audacity of Hope* page 275 – "*My mother's ties to Indonesia would never diminish; for the next twenty years she would travel back and forth, working for international agencies for six or twelve months at a time as a specialist in women's development issues, designing programs to help village women start their own business or bring their produce to market.*"

If you study the Qur'an, you will understand that no Muslim country will allow an American, especially a woman, to help design programs for a Muslim-run business unless that country is absolutely convinced that the individual had converted to Islam, and was a devout follower of Islam. Muslim countries call the United States "the devil." It's inconceivable that Indonesia, or any other Muslim controlled country, would allow an American to train Muslim women.

I would like to leave this chapter with Obama's comment about his trust in his stepfather, Lolo. Barack Obama - *Dreams from My Father* page 38: "*So it was to Lolo that I turned for guidance and instruction. He didn't talk much, but he was easy to be with.*"

CHAPTER THREE

What I am trying to make known by writing this book is the fact that we really do not know anything about Obama. His stories throughout his autobiography don't add up. He gives us just enough information about himself to avoid a thorough background check. Throughout his books Obama flip-flops about his relationship with his real Muslim father and evades questions about his close relationship with his stepfather, Lolo. What about his Muslim friends in Hawaii?

Obama more than likely had his eye on the White House when he wrote his first book in 1995. When he wrote about his relationship with his real father, it was yes "I did know him," no "I didn't know him." So we really can't pinpoint any kind of relationship he might have had with his real father. It makes sense, however, that at this point in his life if he had admitted to having known his real father intimately, he would have been inundated with questions about his Muslim father's, Luo, Tribe's murderous activity in Kenya when it came time for the presidential run. With that kind of background, there would likely have been an insurmountable hurdle in his chance to be a presidential candidate. Here is one flip-flop about his real father. On page 5 of his book he says he only knew his father from stories from his mother; yet, on page 62 of the same book his grandmother is telling him that his father is coming Hawaii to see him! Barack Obama - *Dreams of My Father* page 5:

"At the time of his death, my father remained a myth to me, both more and less than a man. He had left Hawaii back in

1963, when I was only two years old, so that as a child I knew him only through the stories that my mother and grandparents told."

Barack Obama - *Dreams from My Father* page 62-63 – *"Your father's coming to see you," she said. "Next month. Two weeks after your mother gets here." "After a week of my father in the flesh, I had decided that I preferred his more distant image, an image I could alter on a whim – or ignore when convenient." Speaking of his mother: "Like her, my father had remarried, and I now had five brothers and one sister living in Kenya...'"*

Obama, as usual, was evasive about his real father and at what age he learned about his father's background. But he does tell us that his father is of the Luo tribe from Kenya. For most readers, being from a tribe in Kenya might sound fascinating, but for those of us who know that the Muslim Luo tribe in Kenya has a history of massacring Christians and non-Muslims, we find it alarming that we have a President who is related to this tribe of murderers. The people of Obama's father's tribe are carrying out what the Qur'an teaches about killing the infidel. Ted Sampley posted on *The U.S. Veteran Dispatch's* website on June 13, 2008:

"More than 200 people, mainly Kikuyus, the same tribe as President Kibaki, were desperately seeking safety in the Kenya Assemblies of God church when a gang of 2000 armed young men drawn from the Luo, Kalenjin and Luhya tribes stormed and torched the church. Witnesses reported that when people – at least 80 of them children – tried to flee being burned alive, they were hacked to death with machetes."

This slaughter of Christians, and anyone who is not Muslim, is still happening as the Muslims make their way across the world trying to claim it for the glory of their false god, Allah. We already see it happening in the United State with the killings of the Muslim teenage girls who wanted to be "American" and the beheading of a Muslim wife by her Muslim husband because she filed for a divorce. These killings right here in our own country are not going to stop; the Muslims are going to become more aggressive as they gain power in the United States! And how are they going to gain power in our country.....President Obama and the Muslim law, Shari'a Law, which is being pushed for inclusion in our own justice system! Now let's go back to Obama's book. Barack Obama – *Dreams from My Father* page 9-10:

"He was an African, I would learn, a Kenyan of the Luo tribe, born on the shores of Lake Victoria in a place called Alego. The village was poor, but his father – my other grandfather, Hussein Onyango Obama – had been a prominent farmer, an elder of the tribe, a medicine man with healing powers." "I rarely asked for details that might resolve the meaning of "PH.D" or "Colonialism" or locate Alego on the map. Instead, the path of my father's life occupied the same terrain as a book my mother once bought for me, a book called Origins, a collection of creation tales from around the world, stories of Genesis and the tree where man was born. Prometheus and the gift of fire, the tortoise of Hindu legend that floated in space supporting the weight of the world on its back." (Most of this teaching is mythical.)

Why is Obama sharing in a book at this particular time in his life that he is related to these people? Obama mentions religions, but he does not tell the readers that his father and Kenyan relatives are Muslims.

The book is his autobiography, but was he taking the writing of this book to *Muslims* who did not know who he is? Was it a way to get word out to Muslims without broadcasting it to the world that his political agenda is to help the Islamic movement? As a non-Muslim reader, we would probably read the book as a simple autobiography, but to a Muslim, it gives a myriad of information about Obama's heritage in the Muslim world.

Obama appears to be proud of the "religious" books his mother supplied him with. However, Obama's didn't mention his mother giving him a Holy Bible, but only a [collection] of the Book of Genesis. For those who do not know, Genesis is the first Book in the Old Testament of the Holy Bible. This is a book in the Bible that Islam has twisted and used as a basis for their claim that Ishmael was God's blessed son to Abraham. Was there a reason why Obama's mother didn't give him the entire Holy Bible? Was she advancing his education in Islam rather than filling his mind with a religion that the Muslim world teaches against? Remember, his mother was married to a Muslim who took Obama to mosque for worship. It would be very unlikely that he would allow Obama to study the Christian religion which contradicts their teachings.

Let's go back to the above excerpt where Obama said that as a child he only knew his father through stories from his mother and grandparents. I don't know at what age Obama constitutes being a child, but in his first book he talks about the embarrassment he felt about his real father visiting his school classroom in Hawaii. I don't believe anyone researching Obama's life has determined at what age he actually arrived in Hawaii. We know he could have been twelve or thirteen years old when his real father visited his school.

From reading the account of that visit I doubt very seriously that Obama ever forgot any part of his father's life as he claims in both of his books. He describes vividly the expression on his father's face and how he followed his father's every step as he taught him the Luo Tribal dance steps of his native land:

Barack Obama – *Dreams from My Father* page 71:

"Barry! Look here – I forgot that I had brought these for you. (Barry is Obama)[19] *The sounds of [your] continent."*[20] *It took him a while to puzzle out my grandparents' old stereo, but finally the disk began to turn, and he gingerly placed the needle on the groove. A tinny guitar lick opened, then the sharp horns, the thump of drums, then the guitar again, and then the voices, clean and joyful as they rode up the back beat, urging us on. "Come Barry," my father said. "You will learn from the master." And suddenly his slender body was swaying back and forth, the lush sound was rising, his arms were swinging as they*

---

[19] Name Obama added for clarity

[20] Brackets for emphasis

cast an invisible net, his feet wove over the floor in off-beats, his bad leg stiff but his rump high, his head back, his hips moving in a tight circle. The rhythm quickened, the horns sounded, and his eyes closed to follow his pleasure." "I took my first tentative steps with my eyes closed, down, up, my arms swinging, the voices lifting. And I hear him still: As I follow my father into the sound, he lets out a quick shout, bright and high, a shout that leaves much behind and reaches out for more, a shout that cries for laughter."

For someone who said he did not know his father, that he remained a "myth" to him, Obama certainly does give a good description of his father's movement as he danced. Obama also said when he wrote that story in 1995, *"And I hear him still."* [21]

Based on the above positive description of his real father, would it be presumptuous to believe that Obama was, in fact, closer to his father than he leads us to believe. But was his book, *Dreams from My Father* written in memory of his real father? Let's take a closer look at Obama's Muslim father's Luo tribe. This is what Ted Sampley – *U.S. Veteran Dispatch* January 6, 2008 wrote about the Luo Tribe of Africa:

"Since the Kikuyu tribe of President Kibaki was the target of the killings and members of the Obama Jr's Luo tribe were doing the killing, one can image what the Kikuyu tribe thought of U.S. presidential candidate Obama Jr's plea for peace." Sampley goes on to say:

"More than 200 people, mainly Kikuyus, the same tribe as President Kibaki, were desperately seeking safety in the Kenya Assemblies of God church when a gang of 2000 armed young men drawn from the Luo, Kalenjin and Luhya tribes stormed and torched the church. Witnesses reported that when people – at least 80 of them children – tried to flee being burned alive, they were hacked to death with machetes."

The above story was also picked up and posted on the *BAPTIST ASSOCIATED PRESS* website Thursday, 03 January 2008, corroborating the story above with the exception that the

---

[21] *Dreams from My Father* page 71

mob barricaded the church and started the fire with gasoline-soaked mattresses. The observers said they saw disturbing echoes of the 1994 Rwandan genocide in the church burning.

We know from media sources that conflicts between African tribes have been going on for years, but now those conflicts have come to the attention of the United States because the Kenyan Muslim Luo tribe is openly butchering a people that the United States, a Christian nation, can relate to. According to another article in *The U.S. Veteran Dispatch*, Obama visited Africa in 1987, 1992 and 2006. He must have been aware of what was happening with the Luo Tribe when he wrote this book in 1995. Ted Sampley – *The U.S. Veteran Dispatch* June 2008:

"In August, 2006, Sen. Obama Jr. made an emotional visit to Kenya, the homeland of his late father Barack Hussein Obama Senior of the Luo tribe. It was a highly publicized visit, a prelude to Obama Jr's campaign to become President of the United States. He has visited Kenya 3 times, in 1987, 1992, and 2006. His first, while he was in school, second while he was working as a community organizer in Chicago and third as a high profile United States Senator. He was welcomed as a U.S. senator hero, 'the son of a Luo tribesman.'"

Not only do we have a president whose Muslim ancestors have a violent hatred of Christians and non-Muslims, we have one whose name Muslims revere.

Not until his presidential run did we learn that President Obama's middle name was Hussein. That name alone should have raised a flag for us to understand that if we voted him into the Oval Office, we would be facing a challenge like none other in the history of our country. But our country was caught up in the word *change*, not insisting on an answer to what that *change* was all about.

Let's take a close look at what President Obama has done so far about keeping his promise for change. Would you agree that his focus has not been on our country's immediate needs, but has focused on keeping his promise that he would speak to the Muslim world within 100 days after taking office. Sure, he is traveling around the United States visiting various cities, but he is doing exactly what he did during his presidential campaign, he is making promises. And while we listen to his promises again, he is virtually pulling our country down.

Let's just suppose that President Obama *is* a Muslim and he has a scheme to get us into such a financial state that we will run to Arab countries to borrow money to bail us out! If that is true, what would happen to our country? All we need to do is look at other countries who have submitted to Islam. If we borrow money from Arab countries, we will be under pressure from Islamic banks that adhere to the Shari'a Law, and Obama will be the president over a Muslim controlled country.

We are feeling the brunt of our ignorance for failing to see that a potential Muslim would become the most powerful man in the world.

Was Obama a Muslim Implant?

Obama's mother chose to marry two Muslims men, one from Africa and the second from Indonesia, both from countries that are controlled by Muslims who are killing Christians and who hate the United States. Was Obama's destiny to become president of the United States planned by his Muslim stepfather and a mother who gave most of her life to the Muslim world? That idea is not inconceivable! The Muslims who took down the Twin Towers trained for twenty years for that one attack on the United States.

Let's explore the potential of a young American boy raised in a Muslim country, becoming a vehicle through which Islam could gain control of the White House. Why was Obama's stepfather, a devout Muslim, attending a university in the United States? According to Obama's book, Lolo was conscripted from the university in Hawaii back into the military of Indonesia. His mother's first marriage was to a Muslim who already had a wife in Africa, so the marriage ended. The young mother with a four-year-old son provided the perfect candidate who could be raised up to help Islam's infiltration into our Christian nation at some future date.

Obama chose to remain in Hawaii when his mother returned to Indonesia. He would have stayed with his grandmother. Knowing that his mother was out of his life for a while he said, *"The arrangement suited my purpose, a purpose that I could barely articulate to myself, much less to them."* (Speaking of his grandparents.) What was the purpose that he could barely articulate to himself?[22]

This is not a novel, this is not a fairytale. What I am saying is that Islam has been conquering unsuspecting countries for centuries and their degree of success is not because they sit back and wait for the opportune time to step in. No! Those people are still planning and wait for years to position themselves where they can conquer the entire world for Islam. So it *is* conceivable that Obama could have been planted here for just that purpose, especially with his guarded background. You be the judge after reading this book.

Obama admitted in his book that he learned to manipulate people, starting with his own mother while living in Hawaii, giving an impression that he had distanced himself from her when he called himself an *experiment*. Barack Obama - *Dreams from My Father* page 95:

"Don't you think you're being a little casual about your future?" she said. "What do you mean?" "You know exactly what I mean. One of your friends was just arrested for drug possession. Your grades are slipping. You haven't even started on your college applications. Whenever I try to talk to you about it you act like I'm just this great big bother." "I looked at her sitting there, so earnest, so certain of her son's destiny. The idea that my survival depended on luck remained a heresy to her; she insisted on assigning responsibility somewhere – to herself, to Gramps and Toot, to me. I suddenly felt like puncturing that certainty of hers, letting her know that her experiment with me had failed."

Who exactly was responsible for his upbringing if all of the agents above were exempt? It appears that, from the statement

---

[22] Barack Obama – *Dreams from My Father* page 75-76

above, Obama had already distanced himself from his mother while in Hawaii. And what did he mean when he said, "....letting her know that her experiment with me had failed."

Was the *experiment* an act of bringing him up under the tutelage of the Nation of Islam?

Researching Obama's life likens to a puzzle that has been shuffled around and you have to hunt for the various pieces to make the puzzle fit together. His first book is definitely like a puzzle. He reminisces about one point in his life, and then he suddenly switches to an entirely different experience. He kept his relationship with his real father relatively secrete, so we do not know how much influence he had on Obama's life. The only thing we know for certain is that he was raised by two Muslim men who had very strong religious convictions. In the following excerpt Obama is reflecting back to how much time he spent with his real father. Barack Obama - *Dreams from My Father* page 66:

"There was so much to tell in that single month, so much explaining to do; and yet when I reach back into my memory for the words of my father, the small interactions or conversations we might have had, they seem irretrievably lost."

We see another discrepancy about his father. Barack Obama -*Dreams from My Father* page 76.

"My father's letters provided few clues. They would arrive sporadically, on a single blue page with gummed-down flaps that obscured any writing at the margins." "I would respond promptly on a wide-ruled page, and his letters would find their way into the closet, next to my mother's pictures of him."

Obama entitled his first book *Dreams from My Father,* but we find in his book that Obama had very close emotional ties to his Muslim stepfather, Lolo. He writes very little about his real father suggesting that he may have written the book in memory of Lolo rather than his real father, a stepfather who gave him direction in his life as a boy in Indonesia.[23]

---

[23] Lolo's guidance – *Dreams from My Father* page 38

Obama wrote that memories of his *real father* were *irretrievably lost*, but has he forgotten his grandmother, Sarah Obama's strong council to him about Obama's Muslim grandfather's rejection of Christianity and his strong stance on Islam and where Obama's heart should lie? According to Ted Sampley this was Sarah's counsel to Obama. Ted Sampley - *The U.S. Veteran Dispatch* January 6, 2008:

"Sarah Obama, a devout Muslim, was quoted telling Obama Jr. 'What your grandfather respected was strength. Discipline. This is also why he rejected the Christian religion, I think. For a brief time he converted to Christianity, and even changed his name to Johnson. But he could not understand such ideas as mercy towards your enemies, or that this man, Jesus, could wash away a man's sins. To your grandfather, this was a foolish sentiment, something to comfort women. And so he converted to Islam, he thought its practices conformed more closely to his beliefs.' 'Obama Jr's grandfather, for whom he was given the middle name, Hussein, was 'fiercely devoted to Islam.'"

Does Obama's Muslim family have influence in his life? You had better believe they do! In the Introduction Page of his book, Obama expresses his gratitude to his siblings for their support in the writing of his book. We know that Obama was in Africa before this book was written and after it was published. They are his family, but they are Muslim with probable Muslim influence, especially his grandmother. He dedicates his book: Barack Obama - *Dreams from My Father* page Xvii:

"It is to my family, through – my mother, my grandparents, my siblings, stretched across oceans and continents – that I owe the deepest gratitude and to whom I dedicate this book. Without their constant love and support, without their willingness to let me sing their song and their toleration of the occasional wrong note, I could never have hoped to finish. If nothing else, I hope that the love and respect I feel for them shines through on every page."

Ted Sampley - *The U.S. Veterans Dispatch* January 6, 2008:

"Just over a year later, on Sunday, Dec. 30, 2007, all of Kenya was edged closer to tribal warfare when over 100 people were murdered in a church were they had fled for refuge."

That killing was just over a year ago. Has Obama apologized for his real father's tribe's involvement in murdering innocent people? Has he addressed the massacre at all? Am I suggesting that Obama is callous to the machete massacre and torching of people who were trying to hide in a church? No. What I am trying to articulate is that the Muslims who massacred those innocent people were from Obama's father's tribe, the Luo.

Is President Obama sympathetic to the Muslims? I ask this question because in his books he gives tribute to Muslims and expounds on his unsurpassed affection for his Muslim stepfather, Lolo while putting down his white mother[24] and his white grandmother.[25]

[26] From what Obama writes in his first book, he evidently had open range while living with his grandparents. His mother had decided to return to Indonesia, but Obama remained in Hawaii. It appears that this may be the point that Obama was pulling away from his white mother and white grandparents and began his quest for his real identity.

When I read the following excerpt from his first book, I had sympathy for him, but then I read on further in the book and realized that Obama had a choice, and he chose to grow up an angry person, a person who seemed to put forth a lot of energy to find Muslim friends. In the following excerpt, his mother had just left for Indonesia, leaving him behind by his own choice.

Barack Obama – *Dreams from My Father* page 75-76:

"More than that, I'd arrived at an unspoken pact with my grandparents: I could live with them and they'd leave me alone so long as I kept my trouble out of sight. The arrangement suited my purpose, a purpose that I could barely articulate to

---

[24] White mother - Barack Obama - *Dreams from My Father* page 95
[25] White grandmother - WorldNetDaily website posted March 18, 2008
[26] Grandmother's fear – posted on *WorldNetDaily* 2009 – 'Obama speech tackles 'divisive turn on race'

myself, mush less to them. Away from my mother, away from my grandparents, I was engaged in a fitful interior struggle. "

First of all I wonder why an *"unspoken"* pact with his grandparents? How many grandparents would let a grandchild left in their custody fend for his self? Obama said, "I *"could"* live with them as long as I left my *"trouble"* out of sight." What kind of *"trouble"* is he talking about? Then he went on to say, "The *arrangement* suited my *"purpose,"* a *purpose* that *I could barely articulate to myself, much less to them.*" What was the *"purpose"* that Obama could not speak to his grandmother about?

Too many people have turned a deaf ear to the warnings about President Obama. Remember the terrorists who took down the Twin Towers. Those men were trained twenty years for that one terrorist act. So it is not inconceivable that Islam would train someone to manipulate their way into the White House.

Islam is keenly aware that they can't change the United States guiding principles by using military tactics, but can you imagine how much power they will have by putting someone in the White House who will open the doors wide for them? Determine for yourself after reading the rest of this book whether Obama is a legitimate, Christ-loving American or if he is here to help Islam proselyte America. Obama set himself up for such a suspicion when he poured his heart into his first book, *Dreams From My Father.*

Obama became angry over a comment that Jeff, a white friend, had made while at an all black party. He found himself mulling over what his black friend, Ray, had said earlier about white people. The more he thought about what Ray had said, the angrier he became. He searched for an answer and came to a conclusion that Malcolm X, who was also of mixed blood, had found the right resolve to his own questions. Malcolm X, a United States citizen, was a radical black African American Muslim who created havoc in the United States from 1952 until

1965.[27] He has been described as one of the most influential African Americans of the 20th century.[28]

Obama writes about an incident that happened when he was a teen at Punabou School in Hawaii.[29] He appeared to be extracting anger from his past experience and putting in down on paper. Barack Obama - *Dreams of my Father* page 84:

"You know, man," he said, "that really taught me something. I mean, I can see how it must be tough for you and Ray sometimes, at school parties...being the only black guys and all." I snorted. "Yeah. Right." A part of me wanted to punch him right there. We started down the road toward town, and in the silence, my mind began to rework Ray's words that day with Kurt, all the discussions we had had before that, the events of that night. And by the time I had dropped my friends off, I had begun to see a new map of the world, one that was frightening in its simplicity, suffocating in its implications. We were always playing on the white man's court, Ray had told me, by the white man's rules. If the principal, or the coach, or a teacher, or Kurt, wanted to spit in your face, he could, because he had power and you didn't. If he decided not to, if he treated you like a man or came to your defense, it was because he knew that the words you spoke, the clothes you wore, the books you read, your ambitions and desires, were already his. Whatever he decided to do, it was his decision to make, not yours, and because of that fundamental power he held over you, because it preceded and would outlast his individual motives and inclinations, any distinction between good and bad whites held negligible meaning. In fact, you couldn't even be sure that everything you had assumed to be an expression of your black, unfettered self – the humor, the song, the behind-the-back pass – had been freely chosen by you. At best, these things were a refuge; at worst, a trap. Following this maddening logic, the only thing you could choose as your own was withdrawal into a smaller and smaller coil of rage, until being black meant only the knowledge of your own powerlessness, of your own defeat.

---

[27] Date - *Malcolm X – Malcolm X Speaks* - Forward Page of book

[28] *en.wikipedia.org/wiki/Malcolm_X*

[29] Punahou School Hawaii – *Dreams from My Father* page 84

And the final irony: Should you refuse this defeat and lash out at your captors, they would have a name for that, too, a name that could cage you just as good. Paranoid. Militant. Violent. Nigger."

Barack Obama - *Dreams from My Father* page 85-86:
"Over the next few months, I looked to corroborate this nightmare vision. I gathered up books from the library – Baldwin, Ellison, Hughes, Wright, DuBois. At night I would close the door to my room, telling my grandparents I had homework to do, and there I would sit and wrestle with words, locked in suddenly desperate argument, trying to reconcile the world as I'd found it with the terms of my birth. But there was no escape to be had. In every page of every book, in Bigger Thomas and invisible men, I kept finding the same anguish, the same doubt; a self-contempt that neither irony nor intellect seemed able to deflect. Even DuBois's learning and Baldwin's love and Langston's humor eventually succumbed to its corrosive force, each man finally forced to doubt art's redemptive power, each man finally forced to withdraw, one to Africa, one to Europe, one deeper into the bowels of Harlem, but all of them in the same weary flight, all of them exhausted, bitter men, the devil at their heels. Only Malcolm X's autobiography seemed to offer something different. His repeated acts of self-creation spoke to me; the blunt poetry of his words, his unadorned insistence on respect, promised a new and uncompromising order, martial in its discipline, forged through sheer force of will. All the other stuff, the talk of blue-eyed devils and apocalypse, was incidental to that program, I decided, religious baggage that Malcolm himself seemed to have safely abandoned toward the end of his life. And yet, even as I imagined myself following Malcolm's call, one line in the book stayed me. He spoke of a wish he'd once had, the wish that the white blood that ran through him, there by an act of violence, might somehow be expunged. I knew that, for Malcolm, that wish would never be incidental. I knew as well that traveling down the road to self-respect my own white blood would never recede into mere abstraction. I was left to wonder what else I would be severing if and when I left my mother and

my grandparents at some unchartered border. And, too: If Malcolm's discovery toward the end of his life, that some whites might live beside him as brothers in Islam, seemed to offer some hope of eventual reconciliation, that hope appeared in a distant future, in a far-off land. In the meantime, I looked to see where the people would come from who were willing to work toward this future and populate this new world."

Obama said *if* and <u>when</u> he would leave his mother and grandparents at some unchartered border. Doesn't the word *when* sound like he anticipated distancing himself from them? He had just read the devout Muslim, Malcolm X's autobiography when he made that statement. He looked to the Muslim world, to a man he could probably relate to. He was raised in Indonesia where, according to his book, he enjoyed a happy life running free in rice patty fields.[30] Then he came to a whole new culture in Hawaii where he seems to have become obsessed with reaching into the remotest corners of darkness in the world. Barack Obama - *Dreams from My Father* page 102-103:

"Marcus had waved her over to our table, rising slightly to pull out a chair. "Sister Regina," Marcus said. "You know Barack, don't you? I'm trying to tell Brother Barack here about this racist tract he's reading." He held up a copy of Heart of Darkness, evidence for the court. I reached over to snatch it out of his hands. "Man, stop waving that thing around." "See there," Marcus said. "Makes you embarrassed, don't it – just being seen with a book like this. I'm telling you, man, this stuff will poison your mind." I tossed the book into my backpack. "Actually, he's right," I said. "It is a racist book."

The book "*The Heart of Darkness*" is about black slavery. And the book should anguish anyone who reads it, whether black or white. But the fact that Obama was reading such a book looks obvious that he was actually searching for something to incite anger within him. Malcolm X's powerful book *Malcolm X Speaks* exemplifies a need to incite anger

---

[30] *The Audacity of Hope* page 27-279

within himself against Christianity and white people; Christianity in particular. He believed that Christians are more infidel than other non-Muslims because they fight against Islam.

Obama's books indicates that he may be following close behind Malcolm X's concept by voicing his admiration for the way Malcolm resolved his search for peace in his life. Obama called Christianity *religious baggage*, indicating that he agreed with Malcolm X's judgment that Christianity is worthless.

According to Obama's autobiography he, himself, has searched a lifetime for his identity. And while searching Malcolm X's autobiography to find some similarity between his anger and Malcolm X's anger, he concluded that Malcolm X had found his identity and peace within the Islam religion. Obama evidently also found support from another man who lived in Hawaii, one equally as dangerous to the United States.

CHAPTER FOUR

Barack Obama - *Dreams from My Father* page 98, *"It made me smile, thinking back on Frank and his old Black Power dashiki self."*

Obama was preparing to leave Hawaii for college when he went to his old friend, Frank, for advice.[31] Who was the *Frank* that brought a *smile* to Obama's face? In *Dreams from My Father* Obama sought old Frank's advice during his teen years in Hawaii. And notice that Obama capitalized the "B" and the "P" in black power. The writing, throughout his first book, seems to dwell on "Black Power." Let's go back to his mentor, Old Frank, and find out why Obama put emphasis on "Black Power." Jerome R. Corsi said in his book *The Obama Nation* page 85:

"The only poet who fits that description completely is Frank Marshall Davis, a newspaper journalist and poet who was widely known in the 1950s to be a communist. The first identification of "Frank" with Frank Marshall Davis was made by Gerald Horne, a contributing editor to Political Affairs, an openly Marxist political review.[42] In March 2007, Horne gave a speech at New York University on the occasion of the Communist Party USA archive's being placed at an NYU library. In that speech, he discussed Frank Marshall Davis, noting that Davis, who was born in Kansas and lived much of his adult life in Chicago, had moved to Honolulu in 1948 at the suggestion of his good friend, actor Paul Robeson. In the 1940s,

---

[31] Old Frank – *Dreams from My Father* page 97

Robeson was an outspoken critic of segregation and racial discrimination in the United States. At the time, Robeson was a strong advocate of the Soviet Union and a member of the Communist Party USA. Horne also documented Davis's friendship with the Dunham family in Hawaii. "Eventually, he [Frank Marshall Davis] befriended another family – a Euro-American family – that had migrated to Honolulu from Kansas and a young woman from this family eventually had a child with a young student from Kenya East Africa who goes by the name of Barack Obama, who retracing the steps of Davis eventually decamped to Chicago."[43] Horne further documented that Frank Marshall Davis was "a decisive influence in helping him [Barack Obama] to find his present identity as an African-American, a people who have been the least anti-communist and the most left-leaning of any constituency in this nation."[44] After Horne's speech, the identity of "Frank" was never in doubt, nor was his importance in the development of the young Barack Obama."

If Corsi's findings are accurate, this mentor appears to be none other than a communist who worked in Hawaii on behalf of the Soviet Union. If the Frank in Obama's book was indeed Frank Marshall Davis, as Corsi suspects, then Obama was personally involved with and mentored by a communist. The possibility that Obama had a communist friend and mentor in Hawaii at such early age should raise eyebrows, but more importantly is the fact that President Obama may now be planning to become more involved with Muslims in their endeavor to nationalize this world.

Since taking the Oval Office President Obama has not only been *talking* favorably to Arab nations, he has just completed a planned trip to one of the highest Muslim populated countries in the world. Turkey, that is 99.6% Muslim, held a global conference to pull leaders of the world together. This conference pertains to religion, so keep your eye on the country of Turkey, not on Iraq, Saudi Arabia or Iran.

The danger our country is facing right now is much bigger than a political fall-out with those countries, it's the ultimate take-over by Islam and rule under a Muslim nation. This radical takeover will liken to Hitler when he controlled Germany, only citizens of the Unites States will be the ones hiding in basements and ally-ways, running for their lives because they will not succumb to the Islam religion.

I will venture to say the reason for President Obama's trip to Turkey was as he has previously stated, to reboot our relations with the Muslim nation, but is it the kind of rebooting that we want with the Nation of Islam? President Obama met with some of the most influential Muslims in the world. And keep in mind that since Obama is the son of a Muslim and the president of the most powerful nation on earth, it is not an unreasonable leap of logic to say that he could be the most influential Muslim on Earth.

When Hillary Clinton made the announcement that President Obama was going to Turkey she didn't come out and say that he was going to attend the Conference, but she did say his trip would coincide with the Second Forum of the United Nations Alliance of Civilization.[32]

Obama did attend the conference. It was veiled as a good-will mission, but without credible reporting by a neutral media source, how will America truly know the context of these talks?

Keep in mind that our banks are in crisis, and that other nations are ready to step in and offer their help. The Islamic countries are the wealthiest people on earth, and that includes the country of Turkey where this conference of Muslim leaders was held. Don't be surprised if President Obama came back from Turkey with an answer to our economy crisis.

The concept of borrowing our way out of debt has never worked for individuals, families, businesses or governments in the past. In fact, it has been a sure-fire recipe for failure. But how much more disastrous can it be to borrow from countries who are committed to our destruction and looking for some leverage in our political process?

How many of our congressmen and senators have chastised Obama for making impulsive decisions that are worsening our economic collapse? The man remains the mystery man who

---

[32] *Telegraph.co.uk* by Tim Shipman in Washington 07 Mar 2009

appears to keep his cool yet takes to task anyone who does not support his ideas. During his presidential campaign the unknown senator wooed our nation into his ideology. Now that he has control of the White House his wooing has become a command of respect while still keeping his cool.

Is he now trying to manipulate our minds into believing that the trip to Turkey was the trip of a promise that he'd made during his presidential campaign, rather than to receive training to incorporate the Muslim Shari'a Law into our judicial system. He moves about with an almost eerie ease and confident grace, regardless of his situation. When caught in a lie or contradiction, it seems as though he believes he can counter anything simply by the flash of his charm. Sort of reminiscent of another recent slick Democratic president, wouldn't you say?

According to his book, Obama learned at an early age to disguise his thoughts and moods. He writes about a Muslim man by the name of Malik who played basketball with him in Hawaii now and then. Thirty-plus years later when Obama writes this book, he remembered the man's name, that he was a Muslim and that the conversation revolved around Malcolm X.

There must have been a myriad of incidences in his life to write about, but he chose to bring up the Black Muslim, Malcolm X, as an important part of his life. He also recalled that he lost his temper with his friend, Ray, because Ray laughed at a remark that was made about Malcolm X. It was at that point, according to Obama's book, that he learned to disguise his feverish moods. Barack Obama - *Dreams from My Father* page 86-87:

"Ray and I happened to strike up a conversation with a tall, gaunt man named Malik who played with us now and again. Malik mentioned that he was a follower of the Nation of Islam but that since Malcolm had died and he had moved to Hawaii he no longer went to mosque or political meetings, although he still sought comfort in solitary prayer. One of the guys sitting nearby must have overheard us, for he leaned over with a sagacious expression on his face. "You all talking about Malcolm, huh? Malcolm tells it like it is, no doubt about it."

"Yeah," another guy said. "But I tell you what – you won't see me moving to no African jungle anytime soon. Or some @@@@@@[33] desert somewhere, sitting on a carpet with a bunch of Arabs. No sir. @@@@@@@@@@'[34] I noticed Ray laughing and looked at him sternly. "What are you laughing at?" I said to him. "You've never read Malcolm. You don't even know what he says." I decided to keep my own counsel after that, learning to disguise my feverish mood."

Speaking of Obama's feverish moods, I would like to ask the reader to think back to the expression on President Obama's face during some of his speeches or Q&A sessions during his presidential campaign, especially when he was defending Reverend Jeremiah Wright. He was definitely trying to disguise his *feverish* mood as in previous times during his race for the White House.

Rather than recognize Reverend Wright for the America hater that he is, Obama seemed to be angry with American citizens who were defending America, a people who saw right through Reverend Wright sermons against the United States. Obama definitely did not keep his "cool" when the media questioned him about Rev. Wright. I watched the episode on *Fox 2 News*. He was very belligerent towards the reporters, but quickly changed his tone when he realized what he had done.

Let's get back to when Obama adamantly defended Malcolm X. His friend, Ray, had just made a snide remark about Malcolm X. Malcolm X hated America and believed that the only redeemed Americans would be a follower of Islam. Realize as you read the following excerpt that this is the man that President Obama admires. Malcolm X may be dead, but his daughter is evidently in Obama's life. She was scheduled to write an article about him in the Muslim magazine **élan**.[35] George Breitman - *Malcolm X Speaks* page 59-61:

[33] @ Omitted God's Name being used profanely
[34] @ Omitted filthy language
[35] Bob Unruh of *WorldNetDaily January 09, 2009*

"Last night I made my seven circuits around the Kaaba, led by a young Mutawif named Muhammad. I drank water from the well of Zem Zem, and then ran back and forth seven times between the hills of Mt. Al-Safa and Al-Marwah. There were tens of thousands of pilgrims from all over the world. They were of all colors, from blue-eyed blonds to black-skinned Africans, but were all participating in the same ritual, displaying a spirit of unity and brotherhood that my experiences in America had led me to believe could never exist between the white and non-white. America needs to understand Islam, because this is the one religion that erases the race problem from its society. Throughout my travels in the Muslim world, I have met, talked to, and even eaten with, people who would have been considered 'white' in America, but the religion of Islam in their hearts has removed the 'white' from their minds. They practice sincere and true brotherhood with other people irrespective of their color"

He goes on to say, *"True Islam removes racism, because people of all colors and races who accept its religious principles and bow down to the one god, Allah, also automatically accept each other as brothers and sisters, regardless of differences in complexion. Each place I have visited, they have insisted that I don't leave. Thus I have been forced to stay longer than I originally intended in each country. In the Muslim world they love me once they learned I was an American Muslim, and here in Africa they love me as soon as they learn that I am Malcolm X of the militant American Muslims. Africans in general and Muslims in particular love militancy. There is nothing in our book, the Koran, that teaches us to suffer peacefully. Our religion teaches us to be intelligent. Be peaceful, be courteous, obey the law, respect everyone; but if someone puts his hand on you, send him to the cemetery. That's a good religion."*

Obama had been searching for his identity because of his mixed blood. Evidently he could not determine which ethnic group he should follow. Malcolm X determined he could solve the race problem through Islam. Is that Obama's goal today, to bring everyone under Islam? That religion calls for *all* people to bow down to the *one god, Allah.* Malcolm also said, *"Africans in general and Muslims in particular love militancy."* We saw earlier in this book where Obama's Muslim father's African Luo tribe demonstrated that militancy. There *should be* a fear that one day President Obama will not disguise his feverish moods. I am not saying that Obama, himself, will turn violent against us, but we do need to remember that Malcolm X's goal was to bring the whole world to the religion of Islam..... with violence if necessary. And Obama, our President, has defended this radical man, thereby illustrating that he shares the same values, (or lack of), and hatred as Malcom X.

You might say, "But Malcolm X is dead. We don't have to worry about Obama seeking *his* counsel." And you would be absolutely right, except that Malcom X's words and ideology live on in written form for future haters to emulate.

And keep in mind that the Muslim, Louis Farrakhan, hater and Leader of The Nation of Islam is very much alive and active in our country today. He is a friend and associate of Rev. Jeremiah Wright and his Nation of Islam headquarters is in Chicago where Obama lived and did his community work; and the man has openly praised Obama and has called him the Messiah.[36]

---

[36] Farrakhan called Obama Messiah – taken from *WorldNetDaily* posted October 09, 2008

CHAPTER FIVE

President Obama learned to bring into play people and opportunities that very well could have helped him achieve his agenda.

This is Osama bin Laden's *"Letter to America"* posted on *guardian.co.uk website posted on 24 November 2002.* The letter was originally broadcast in Arabic, but the letter has been picked up by several U.S. networks.

Bin Laden is giving a warning to the American people. The letter was very lengthy, so given the length of the letter I will quote a section where he warns America what is going to happen to us through the Islamic world:

"If the Americans refuse to listen to our advice and the goodness, guidance and righteousness that we call them to, then be aware that you will lose this Crusade Bush began, just like the other previous Crusades in which you were humiliated by the hands of the Mujahideen, fleeing to your home in great silence and disgrace. If the Americans do not respond, then their fate will be that of the Soviets who fled from Afghanistan to deal with their military defeat, political breakup, ideological downfall, and economic bankruptcy."

Osama bin Laden is giving us an example of what happened to the Soviets. Now I don't know the history of what happened between the Soviets and Islam, but nevertheless Osama is saying that we, America, will experience economic bankruptcy. Does that sound familiar? What is happening right now in the United States? We are just about bankrupt. And who has put us there? President Obama has managed to get approved one of the biggest stimulus packages the United States has ever seen, and he has some Democrats and some Republicans alike scurrying to figure out what it is all about.

Allow me to tell you what I suspect is happening! And it is the purpose for writing this book. Most people are still considering the "political" aspect of this phenomenon. Citizens of the United States are not seeing that we are headed right into the direction of socialism with Islam the ruling entity. Osama bin Laden gave us a warning in 2002. Yet, Barack Obama had the audacity to tell the world in his second book *The Audacity of Hope* written in 2006 that the country he was raised in (Indonesia) had a higher opinion of Osama bin Laden than they did President Bush. There are other countries (Arab countries) that had a higher opinion of Osama bin Laden than they did President Bush, like most of the Arab nations? Why did Obama choose to bring it to the world's attention that Indonesia, a Muslim country and his home at one point in his life, endorsed Osama bin Laden?

The whole world must know that Osama bin Laden, a Muslim, was the mastermind of terrorist attacks on the United States September 11, 2002 when the Twin Towers were taken down; he remains the most wanted terrorist in the world! The only difference between Osama bin Laden and Malcolm X's agenda was that bin Laden was trying to convert America to Islam by threats from outside our boarders; Malcolm X was a citizen of the United States and exercised his freedom of speech to lead strong protests and incite violence against America for the sake of Islam from within our borders.

The majority of Americans know from reading newspapers and watching television that Obama has close relationships with Muslims in the United States, such as Louis Farrakhan the Leader of Islam who endorsed him. Does the majority of our country know anything about Louis Farrakhan? Probably not!

So during your reading of this book you may find that I have repeated a phrase or excerpt with reference to Louis Farrakhan. This of course will be to reinforce what I am trying to convey. And at times I may sound political, but keep in mind that this book is being written to warn our nation about Islam, and that *today* Islam is pursuing a political agenda in our country.....a first step to take-over.

Whether Obama denies being Muslim or not is beside the point. We can't ignore the fact that his association with Muslims brings a weighty cause for concern that *he is* a Muslim. Obama appears to ignore questions asked about Louis Farrakhan, but the following article certainly draws a lot of skepticism about that relationship. Kenneth R. Timmerman - *Newsmax.com* November 1, 2008:

"A former top deputy to Nation of Islam leader Louis Farrakhan tells Newsmax that Barack Obama's ties to the black nationalist movement in Chicago run deep, and that for many years the two men have had 'an open line between them to discuss policy and strategy, either directly or through intermediaries.' He goes on to say, 'Remember that for years, if you were a politician in Chicago, you had to have some type of relationship with Louis Farrakhan. You had to. If you didn't, you would be ostracized out of black Chicago,' said Dr. Vibert White Jr., who spent most of his adult life as a member and ultimately top officer of the Nation of Islam."

Is there a legitimate concern here about Obama being involved with the Leader of the Nation of Islam? There is too much evidence of Obama's association with Muslims to ignore these warnings. In the following excerpt, Farrakhan tells us that judgment will come first in America. Farrakhan is talking about Islam's takeover. George W. Braswell, Jr. - *What You Need to Know About Islam & Muslims* pages 66-67:

"Elijah Muhammad brought a central belief that blacks were the first of creation, that whites were devils, and that the black race was to gain its rightful leadership when God destroys the white race. He preached that Christianity was the white man's religion. Farrakhan vowed to continue the tradition of Elijah Muhammad in the Nation of Islam. Farrakhan's brand of Islam continued the major tenets of his mentor Elijah Muhammad, which include the following: There is one God, Allah. The Qur'an and the truth of the Bible are to be believed, though the present Bible is corrupt and must be

reinterpreted. Allah's prophets and their scriptures must be accepted. The judgment of Allah will take place first in America."

The following excerpt is taken from Louis Farrakhan's book, *Prophet of Rage* page Xvii:

"Farrakhan has always had outsized assumptions about himself, and now, with Garvey and Muhammad long gone and the African-American community in disarray and distress, he speaks truths, he is allied with the power of God, he can redeem his people and lead them to the Promised Land through his Nation of Islam, the conduit for respect and esteem. In 1982, Farrakhan may have said, with a half-smile, alluding to the Nation of Islam's trademark fashion statement, 'We are not a bow-tie-cult,' but the NOI's bow tie confers status, power, authority, and civility on a community hungry for all four."

President Obama should be familiar with the Nation of Islam's "bow tie" status of power. In *Dreams from My Father* he described Farrakhan's men dressed in suits and bow ties standing on a street corner in Chicago.[37] Our country experienced Obama's show of power when he managed to manipulate our country into voting for him with a promise of "change" as his platform, but never really telling us what that "change" was going to be. He has the power to deceive people.

To those who have read Obama's first book, Obama will appear to be a boy who simply comes from a dysfunctional family and blames the world for his misfortune. But researching deeper into the book it seems to be more of a power struggle than a search for identity. I do believe that President Obama needs power, and you can be sure that we will see more and more power exercised as he *"demands"* that we be different. In a newspaper article his wife, Michelle, was quoted as saying, *"The change Barack is talking about is hard,"* she insists, *"so don't get too excited, because Barack is going to demand that you, too, be different."* [38]

---

[37] *Dreams from My Father* page 201
[38] Jonah Goldberg,- *St. Louis Post Dispatch* Monday June 9, 2008

That word *"different"* should scare anyone who knows about Obama's Muslim background. I doubt that the change he is going to demand of us is going to be strictly *"political"*. Our country has experienced some of the most difficult changes in our history, but we have always managed to overcome those obstacles. The *"changes"* or *"obstacles"* in our country have not been anything *"different"* just difficult. So what did Michelle mean by that statement? It scared me a little, too, when Obama was asked what sin is and he answered, *"Being out of alignment with my values."*[39] What did he mean by *"my"* values? When the words *"sin"* and *"values"* are used in a narrative it usually refers to religion. He just about equated himself to a messiah. Didn't Louis Farrakhan call him a messiah to the Muslims? *Will we be different? Will we be a Muslim country with Obama as our messiah?*

Read the following excerpt taken from his book and decide for yourself whether he meant *"political"* values or *"religious"* values. He appears to be bragging about bluffing his way around questions his college classmates asked. Notice that, even as a college student, he used the word *"change"* to get around what he couldn't do. Barack Obama - *Dreams from My Father* page 133:

"When classmates in college asked me just what it was that a community organizer did, I couldn't answer them directly. Instead, I'd pronounce on the need for change. Change in the White House, where Reagan and his minions were carrying on their dirty deeds. Change in the Congress, compliant and corrupt. Change in the mood of the country, manic and self-absorbed. Change won't come from the top, I would say. Change will come from a mobilized grass roots."

What about the *"mobilized grass roots"* Obama mentioned in his book? If you can't guess, I will tell you that Malcolm X has a chapter about *"Grass Roots"* on page three of his book, *Malcolm X Speaks*. Did Obama copycat Malcolm X, the man he admires? And did President Obama use the same word

---

[39] Jonah Goldberg,- *St. Louis Post Dispatch* Monday June 9, 2008

"change" as a strategy to fool the United States as he did his college classmates? Did he "hoodwink" the United States citizens into voting him into the presidential office by simply promising a *"change"*?

Evidently, according to his book, in his college days he had plans to become a community organizer, but didn't appear to be interested enough in politics to have answers for his college classmates. So, if he was not interested in politics in his college days, could the *[change]* he talked about in his presidential campaign have been an avenue to change the religious freedom we have in our country today?

Many Christians are concerned that President Obama is on his way to making a decision to do away with "faith based" programs as we know them. It would mean that we can continue to do "good" to help people, but we can't use a particular religion as an avenue to help people. That would be devastating for Christians who are reaching out with the Gospel of Jesus Christ to try and help people understand that peace comes only with a personal relationship with Jesus Christ.

The changes are coming! Just six weeks into his administration he made one of the most disastrous decisions ever made in the history of our country. He managed to pass a $787 billion stimulus package, seemingly to restructure the entire Country to his way of thinking, heading us into bedlam. Was this what his wife Michelle meant when she said that Obama would *"'demand' that we, too, be 'different'"*? Is this going to be the *"change"* he promised. How will the United States be restructured after two hundred-plus years of growing into one of most prosperous nations in the world; one of the most powerful militarily nation in the world, and a nation known as one of the most powerful Christian nations in the world. We have it all because we, as a free nation under God's hand, worked hard to become the most powerful country in the world. The restructuring that President Obama has done thus far is heading us right into socialism. Is President Obama trying to destroy our nation as we know it because he hates the United States? While on a talk show this week he was laughing during the entire serious Q&A segment of the show. Even the talk show host stopped and looked at him and asked, "Why are you laughing!? You are laughing, why?" He was sitting back in his chair as if laughing at our country because he is in control!

Let's revisit "restructuring" of our country. How many Americans, knowingly, would have given up their freedom to pull the entire world together as one if they knew it would mean a complete restructuring of our country and of our values? Obama wasn't telling us the truth about what the *"change"* would be. We had a chance to stop him....but we didn't! He caught us off guard with his charisma. Look how quickly he is acting out his idea for *"change."* His change, if he continues making decision such as he has made in the first weeks of his administration, will destroy our country as we know it.

He tried to silently sign a bill that would continue to kill innocent babies. The following story comes from the same *Media Research Center* Volume 16 issue:

"'Brutal Pro-Lifers – After President Obama quietly reversed a policy launched by President Reagan to prevent taxpayer money from going to groups overseas that provide abortions – the Mexico City Policy – CBS and NBC barely mentioned the news on Jan. 23 while ABC totally ignored it. Then, apparently to make up for its negligence, ABC aired a segment on Jan. 25 highlighting the 'brutal' reaction of conservatives to Obama's action."

Doesn't it sound like some media are controlled by President Obama's Administration? I believe so! The closing of the terrorist prison camp Guantanamo is another quick action he took. It hasn't been closed yet, but the bill to close it has been signed. The question everyone is asking, "Where are those terrorist who terrorized our country going?" It's rumored that President Obama will bring some to prisons in the United States and release others *into* the United States. Do you get the drift of what I am trying to convey in this book? With all of this quick decision making it appears that he has a scheduled agenda with a deadline. Whether by accident of design this man is doing everything he can to destroy our country!

Maybe you think I am overreacting about President Obama's agenda, but we have to remember that Obama's world has intermingled with his Muslim father's world in Africa; a Muslim stepfather's world in Indonesia; Malcolm X's world through his autobiography and Louis Farrakhan who said, *"Judgment will start in America."*[40] These are just a few prominent Muslims mentioned in this book who have life-threatening ideas for our country.

As a Christian and a concerned citizen of the United States, I can't see that I have a choice but to present, with all the evidence that points to Obama being a Muslim, the facts that I have uncovered about the Muslim movement in our country and Obama's association with Muslims who have voiced that *"Allah's judgment will begin in America."* You may ask, "If the Almighty God of Christianity is not the Muslim's god, then who is their god?"

I will answer that legitimate question below and in other chapters of the book:

Muslims' prayers of worship are directed towards a 50-foot cubic structure of stone and marble called Kaaba, the house of Allah [where their false invisible god lives]. It is positioned in Mecca [Saudi Arabia]. At one time the Muslims claimed the Kaaba contains 360 gods – one for each of the lunar calendar days. Their sacred black stone is a meteorite of ancient origin and is the cornerstone of the Kaaba. Muslims believe it has the power to protect them. The Scripture below from the Holy Bible's warns about these false gods:

The Holy Bible – Exodus 20:3-5 – *"You shall have no other gods before me." "You shall not make for yourself a carved* image-any likeness of anything that is in Heaven above, or that is in the earth beneath, or that is in the water under the earth; you shall not bow down to them nor serve them. For I, the LORD your God, am a jealous God, visiting the iniquity of the fathers upon the children to the third and fourth generations of those who hate Me." NKJV

---

[40] Quote from: *What You Need to Know About Islam & Muslims* page 67

Obama was not raised in Saudi Arabia where the sacred Kaaba stands, but he was raised in a country where Muslims prayed eastwardly toward Mecca. Throughout his books Obama expounds either on his life in Indonesia as a child, or on Indonesia itself as a country. It's a country of 237 million Muslims, a country with Muslims who hate Christians and the United States; yet, in his book, *The Audacity of Hope,* published in 2006, Obama still expressed his desire to return to Indonesia with his wife and daughters to share with them his life experience while living in that Muslim country. Barack Obama - *The Audacity of Hope* page 278-279:

"In 2002, an explosion in a Bali nightclub killed more than two hundred people; similar suicide bombings followed in Jakarta in 2004 and Bali in 2005." "It was on a beach just a few miles from the site of those bombings that I stayed the last time I visited Bali. When I think of that island, and all of Indonesia, I'm haunted by memories – the feel of packed mud under bare feet as I wander through paddy fields; the sight of day breaking behind volcanic peaks; the muezzins's call at night and the smell of wood smoke; the dickering at the fruit stands alongside the road; the frenzied sound of a gamelan orchestra, the musicians' faces lit by fire. I would like to take Michelle and the girls to share that piece of my life, to climb the thousand-year-old Hindu ruins of Prambanan or swim in a river high in Blinese hills."

Obama recalls the bombing of Jakarta in 2004 and Bali in 2005. Again, Obama is very vague in his books about dates. We don't know if he was in Jakarta *before* the bombings or *after* the bombings. Either way it appears that Obama has visited Indonesia. And why is he haunted by memories of the muezzins and the sounds of a gamelan. [A muezzin] is a male Muslim crier who calls Muslims to prayer five times a day. A [gamelan] is a Javanese instrument resembling the xylophone; a flute string of Southeast Asia in Muslim country. [Javanese] is a member of an Indonesian people inhabiting the Island of Java which is 90% Muslim. Obama seems to remember clearly the musicians' faces lit by fire, and refers ardently to the thousand-year-old Hindu ruins of Prambanan.

For someone who claims to have lived in Indonesia for only a few years, his focus on Indonesia in his two books gives the impression that the *supposedly* few years he lived there were extended years; perhaps trips made during the twenty-year period his mother returned to Indonesia. He writes in his book as though his heart is in Indonesia. He, himself, said he is haunted by memories of that country. Indonesia must have made a tremendous impact on his life because in 2006 he wrote that he was haunted by those memories and had a desire to return to the country.

Something about Indonesia seems to draw Obama's attention and memories back to his childhood there. Was it the life he lived with his stepfather? Did his love for his stepfather outweigh his love for his real father? His book *Dreams from My Father* appears to have been written in memory of his real father, but a statement he made in the book leads to a different view. Barack Obama – *Dreams from My Father* page 278:

"That was one of the lessons I'd learned these past two and a half years, wasn't it? – that most black folks weren't like the father of my dreams, the man in my mother's stories, full of high-blown ideals and quick to pass judgment. They were more like my stepfather, Lolo, practical people who knew life was too hard to judge each other's choices, too messy to live according to abstract ideals."

Where are Obama's dreams coming from? He called his father's life *"full of high-blown ideals,"* and esteemed his Muslim stepfather who mentored him through the formative years of his life. He called his stepfather's people *those practical* people." Those *practical* people were Muslims in Indonesia.

Obama appeared to have sought out people in Chicago who would accept his background. While visiting different churches in Chicago trying to find a church to back his ideas, he evidently found people who acknowledged Muslims. Barack Obama - *Dreams from My Father* page 279:

"Whenever I first reached them on the phone, they would often be suspicious or evasive, uncertain as to why this Muslim – or worse yet, this Irishman, Obama – wanted a few minutes of their time. And a handful I met with conformed to the prototype found in Richard Wright novels or Malcolm X speeches." "For the most part, though, once I'd had a chance to meet these men face-to-face, I would come away impressed. As a group, they turned out to be thoughtful, hardworking men, with a confidence, a certainty of purpose, that made them by far the best organizers in the neighborhood."

Did you catch Obama's own words in the above quote, *"….uncertain as to why this **Muslim**….."* Did you also notice that he did not deny that he was Muslim or that they had misunderstood his faith. He also said *"Whenever I **first** reached them **on the phone** they would often be suspicious or evasive, uncertain as to why this **Muslim**…"* He evidently told them up front that he was a Muslim. How do you know that? you may ask. Because Obama said *"Whenever I **first** reached them on the **phone** they would often be suspicious…."* He also said, *"Once I'd had a chance to meet with these men **face-to-face**…."*

Also notice that the men he met with were conformist to the prototypes found in Richard Wright novels or Malcolm X speeches. We saw that Obama defended Malcolm X on page 84 of the same book; now he is comparing the men he met in Chicago to Malcolm X. He said *some* conformed to Malcolm X's speeches. Malcolm X died in February 1965. Obama was born in 1961, so Obama had to have *read* Malcolm X's book; otherwise, he could not have known that those men conformed to the prototype of Malcolm X's speeches. Malcolm X's book "Malcolm X Speaks" is a *book* of Malcolm's *speeches*. Obama said he came away from the men impressed. Those men who conformed to Malcolm X, according to Obama, turned out to be hard-working men. What were these men who were prototypes found in Malcolm X's speeches working hard toward?

We can see from Obama's history in the news media that he evidently continued to seek out other pastors who would agree with his philosophy. One of the pastors was Reverend Jeremiah Wright, Obama's radical pastor who preached *"God Damn*

America." Obama knew what Reverend Wright stood for from the very beginning of his relationship with him.

Obama wrote this in his book *Dreams from My Father* page 282-283:

> *"I'll try to help you if I can," he said. "But you should know that having us involved in your effort isn't necessarily a feather in your cap." "Why's that?" Reverend Wright shrugged. "Some of my fellow clergy don't appreciate what we're about. They feel like we're too radical. Others, we ain't radical enough."*
> *"He had grown up in Philadelphia, the son of a Baptist minister. He had resisted his father's vocation at first, joining the Marines out of college, dabbling with liquor, Islam and black nationalism in the sixties."*

Obama had learned up front in his first days with Reverend Wright that Wright had *"dabbled in Islam"* and *"Nationalism"*, and that Wright was not apposed to Muslims attending his church. Wright's church was radical by his own admission; still, Obama chose to join that church and spend twenty years listening to Wrights radical preaching. It appears that Obama had found a church to lean on while he moved forward, using Wright's connections for his agenda.

CHAPTER SIX

Being on the mainland appeared to heighten Obama's struggle to find his identity rather than alleviate his anger against the world.

Not only did Obama's pastor dally in Islam, Reverend Wright is a friend of Louis Farrakhan, Nation of Islam Leader.[41] This is what Jerome R. Corsi wrote about the relationship between Wright and Farrakhan: *The Obama Nation* page 190-192:

"In 1984, Wright accompanied Farrakhan to Libya, where they met with Muammar Qaddafi." (Qaddafi is a strong supporter of the Nation of Islam.) "In a speech the previous year Farrakhan had proclaimed, "The Jews don't like Farrakhan, so they call me Hitler. Well, that's a good name. Hitler was a very great man."

Obama's ex-pastor is not only associated with Muslims, he is associated with one who likens himself to Hitler, calling Hitler a great man. I don't want to go into World War II history, but Farrakhan's statement about Hitler would make sense to the Nation of Islam. During Hitler's totalitarian dominance over Germany he befriended and sought counsel from a Nation of Islam leader. Find a good documentary on Hitler's life....it's all there. Howard Gordon put out a good CD that was circulated throughout the United States. It showed segments about Hitler

---

[41] Louis Farrakhan's title - John L. Esposito – *The Oxford History of Islam* page 721

and the Muslim people. The following is a quote from the CD *"Obsession – Radical Islam's War Against the West"* 2008:

"From the mid 1920's – 1936 - Haj Amin al-Husseini, Muslim Grand Mufti of Jerusalem. Hitler tried to win over the Arab people. Hitler revealed to Husseini in secret that his war was to exterminate the Jews – Muslim soldiers fought along with Hitler to annihilate the Jews."

As you can see, Louis Farrakhan probably knew the history of Hitler and the Jews. According to the Muslims Qur'an, the Muslims are commanded to hate the Jews.[42]

How familiar is Obama with Farrakhan? Louis Farrakhan led the Million Man March as a Nation of Islam on Washington D.C. in 1995 making national news. Barack Hussein Obama participated in the march.[43] The Million Man March was a "Black Muslim" event, and Farrakhan was the leader. February 25, 2008, thirteen years later, Farrakhan publicly endorsed Obama for president, telling the crowd of thousands at a Nation of Islam annual convention in Chicago, *"We are witnessing the phenomenal rise of a man of color in a country that has persecuted us because of color."*[44]

Why would Farrakhan praise Obama? Maybe it was because he had read Obama's book. In his first book Obama spoke in awe of Louis Farrakhan and Farrakhan's Nation newspaper *Final Call* in his 1995 book *Dreams from My Father* page 200-201:

"Among the handful of groups to hoist the nationalist banner, only the Nation of Islam had any significant following: Minister Farrakhan's sharply cadenced sermons generally drew a packed house, and still more listened to his radio broadcasts. But the Nation's active membership in Chicago was considerably smaller – several thousand, perhaps, roughly the size of one of Chicago's biggest black congregations – a base that was rarely, if ever, mobilized around political races or in

[42] Hate the Jews - *The Holy Qur'an* 5:51
[43] *The Obama Nation* page 189
[44] Farrakhan - Margaret Ramirez – *Chicago Tribune* February 25, 2008

support of broad-based programs. In fact, the physical presence of the Nation in the neighborhoods was nominal, restricted mainly to the clean-cut men in suits and bow ties who stood at the intersection of major thoroughfares selling the Nation's newspaper, The Final Call. I would occasionally pick up the paper from these unfailingly polite men, in part out of sympathy to their heavy suits in the summer, their thin coats in the winter; or sometimes because my attention was caught by the sensational, tabloid-style headlines (CAUCASIAN WOMAN ADMITS: WHITES ARE THE DEVIL). Inside the front cover, one found reprints of the minister's speeches, as well as stories that could have been picked straight off the AP news wire were it not for certain editorial embellishments."

Obama did his community work in Chicago, where Farrakhan's mansion and the headquarters of Islam is located. It's ironic how eloquently he describes Farrakhan's men and his newspaper *"The Final Call."* And why did the tabloid headline *"Caucasian Woman Admits Whites Are the Devil"* catch his eye? He called the tabloid depiction of white people as devils *"sensational"*.

Obama has certainly given us food for thought about his search for Muslim associates during his lifetime. Was it a coincidence that he chose to move into a neighborhood where Farrakhan lives; someone who is very influential in the Islamic world? We also learned through media that Obama's supporters in Chicago include a white priest, Father Pfleger, who has links to Louis Farrakhan. This same Father Pfleger allowed Farrakhan to speak from his pulpit. Father Pfleger is also the same radical priest whom Reverend Wright, Obama's pastor, invited to preach from his pulpit. Most of us know from watching Father Pfleger's sermon on national television that it was a hate sermon against the United States.

Obama does not say much about his being in L.A., so we go to New York where he has just arrived and seeks out an illegal immigrant Muslim friend. Barack Obama - *Dreams from My Father* page 113 -118 & 120:

*"I knew one person in New York, a guy named Sadik whom I'd met in L.A." "He greeted me on the street, a short, well-built [**Pakistani**] who had come to New York from London two years earlier and found his caustic wit and unabashed desire to make money perfectly pitched to the city's mood. He had overstayed his tourist visa and now made a living in New York's high-turnover, <u>illegal immigrant</u> workforce, waiting on tables."*
"When Sadik lost his own lease, we moved in together. And after a few months of closer scrutiny, he began to realize that the city had indeed had an effect on me."

Obama had met this Muslim friend first in L.A. and then looked him up in New York. Why did Obama *choose* to move in with a Pakistani whose country is 86% to 100% Muslim and is known to be training terrorists to send out into the world? There are two things here that *should concern America*. One is that Obama *chose* to move in with an illegal Pakistani; second, he did not feel obligated to report someone who might be in the United States illegally for terrorist activity. Obama admits to rooming with the Pakistani for months. I have not heard anything through the media about Obama's connection with a *Sadik*. That leads me to wonder just where that illegal Pakistani is now, and if Obama was influenced by another Muslim.

Here again, Obama's interest focused on someone who identifies with Muslims. He writes about his first days in New York, how he imagined what his life would be like. He imagined that he would stop and hear Jesse Jackson make a speech on 125th. Barack Obama – *Dreams from My Father* page 121:

"I might wander through Harlem – to play on courts I'd once read about or to hear Jesse Jackson make a speech on 125th."

I don't know whether Jesse Jackson is a Muslim or not, but he definitely has ties to the Muslim world. The Oxford History of Islam has an article about the Muslim Political Action Committee hosting Jesse Jackson during his presidential campaign in 1988 raising $700,000 for his campaign. The article below displayed a photograph of Jackson with the

Muslims sitting behind him as he made his speech. John L. Esposito - *The Oxford History of Islam* page 637-638:

"Muslims in the West are increasingly beginning to see the usefulness of participating in interfaith dialogue and political activities that promote common causes. In 1988, for example, the Muslim Political Action Committee hosted the Reverend Jesse Jackson when he ran for President. The Arab American Institute (AAI) was established in 1984 by James Zoghby, who was appointed as national co-chair of the campaign and was able to raise $700,000 for Jackson's campaign. The AAI encourages participation in the political system and is eager to get Arab Americans (either here legally or born in the U.S.) to run for office. The institute establishes Democratic and Republican clubs in various parts of the country. These political action committees have been recognized as representative institutions of the Muslim community. The leadership has been invited to the White House for Islamic celebrations...."

What did the above excerpt say! *"The AAI encourages participation in the political system and is eager to get Arab Americans (either legally here by law or born in the U.S.) to run for office."* And Obama imagined going to hear one of Jackson's speeches! And did you notice, the *leadership* has been invited to the *White House* for Islamic celebrations. Isn't the fact that Muslims are invited to the White House a little daunting knowing that Obama already has connections with Muslims and terrorists? Can you see that the trend was *slowly and quietly set* by Islam for obtaining an audience with Obama in the White House? The above quote was published in 1999. The Muslims have come a long way in the past nine years.

We knew very little about President Obama before he was elected, and we still don't have a clue about the real history of his life in Indonesia and Hawaii, only what he has told us in his books and what the media has picked up on him. How many of our presidents, before President Obama, were elusive about their past? They were open and above board about their personal lives and they had no reservations about allowing their lives to be an open book to the American people. And we unquestionably did not have a president who, in his private life, was so closely associated with Muslims; or one who knowingly appointed a man to United States Attorney General who helped pardon from prison one of the most notorious enemies of the United States. That appointment came quickly suggesting that Obama planned carefully before the election who he would appoint to his staff.

"Will our nation belong to Obama"? Jerome R. Corsi wrote the book, *The Obama Nation.* Recently I saw a blurb on the net that read, *"Obama's nation has begun. Join the Resistance."* How many people agree that Obama is on his way to try and overtake our nation? And it wouldn't make sense that he wants to control it himself. He can't run it alone. And not even our congress, Republican or Democrats, would allow him to have free dictatorship over the United States without a fight. So who would be a logical people-group to hold a vice-like grip on America? You can mark my word…..Islam. Muslims, whose will is to fight their holy war against the United States and Christianity, will be the ones who gladly carry the burden.

I mentioned at the beginning of this book that at times I will repeat facts in this book. The purpose is to bring to light a particular point that I am trying to make. This is one of those revisits.

Jesse Jackson received $700,000 from an Islamic organization whose objective was probably to get a passport into the White House. Of course we know that Jackson lost the primary, but through this information about Jackson, we can see that Islam's tremendous money power exists in the politics of our country. Jackson's run was unsuccessful. Twenty years later, however, Islam has found another avenue of a never-ending struggle to find a way to eventually incorporate their Shari'a Law into our justice system - the first step to take over. I say *never-ending* because Shari'a law means to fight until it has been accomplished.

If we search it out, we will find that Muslims have found another way to infiltrate the United States without having to fight us with jihad the way they have in other countries. From media reports in the past, we know that Muslims have been strategically planted in the United States at a young age or from birth as a citizen to eventually infiltrate our country for the purpose of bringing terrorist attacks against the United States; or, in some cases (as in Detroit Michigan) simply to become part of the political power in our country to advocate the Islamic law. With this in mind we can't rule out the possibility that President Obama was a candidate selected and nurtured through life by Islam right up to the presidential election.

This brings us back to Obama and his Muslim ties. I flipped the channel to *Fox News* one night and came in on the middle of an interview with a man who said that in 1988 he was asked to write a letter of recommendation for a young man to attend Harvard Law School; and that young man turned out to be Barack Hussein Obama. Curious myself about how Obama managed to get to the top so fast, I searched the net to corroborate what the man in the interview had said. I have no problem with students accepting financial support to help him/her achieve a dream; however, I do have a problem with the fact that President Obama, as a student of Harvard, accepted financial help from a Black Muslim, an advisor to the Saudi prince Alwaleed bin Talal.

Kenneth R. Timmerman, *Newsmax.com* Tuesday September 23, 2008 reported the following:

"The allegations first surfaced in late March, when former Manhattan Borough president Percy Sutton told a New York cable channel that a former business partner who was 'raising money' for Obama had approached him in 1988 to help Obama get into Harvard Law School. In the interview, Sutton says he first heard of Obama about twenty years ago from Khalid Al-Mansour, a Black Muslim and Black Nationalist who was a 'mentor' to the founders of the Black Panther party at the time the party was founded in the early 1960s. Sutton described al-Mansour as advisor to 'one of the world's richest men,' Saudi prince Alwaleed bin Talal. As Sutton remembered, Al-Mansur was raising money for Obama's education and seeking recommendations for him to attend Harvard Law School. I was introduced to (Obama) by a friend who was raising money for

him," Sutton told NY city hall reporter, Dominic Carter. *"The friend's name is Dr. Khalid al-Mansour, from Texas."*

Timmerman goes on to say, *"Where did he find the money? Did it come from friends of Khalid Al Mansour? And why would a radical Muslim activist with ties to the Saudi royal family raise money for Barack Obama?"*

Most of us have listened to Obama's speeches. The man has a Harvard degree, but is he Harvard educated? His rhetoric is elegant, but his words seem to say nothing. Did Obama "slide" through Harvard Law School with the backing of a Muslim activist with ties to Saudi? Was Obama set up for a purpose? And wasn't there somewhat of a controversy about President Obama's place of birth and even being eligible to be the president of the United States? Yes there was! This was posted on *WorldNetDaily* by Bob Unruh on November 20, 2008:

"Former presidential candidate Alan Keyes and others filed a court petition in California asking the secretary of state to refuse to allow the state's 55 Electoral College votes to be cast in the 2008 presidential election until Obama verifies his eligibility to hold the office."

It has been rumored that the efforts to pin Obama down as to his eligibility to hold the office were halted by Obama's presidential influence. This allegation has just recently surfaced again and supposedly has Obama's attorneys scurrying to put a halt to the rumor that an organization called Americans for Freedom of Information has released copies of President Obama's college transcripts from Occidental College showing that received financial aid as a foreign student.

This article was pulled from Fourwinds10.com (AFPN) May 4, 2009: AP- WASHINGTON D.C. – *"In a move certain to fuel the debate over Obama's qualifications for the presidency, the group "Americans for Freedom of Information" has released copies of President Obama's college transcripts from Occidental College. Released today, the transcript indicates that Obama, under the name Barry Soetoro, received financial aid as a foreign student from Indonesia as an undergraduate at the school. The transcript was released by Occidental College in compliance with a court order in a suit brought by the group in the Superior Court of California. The transcript shows that Obama (Soetoro) applied for financial aid and was awarded a fellowship for foreign students from the Fulbright Foundation Scholarship program. To qualify, for the scholarship, a student must claim foreign citizenship. This document would seem to provide the smoking gun that many of Obama's detractors have been seeking."*

Whether the above article is correct or not, we do have to give credence to the fact that, according to Aaron Klein © 2009 WorldNetDaily Posted: March 08, 2009, the *"Wikipedia, the online "free encyclopedia" has been deleting anything that comes on their website about Obama's eligibility to be president. Aaron Klein: "Wikipedia, the online "free encyclopedia" mega-site written and edited entirely by its users, has been deleting within minutes any mention of eligibility issues surrounding Barack Obama's presidency, with administrators kicking off anyone who writes about the subject, WND has learned."*

If the *"Americans for Freedom of Information"* is correct and President Obama is not eligible to be president, was Obama's college preparation just another stepping stone for the Islamic world to get their foot into the White House? Howard Gordon's CD *"Obsession – Radical Islam's War Against the West"* 2008 had an alarming segment about how Islam plans to take over the White House. The following was an interview with Dr. Ahmad Dwidar, Muslim Cleric. The interviewer's name was given:

Dr. Dwidar – *"In 1995 I heard some sermons saying that Muslims should march on the White House from some of the mosques."*

Interviewer – *"What do you mean march on the White House?"*

Dr. Dwidar – *"One cleric said in his sermon, we are going to the White House, so that Islam will be victorious – Allah willing - and the White House will become a Muslim House."*

Interviewer – *"Are they going to occupy the White House—or what?"*

Dr. Dwidar – *"No. They say that through the domination of Islam and its ideas the White House will be changed."*

Was there a motive behind the Islamic world financing Obama's education at one of the most elite schools in the United States? Did Obama feel honored to be a part of a high-status university? Or was it simply a prelude to the presidency, to get into a position to advance the Muslim religion. Wasn't that what Dr. Ahmad Dwidar, the Muslim cleric, boasted about to the interviewer in the *Obsession* CD? He said that *[through the domination of Islam]* and its ideas the White House will be changed. Can we surmise from the following excerpt from Obama's book that he wasn't particularly interested in what Harvard Law School had to offer, that it was possibly a springboard to the White House?

This is Obama's sentiment of a school that gave him a prestigious honor. Most people think of Harvard as a scholarly school. The following is Obama's opinion of Harvard Law School's curriculum. He is speaking of his election as the first black president of the *Harvard Law Review*, a legal periodical. Barack Obama - *Dreams from My Father* page Xiii:

"A burst of publicity followed that election, including several newspaper articles that testified less to my modest accomplishments than to Harvard Law School's peculiar place in the American mythology..."

We might miss Obama's phraseology here. Does Obama know the difference between *mythology* and the *real* world? Let's see what Obama's credentials are for passing judgment. What does he actually know about American history? Let me quote what he said in his book. Barack Obama - *The Audacity of Hope* page 8:

"Even the standard high school history textbook notes the degree to which, from its very inception, the reality of American life has strayed from its myths."

The reality of American life has strayed from its "myths!" Is he telling us that American history is a fable that we have forgotten; a fairy tale; a saga; a parable; an allegory; a falsehood; is fiction; is an illusion; was an invention; is a fabrication; is an untruth? All of the above are definitions of the word "myth." His innermost concept of American history seems to be *mythology*. Does he really understand what he is saying? Is he comparing our history with what he was taught in Indonesia? Multiple mythical-type religions, a philosophy that his mother thought he should experience?

Where did Obama get his American education while in Indonesia? From U.S. correspondence courses. Barack Obama - *Dreams from My Father* page 47:

"Without the money to send me to the International School, where most of Djakarta's foreign children went, she had arranged from the moment of our arrival to supplement my Indonesian schooling with lessons from a U.S. correspondence course."

He said he was taught through U.S. correspondence courses, but where did his Muslim education come from? Did it come from a Muslim stepfather who took him to mosque,[45] and a Muslim school in Indonesia where they also teach the mythical concept of their religion? Did the Muslim school teach him about American history? According to the following article, Muslim students receive a solid education about killing Americans, the infidels. Ted Sampley – *The U.S. Veteran Dispatch* June 13, 2008 wrote this in his column:

"Almost from birth, Muslim children are taught to hate Christians and Jews – to glorify 'jihad' (holy war) and to embrace violence, death and child martyrdom. In their schools and mosques, young Muslim's are taught songs about wanting

---

[45] Obama (aka Barry) at mosque - Jerome Corsi -*The Obama Nation* page 56

to become 'suicide warriors' and taking up guns and bombs to kill non-believers. Such indoctrination is an essential part of Islamic prescribed destiny which is to destroy all non-Muslims (infidels) and thereby achieve their Quranic vision of one world under Islam."

The U.S. Veteran Dispatch is not the only source who publishes stories about Muslim children being taught to hate Americans. I encourage you to pull up *Haaretz.com/Channel 10* on the net. Haaretz shows live footage of kids in a Gaza summer camp being taught to hate the Americans and Jews and to kill us. This was posted by - Haaretz Staff and Channel 10 January 9, 2009:

"The educational activities provided to children on a Hamas paramilitary camp in Gaza are probably unlike those of any other summer schemes in the world. The camp is aimed at indoctrinating the children to hate Israel and the United States, as well as to take pride in Hamas, the Palestinian militant group that controls the Gaza Strip. While Israel and Hamas maintain a fragile cease-fire in the coastal territory, the camp teaches the children to strive towards being militants and continue the conflict."

Watching the Haaretz video and seeing how easily young people are influenced brought to mind an article that was posted on *WorldNetDaily* about Obama's uncanny ability to attract the youth of our country. The article shows Louis Farrakhan speaking from a podium giving a strong speech about the youth that Obama was attracting. He was congratulating Obama's ability to draw such a crowd. John Under - *WorldNetDaily* November 07 writes:

"Addressing a large crowd behind a podium Feb. 24 with a Nation of Islam Savior's Day 2008 sign, Farrakhan proclaims, 'You are the instruments that God is going to use to bring about universal change, and that is why Barack has captured the youth. And he has involved young people in a political process that they didn't care anything about. That's a sign, when the

Messiah speaks, the youth will hear, and the Messiah is absolutely speaking.'"

Obama's ability to attract our youth is a daunting thought knowing that the youth of today will be our leaders of tomorrow. And will they be leaders of a Muslim country in a Muslim White House?

If we, as a free nation with Christian values, do not stand up and fight against this apparent on-going idea of President Obama's to bring the Muslim world and the United States together, we are going to lose our county to a foreign nation. The Muslim world has already expressed their idea in the *"Obsession"* CD that we will succumb to their ideology when someone in the White House changes things. And where could Obama find a better source to start Islamizing our country than through our youth? [Is] Obama toying with the minds of our young people, trying to put their thought process into a mindset that [his] way for change is better than our history; that our history is not applicable to our lives today? Is it possible that Obama's remark, about our history books being a myth, is a lead-in to announcing that the history of the world is as Islam sees it? Obama is still drawing our youth to his ideas, some still following the ides that he is the messiah, Jesus Christ returning to earth. Listen to him closely.....our youth and young adults are listening to him!

With this in mind, we need to remember God's warning in the Holy Bible about false teachers coming into the world. As you read the Scripture below, keep in mind that Muslims do not acknowledge Jesus Christ as the Savior and that Obama was raised by a Muslim stepfather in Indonesia. Muslims teach that Jesus was a mere man. Since Obama's stepfather was a Muslim, could we assume that he taught Obama that Jesus was a mere man?

The Holy Bible – 1 John 4:1-3 – "Beloved do not believe every spirit, but test the spirits, whether they are of God; because many false prophets have gone out into the world. By this you know the Spirit of God: Every spirit that confesses that Jesus Christ has come in the flesh is of God, and every spirit that does not confess that Jesus Christ has come in the flesh is not of

God. And this is the spirit of the Antichrist, which you have heard was coming, and is now already in the world." NKJV

Someone who is not knowledgeable of the Holy Bible might misunderstand and think that Obama knows Jesus because he has mentioned His name. There is a difference between *knowing about* Jesus and having a *personal relationship* with Him. The Qur'an does talk about Jesus, but to Muslims He was but a man, not someone in whom they put their trust. Muslims put their trust in their man-made false god, Allah and the false prophet Muhammad in place of Jesus Christ. Therefore, Obama can legitimately claim to know Jesus.

We should warn our young people about Obama's deception. Tell them to *listen* to Obama when he speaks, *watch* his body language and his eyes when they turn darker in anger as he moves about, an anger that he, himself, said he has learned to control. Suggest to them that they read Obama's first book written in 1995 then rewritten in 2004 with a critical eye. They will see that the book itself unveils his true character and reveals his anger. The book will open the eyes of youth who are willing to listen and think logically. In one of the chapters he vents his anger and frustration with life after talking with his Muslim friend, Rafiq. Barack Obama - *Dreams from My Father* page 197:

"Ever since the first time I'd picked up Malcolm X's autobiography, I had tried to untangle the twin strands of black nationalism, arguing that nationalism's affirming message – of solidarity and self-reliance, discipline and communal responsibility – need not depend on hatred of whites any more than it depended on white munificence. We could tell this country where it was wrong, I would tell myself and any black friends who would listen, without ceasing to believe in its capacity for change. In talking to self-professed nationalist like Rafig, though,[46] *I came to see how the blanket indictment of everything white served a central function in their message of uplift; how, psychologically, at least, one depended on the*

---

[46] Underscore for emphasis

other. For when the nationalist spoke of a reawakening of values as the only solution to black poverty, he was expressing an implicit, if not explicit, criticism to black listeners: that we did not have to live as we did."

Perhaps Obama's life would have been less complicated had he not continually sought solace from Malcolm X's writings. The quote below gives us more insight to what Obama would have learned about Malcolm X's philosophy by reading his works. George Breitman -*Malcolm X Speaks* page 4:

"So we're all black people, so-called Negroes, second-class citizens, ex-slaves. You're nothing but an ex-slave. You don't like to be told that. But what else are you? You are ex-slaves. You didn't come here on the 'Mayflower'. You came here on a slave ship. In chains, like a horse, or a cow, or a chicken. And you were brought here by the people who came here on the 'Mayflower'; you were brought here by the so-called Pilgrims, or Founding Fathers. They were the ones who brought you here."

Doesn't Rev. Wright's radical sermons against the United States line up with Malcolm X's philosophy? Even today Obama seems to be attracted to people who have unfounded militant opinions of our country and refuses to alienate himself from them. Obama fervently defended his racist pastor Reverend Jeremiah Wright during a Q&A session aired on television saying that disowning Wright would be like disowning his white grandmother. That critical comment Obama made about his white grandmother grabbed the attention of news media. *WorldNetDaily* posted the speech on their website March 18, 2008. This is what Obama said during his speech while defending Wright:

"I can no more disown him than I can disown the black community. I can no more disown him that I can my white grandmother – a woman who helped raise me, a woman who sacrificed again and again for me, a woman who loves me as much as she loves anything in this world, but a woman who once confessed her fear of black men who passed by her on the

street, and who on more than one occasion has uttered racial or ethnic stereotypes that made me cringe."

Obama's grandmother was still alive when Obama made that statement and, from what media reports say, kept a watchful eye on his speeches. In that speech he clearly expressed a deep affection for his pastor; but if you notice he didn't say *"a grandmother that I love,"* but simply referred to her as a *woman who* and reinforced the fact that she made him *[cringe]*. Does that sound like a grandson who loved his grandmother? Had Obama already distanced himself from his white grandmother? Was Obama rebelling against his white grandmother when he chose his friends? He appears to show scorn towards his grandmother when he writes in his book, *Dreams from My Father* about his grandmother's objection to his mother's relationship with his African (Muslim) father.[47] Later in his book he expressed hate and resentment against white people after asking his friend, Joyce, who was of mixed blood, if she was going to the Black Students' Association meeting, and she informed him that she was not [black]. Barack Obama - *Dreams from My Father* page 99 -101:

"I'm not black," Joyce said. "I'm multiracial." "To avoid being mistaken for a sellout, I chose my friends carefully. The more politically active black students. The foreign students. The Chicanos. The Marxist professors and structural feminists and punk-rock performance poets." "When we ground out our cigarettes in the hallway carpet or set our stereos so loud that the walls began to shake, we were resisting bourgeois society's stifling constraints. We weren't indifferent or careless or insecure. We were alienated." "No, it remained necessary to prove which side you were on, to show your loyalty to the black masses, to strike out and name names."

It appears that, today, Obama is still choosing his friends and associates carefully, but they are not all politically active to show loyalty to the black masses. It appears that he has chosen another group with whom he can identify in their hatred of

---

[47] *Dreams from My Father* page 17-18

whites, Christians and America. The Muslims! Mark Hemingway writes in the *National Review* – May 2008 page 22:

"*'A recent report in the Los Angeles Times detailed Obama's close relationship with Rashid Khalidi, a professor of Arab studies at Columbia University. In the late 1970s Khalidi worked with WAFA, the official news agency of the Palestinian Liberation Organization; during this period, the PLO and its factions engaged in acts of terrorism.' 'In 2003, Obama attended a tribute dinner for Khalidi where, according to the Los Angeles Times, a speaker likened 'Zionist settlers on the West Bank' to Osama bin Laden.'*"

The *National Review* magazine is a popular magazine and a lot of people will see from this article that Obama is associated with a Muslim Rashid Khalidi. But how many people will pick up the magazine *Trumpet?* Obama's Reverend Jeremiah Wright – Racist black pastor where Obama attended church for twenty years – owns the racist magazine. The racist Magazine *Trumpet* featured top Muslim leaders on the front cover page of the magazine. And guess whose picture was featured [with] top Muslim leader Louis Farrakhan; Elijah Muhammad, Nation of Islam and Reverend Wright along with others? It was Obama! The title under the picture was, *"The Legacy Lives on."* Obama also appeared on the cover page of three other issues of the magazine. [48]

Obama's book *Dreams from My Father* was written before Obama's picture appeared on the front cover of Wright's magazine, but in order to realize that a legacy is *"living on"* there had to have been prior action to prove that the legacy is alive. I can't be a judge of what the statement meant, but doesn't Obama's picture being featured with Louis Farrakhan's and Elijah Muhammad on the cover of a racist magazine give strong support that Obama is a closet Muslim? Even if he is not, for someone with as strong political aspirations as Obama has had to allow himself to appear with haters the likes of Farrakhan and Muhammad displays such a lack of foresight and common

---

[48] Stanley Kurtz – Contributor of *National Review*

sense that one has to wonder about the quality of his judgment when faced with the wide range of politically sensitive and potentially catastrophic scenarios that he will face in the oval office.

Obama writes about one of his Muslim friend's concepts of loyalty to his culture. Does the following excerpt from Obama's book suggest that the legacy that lives on is one of holding the Muslim world together? Barack Obama - *Dreams from My Father* page 196-197:

"When the two of us were alone, though, Rafiq and I could sometimes have normal conversations. Over time I arrived at a grudging admiration for his tenacity and bravado, and, within his own terms, a certain sincerity. He confirmed that he had been a gang leader growing up in Altgeld; he had found religion, he said, under the stewardship of a local Muslim leader unaffiliated with Minister Louis Farrakhan's Nation of Islam. "If it hadn't been for Islam, man, I'd probably be dead," he told me one day. "Just had a negative attitude, you understand. Growing up in Altgeld, I'd soaked up all the poison the white man feeds us. See, the folks you're working with got the same problem, even though they don't realize it yet."

Obama's response to Rafiq's reasoning, *"That was the truth as Rafiq saw it, and he didn't waste energy picking that truth apart. His was a Hobbesian world where distrust was a given and loyalties extended from family to mosque to the black race – whereupon notions of loyalty ceased to apply. This narrowing vision, of blood and tribe, had provided him with a clarity of sorts, a means of focusing his attention. Black self-respect had delivered the mayor's seat, he could argue, lust as black self-respect turned around the lives of drug addicts under the tutelage of the Muslims. Progress was within our grasp so long as we didn't betray ourselves."*

Could it conceivably be — based on the excerpt above and Obama's allowing his picture to be featured on the magazine, *Trumpet,* with Louis Farrakhan and Elijah Muhammad, that he is — in his own way — communicating to the Muslim world that his loyalty to them is still strong?

Was the legacy a loyalty that goes from mosque-to-the-black-race? And what did Obama mean by *"Progress was within our grasp so long as we didn't betray ourselves."* Progress under the tutelage of Muslims? As usual, he didn't expound on the meaning behind what he said…another elusive statement. But it sounds as though he found a way to pull people into Islam as long as he and Rafig didn't forget that Islam was the real answer, alluding to his resolve that Malcolm X had found peace in Islam. Obama had said, *"I looked to see where the people would come from who were willing to work toward this future and populate this new world."*

Is the *change* that President Obama is trying to put into place right now a beginning of finding those people to populate the *new* world? Aren't we right back to where the Muslim cleric Dr. Dwidar said the Islamic religion will take over the White House through the domination of Islam and its ideas?

When we listened to Obama's ideas of the huge stimulus package that was suppose to stabilize our economy, did anyone stop to think that he may be intentionally putting our country into a position where we would need to borrow money from other sources? Despite warnings from conservatives and liberals alike that massive borrowing would lead to disaster at a time when we were teetering on the brink anyway, Obama pushed the legislation through.

And to clear the air about the stimulus package, is there anyone who thinks that borrowing money to try to buy your way out of debt is an idea originated by Obama? Every governmental entity, business owner and household head has considered the ramifications of such an unwise venture since man first found the need to manage a budget. This *"change"* is nothing new. History is littered with the remains the failed marriages, businesses, and governments that tried this same approach. And yes, I realize that the stimulus package is to be strategically stitched throughout the fabric of our economic structure to most effectively stimulate commerce and job growth, but on the back side, there is all that money and interest to repay.

And who will administer the dispersal? It will likely be the same people who were foolish enough to undertake such a catastrophic program in the first place. So how can we have any faith that the stimulus will be effective when we can't trust the judgment of the administrators? Then when you factor in the billions in pork-barrel earmarks that the package contains as bribe money to Congressmen and Senators for their pet projects as motivation to vote for the overall package, and the millions that corporations paid out to executives in the form of bonuses, and the fact that there was little or no accountability built into the dispersal which allowed the same corrupt and greedy CEOs who caused the crisis in the first place to remain in office, one has to wonder: what have we done? Have we merely taken on billions in debt only to line the greedy pockets of the already-rich with little or none finding its way into the pockets of the middle and lower working class who needs it most? Forgive my digression. A few deep breaths and I'll be fine.

Who will step in with the money – wealthy Arab countries? Theoretically what happens when two companies merge? The owner who is contributing the most money controls the company. The same concept will apply to the United States if Arab nations step in with financial help. They will control what happens in the United States….and as Dr. Dwidar said, they will take the White House!

Is Obama leading us there now? He is speaking out to us, telling us that we need to bring the Muslim nations into our fold! Follow on with this book, and then you be the judge!

Reader, please hear what I am saying. The Muslims know what they are doing. If they come into our country as immigrants, it is with one thing in mind, and that is to integrate into our society unnoticed. Regardless of how they get here, their religious teaching follows as if they are in Saudi Arabia, Indonesia, Africa or some other foreign nation controlled by Islam. Even if it is by birth, most of them are taught from infancy not to associate with the American infidel (that's us).

Saudi Arabia (where the Islamic sacred black stone "Kaaba" is located) actually has a corporate office in New York City set to monitor the Muslim activity here in this country. Please understand that these people are not migrating to our country to get away from oppressed countries as some immigrants do. They certainly do not need our money. John L. Esposito – *The Oxford History of Islam* page 621:

"Also involved in the process are foreign governments who seek control of the mosques to manage their affairs and to keep their ideologies in conformity to those advocated overseas. Saudi Arabia established a European office of the Muslim World League in Belgium and two offices in North America (in New York and Toronto) in an attempt to supervise the mosque's leadership and its message by recruiting mosques to register as members of the Council of Masajid in Europe or North America."

You might ask, "What does this have to do with President Obama?" We need to wake up to the fact that it has a lot to do with him. Obama has too many Muslim contacts in the United States not to be influenced by this movement. Why would Obama [a lawyer], give up a near-certain Supreme Court clerkship and move to Chicago to do community work? This is what Stanley Kurtz - *National Review* page 24 had to say about Obama's move to Chicago:

"It could be argued that the new and supposedly moderate Obama of 2008 is the real Obama. Unfortunately, that argument is unconvincing. As De Zutter notes, Obama gave up a near-certain Supreme Court clerkship to come to Chicago and do community organizing."

So why would Obama give up a near Supreme Court clerkship to go to Chicago? And why would he seek out Muslims in that city to start his so called community work? Is it possible that Obama already had an agenda for Chicago, knowing that Louis Farrakhan's mansion and the Nation of Islam Headquarters is located in Chicago? Living there would give him prominence and strong support from the Muslim leader.

It looks as if Obama is following Malcolm X's agenda, but Obama learned at an early age that being radical the way Malcolm X was would not get him to where Malcolm was headed, and I suspect that that was to turn the United States into a Muslim country to reconcile whites and blacks.

To see when Obama may have realized that radicalism wasn't the answer to obtaining power, let's go back to his book when his best friend was arrested for drugs and his mother questioned him about his friend's arrest. Barack Obama - *Dreams from My Father* page 94:

"I had tried to explain some of this to my mother once, the role of luck in the world, the spin of the wheel. It was at the start of my senior year in high school; she was back in Hawaii, her field work completed, and one day she had marched into my room, wanting to know the details of Pablo's arrest. I had given her a reassuring smile and patted her hand and told her not to worry, I wouldn't do anything stupid. It was usually an effective tactic, another one of those tricks I had learned: People were satisfied so long as you were courteous and smiled and made no sudden moves."

Taking the excerpt above as gospel, would you surmise that Obama demonstrates that kind of demeanor today? He is courteous and makes no sudden moves. However, if you have watched Malcolm X's radical speeches and Farrakhan's speeches, you can see that Obama has the exact mannerism of both men when he is addressing a crowd. Like Malcolm X, his voice raises, his hands fly and his fingers point; yet, he still has the composure of Louis Farrakhan.

A former deputy to Nation of Islam Leader, Louis Farrakhan, recognized the similarity between Malcolm, Farrakhan and Obama. He tells it all to *NEWSMAX*. Kenneth R. Timmerman – *NEWSMAX* on November 1, 2008:

"Even though Chicago is the third-largest city in the country, within the black community, the political and militant nationalist community is very small. So it wouldn't be uncommon for [Obama and Farrakhan] to show up at events

together, or at least be there and communicate with each other, White told."

Let's go back to where Obama made the statement, *"I looked to see where the people would come from who were willing to work toward this future and populate this new world."*

There are others who are watching people who *want to* populate the new world. The excerpt below is a <u>concern</u> and a <u>warning</u> against that new world. John L. Esposito - *The Oxford History on Islam* page 641:

"What kind of a society will Europe and America become as a consequence of the introduction of the new mix of peoples and cultures who affirm a vibrant religion that they insist transcends borders and supersedes all other claims to truth?"

Yes, Islam claims that *their religion supersedes* all other claims of religion. They are going to fight to win the world to Islam because that is what their Allah (not the true God of Christianity) commands them to do. Conquer the world for Allah even if it means jihad [holy war] in every country.

Farrakhan said Allah's judgment will take place first in America. It's happening now, my friends. The Muslims are silently moving into place, and we need to find out where Obama fits into the picture. Can we piece together the puzzle of Obama's life, a charismatic man raised in a Muslim country that literally came out of nowhere and captivated our entire country, and made an unprecedented rise to the presidency? And he managed to do it all without telling anyone who he really is? Now that he is the President of the United States, however, he is allowing us to see where *some* of those puzzle pieces fit. And it is an ugly puzzle!

Would our country have voted him into the presidential office had we *known early* in his presidential campaign that he had the same name as Saddam Hussein? By the time the secret was out, he had already captivated the people of America with his charm. They could not see beyond his charisma and his promise for *"change."* But he didn't fool the Jewish people.

They apparently, from what the story below tells, were concerned about Obama's run for the presidential office. *St. Louis Post Dispatch* May 24, 2008 after Obama's visit to a synagogue in Florida:

"This week Barack Obama went to a Jewish synagogue in Florida with a promise to Israel. Barack Obama on Thursday promised 'an unshakable commitment to Israel's security' as he sought to reassure doubtful Jewish voters. He also said he hopes to help improve relations between American blacks and Jews."

If that *"unshakable commitment to Israel's security"* was manifest in the form of millions of dollars to Israel's mortal enemy, Hamas, how will his commitment to America manifest itself?

Let me skip down in the article to the Jewish people's response: *"Some Jews fear Obama's willingness to speak with Middle Eastern nations that oppose Israel, while others wonder whether he is a closet Muslim."*

This fear was pre-election. Since Hillary Clinton's visit to the Middle East and Obama's $900 million dollar proposed gift to the Palestinians (includes Gaza and Hamas), Jews worldwide now understand Obama's commitment to the Israel. It is to their total destruction.

Although the article is lengthy, an accurate account of Obama's efforts to contribute to a multi-national effort to funnel funds into Gaza is written by: Sylvie Lanteaume, Sharm el-Sheikh *(ANTARA News/AFP)*.

US Secretary of State Hillary Clinton arrived in Egypt on Sunday for an international donor conference the Palestinians hope will raise billions of dollars to help rebuild war-torn Gaza.

The former first lady is on her first trip to the Middle East as America's top diplomat since US President Barack Obama took office in January pledging a new spirit of global cooperation.

The United States is reportedly mulling a 900-million-dollar aid package to rebuild Gaza, which was devastated by Israel's three-week war against its Hamas rulers in December and January and a continuing blockade.

Clinton will have to respond to the worries of European leaders who want Washington to pressure its top ally Israel to improve aid distribution to the Palestinian enclave.

She said on Friday the aid would depend on how well the Palestinians meet the conditions of the diplomatic Quartet of the United States, the European Union, the United Nations and Russia.

"I will be announcing a commitment to a significant aid package, but it will only be spent if we determine that our goals can be furthered rather than undermined or subverted," she told Voice of America radio.

About 75 countries are taking part in the aid conference being held in the Red Sea resort of Sharm el-Sheikh on Monday, six weeks after the guns largely fell silent around the impoverished enclave.

The Palestinian Authority seeking 2.8 billion dollars for rebuilding the territory of 1.4 million people, most of whom depend on aid from the United Nations.

But major donors are demanding that Gaza`s Islamist rulers agree to play no role in spending the cash, which they insist be handled by the Western-backed Palestinian Authority of president Mahmud Abbas.

Clinton is due to hold bilateral meetings on the sidelines of the conference and join a meeting of the Middle East peace Quartet.

From Egypt, she is due to visit Israel and the West Bank to try to advance peacemaking which ground to a halt after Israel launches it war on Gaza in late December which the aim of stopping militant rocket fire.

Israel's 22-day onslaught destroyed homes, hospitals, schools and other infrastructure as well as killing more than 1,300 Palestinians.

In Egypt Clinton will be joined by a host of top world officials including UN chief Ban Ki-moon, Russian Foreign

Minister Sergei Lavrov and EU foreign policy envoy Javier Solana.

"We expect rapid international aid from all parties to completely rebuild Gaza," Abbas told reporters on Saturday. "We also expect that as in the past there will be one mechanism, the Palestinian Authority."

The Palestinian Authority and Hamas each want to lead the rebuilding effort, but Western countries – which blacklist the Islamists as terrorists – have said they will work only with Abbas.

"I would like to insist that the mechanism used to deploy the money is the one that represents the Palestinian Authority," Solana said on Friday. "I don't think there is a need for new mechanisms."

However, the Palestinian leader's control extends only to the West Bank since Hamas violently seized Gaza in June 2007, ousting Abbas loyalists after days of vicious factional fighting.

The Gaza economy was brought to its knees by the punishing blockade imposed by Israel after Hamas seized the enclave, whose borders, air space and territorial waters remain under Israeli control.

Neither Israel nor Hamas will be represented in Sharm, but the international community is pushing for Israel to lift its blockade and for Hamas to reconcile with Fatah, backbone of the Palestinian Authority.

The rival Palestinian factions last week agreed to start working towards the creation of a national unity government.

In Sharm, Saudi Arabia is expected to reaffirm a commitment for one billion dollars, and the European Union has said it will grant 554 million dollars to the Palestinian people in 2009.

Donor countries from the January 2008 Paris conference will reiterate a pledge of 7.4 billion dollars in aid over 2008-2010, of which three billion has so far been distributed.

Clinton said that she doesn't think any other distribution mechanism needs to be in place as long as the Palestinians handle it. But with Abbas and Hamas struggling for power over the Palestinian territories, how can we trust the distribution mechanism that we have no assurance will be in power after the money is transferred?

I know we have rendered financial aid to countries that we have destroyed in past wars, but at least we had defeated the hostile factions and had installed some stability in the government. And we never would have sent millions in aid to a country until our enemies were defeated. Could you imaging Presidents Truman or Roosevelt sending $900 million to Japan or Germany before they had been defeated in World War II? I can understand the Arab countries sending money to Gaza, because they have the same ideology and hatred for Israel. I can even understand the aid by some of the European Union countries because through their own cowardice and complacency they have sheepishly forfeited control of their country to Islam, who is also dedicated to Israel's destruction. But not the U.S., who has previously made a *"commitment to Israel's security."*

Luckily, President Obama is not fooling the Jewish people or Israel. The Jewish people in Israel are taking up arms against Hamas, militant Muslims who are firing rockets into Israel in an attempt to destroy them. The United States has always had a peace agreement with Israel and we have not only kept that peace agreement, but we are honored to be a friend of this tiny country who has its roots in the biblical Land of Israel, and who has managed to stay alive through hundreds of years of fighting for their freedom. This is a country that has stood firm in their relationship with the United States even though their country is in the middle of our conflict against the Middle East.

Can you imagine how the prime minister of Israel felt when he heard that Hillary Clinton announced that a $900 million U.S. aid package will go to the Palestinians with $300 million of the aid package going to Gaza for "humanitarian aid?" NOW! I ask, is President Obama working for *our* country *or* for Hamas? How many of us can comprehend that President Obama, knowing that Gaza is instigating war against Israel and is training terrorist to send out into the world, is suggesting millions of dollars be sent to that country.

Once the money leaves our hands, we'll have no control over how it is spent. It is up to the leadership of that country to determine where it will go, and we have seen our share of corrupt leaders, (both government and corporate), who say one thing to get funding, then do something completely different once they get the money. If we give money to a country who hates the U.S. and Israel and are waging war against Israel, is it reasonable to assume that the money will not go to humanitarian relief efforts, but rather to train more terrorists and to buy more weapons to use against us and Israel? And since the future leadership of that country has not been finally determined, how can Obama propose such a thing? How much more evidence do we need to see that we may have a Muslim president?

It is my sincere hope that this book finds its way into the hands of Jews and Israelis from all over the world. So please, Israel, take notice! Even though Obama's definitions of concepts like truth, God, change, commitment, love of country and globalization cannot be trusted, conservative, God-loving Christians of America love you and support you. Whatever our national policy is toward you, remember that national policy is shaped by the people who hold power at the time. America as a nation loves and supports you even if our president and the rest of the Muslim world do not.

All of us, even the people who voted for President Obama, can see that there is an unprecedented phenomenon taking place in the United States, and Barack *Hussein* Obama is the central component in this phenomenon. We have put someone virtually unknown into the highest office in the United States and we are facing a possible dictatorship that will render our people helpless.

A historical analysis of former regimes who mesmerized a nation with their charm, then led the people to utter destruction reveals a consistent pattern, one that modern Americans seem to forget all too soon. What did the Hitlers and Husseins in history do? They charmed a populace that was in dire straights, then disarmed them. Once disarmed, they were free to victim their citizenry as directed by their own agenda and personal greed.

They made alliances with ungodly factions who had values and interests contrary to those of the citizenry, then led their nation to war and ultimately collapse. The ostriches of America would stick their heads in the sand and say, *"No way! This is the United States. That could never happen here. These are merely the ramblings of a deranged right-winged extremist. You right-wingers and Christians are the real threat, not people as charming and charismatic as the Clintons, Gores, Pelosis, Reeds and Obama's of the world."*

That's the same argument that societies have used for centuries. Then when the worst case scenario happens, everyone shakes their heads and says, *"The warning signs were there. Why didn't we see them? It's happened so many times throughout history. Why did we allow ourselves to be conned by one more in a long line of devious frauds?"*

Well, my friend, the answer is simple. When selfish, life-long, non-producing consumers (*Have-Nots*) in a democracy realize that they can vote themselves money and benefits that they don't have to pay for, and that will come out of the pockets of hard-working taxpayers, then political slicks hit the campaign trail, promising them the world on a silver platter, (promises by the way that none of them can deliver), and at the taxpayer's expense. Then when the *Have-Nots* finally outnumber the producers (*Haves*), the producers can no longer produce enough to support themselves and all the out-reached hands of the *Have- Nots*. It matters not that the makers of these impossible promises are caught in lies and unfulfilled campaign promises. By the time we find out that they are a fraud, they are already in office and their one consuming motivation is to get rich and re-elected for as many terms as possible so they can get richer.

It should also be noted that when the liberals speak of redistribution of wealth in the interest of social equality, the legislation that they propose always seems to touch the income brackets below them. Aside from a few individual humanitarian outreaches in times of disaster, around the holidays or close to election time, you never see the rich proposing the broad-sweeping, consistent, ongoing redistribution of wealth at their own expense. And before long, the tax and spend policies of the

Democrats outpace the ability of working class and lower middle class Americans to maintain the standard of living that they have worked so hard to maintain.

The political arena is no longer a noble endeavor to serve our country and do what is best for the nation as a whole. It is a scam to see which salesman can most effectively peddle his variation of the same old dog and pony show, and con that sector of the voters who are solely concerned for what the country can give them and not what is best for the nation as a whole. It's time, folks, for a reformation, in all arenas; political, religious, economic and cultural, if it is not already too late.

Let's return to the first step in taking over a nation, disarming the populace. It made the news. People are buying up guns in fear that President Obama will pass a gun control law prohibiting individuals to have guns for protection. Without guns to protect ourselves, where does that leave us? Certainly our enemies and the criminal element already here are not going to comply with any gun-control laws. Who does that leave in control of our country?

Have you seen the CD *Obsession* that I quoted from? If you haven't, you need to watch it! It's an actual undercover film showing a crowd of hundreds of Muslims thrusting guns into the air and shouting "kill the Americans." That footage was filmed in a Muslim country, not in the United State, so how are they going to kill us?

We have an estimated twenty-one million Muslims right here in the United States. And I doubt that they will give up their guns regardless of gun control. And another thing, Hamas and the rest of the Muslim world are rallying at the presidential power Obama has over the United States. To Muslims, President Obama's power represents a license for the Islamic movement to rise up in our country. They are just waiting for the "O.K." The article below is just one of many presidential congratulatory messages to President Obama from the Islamic world. President Almadinejad of Iran voiced his enthusiasm about President Obama's presidential win. The letter, carried by the official *Islamic Republic News Agency* and e-mailed to *The*

Washington Times was posted by Barbara Slavin November 6, 2008:

"I would like to offer my congratulations on your election by the majority of the American electorate, the Iranian wrote. 'I hope you will be able to take fullest advantage of the opportunity to serve and leave behind a positive legacy by putting the real interest of people as well as equity and justice ahead and above the insatiable demands of a selfish and unworthy minority.'"

WorldNetDaily posted on November 6, 2008. Ahmadiniejad encouraged Obama:

"If you take steps on the divine path and follow the teachings of divine prophets, God, the Almighty, will help you to make up in part for the heavy damage inflicted [by the U.S] in the past."

Did you notice that Ahmadiniejad said he hoped Obama would leave behind a *positive legacy?* The similarity to the caption *The Legacy Lives On* featured under the pictures of Obama, Farrakhan and Muhammad on the cover page of Wright's magazine *Trumpet* is striking, don't you think? Of course the *almighty god* that Almadinejad encourages President Obama with is their false god, Allah, and the divine prophet is the false prophet, Muhammad.

With this kind of congratulatory messages from our enemies to President Obama, shouldn't the eyes of our country be opened to the fact that Islam is watching our every move and is waiting for an opportunity to step in and take control for Islam? To give you an idea of what the Muslims believe about the world, how they intend to bring it together as *the one and only religion,* let's go the following excerpts. George W. Bradswell Jr. - *What You Need to Know About Islam & Muslims* page 3:

"Classical Islam divides the world into two areas: (1) the world of peace, where Islam is practiced and the Quran is observed; (2) the world of warfare and ignorance, dominated by non-Muslims. The mission of Islam is to bring this second world under Islam." *"Islam is a religion with missions at its*

heart. Every Muslim should strive to please Allah and to offer Allah's religion to others."

With the above quote still in mind, let's go to another source. John L. Esposito – *The Oxford History of Islam* page 554:

"The Organization of the Islamic Conference (OIC) is the major face for unity among the diverse collection of nation-states in the modern Muslim world. Modeled after the United Nations, it has 55 members, whose heads of state meet every three years in different countries to review conditions in the Muslim world and consider international political developments."

John L. Esposito - *The Oxford History of Islam* page 60: *Muslim World League (New York City)*

"Also involved in the process are foreign governments who see control of the mosques to manage their affairs and to keep their ideologies in conformity to those advocated overseas. Saudi Arabia established a European office of the Muslim World League in Belgium and two offices in North America (in New York and Toronto) in an attempt to supervise the mosque's leadership and its message by recruiting mosques to register as members of the Council of Masajid in Europe or North America."

Yes, they already have offices here in the United States monitoring their progress here. And yes, this action should cause us to take a closer look at their agenda. How has such a movement started in our country? It is happening because we have become complacent to foreign religions moving into the United States.

We have enacted liberal immigration laws that support the belief that we in America owe the entire world access to our country, and that we owe it to the poor and disadvantaged to redistribute the wealth in America so that everyone is on the same economic level. (It should be noted that when liberals advocate the redistribution of wealth, those enlightened liberals are usually enjoying incomes much higher that those of working class America and they typically mean a redistribution of the middle-class wealth so that the poor and welfare-dependant rise to the economic level of the working middle-class. The liberals never propose a redistribution of their wealth that would permit the working class to rise to the income level of the rich. Democrats are quick to suggest that we take from the poor to give to the poorer, but they never propose legislation that will dip into their pockets and investment portfolios to give to the struggling working class.)

But getting back to the issue being discussed before I digressed, we have allowed people to enter who are unable or unwilling to contribute to our culture and are here solely for the educational, economic and social benefits that they can obtain from the sweat of hardworking taxpayers. In addition, we have allowed people to enter who have values and religious beliefs that are not only contrary to our Christian heritage, but who outright hate us and are committed to our destruction.

What really prompted Obama to seek out people who are either Muslim or have close ties to the Muslim world? Was it because of his training in a Muslim school in Indonesia and his Muslim stepfather's influence and his stepfather's Muslim family? His autobiography about his life in Hawaii revealed that he searched out Muslims after leaving Indonesia. Obama was from a Muslim world, and he appeared to have searched for someone that he could identify with in Hawaii.

He clearly admitted in his book that Malcolm X had influenced his life, how he understood Malcolm X's view that whites might live beside him as brothers in Islam.[49] According to Obama's book he researched Malcolm X's life.[50] This short excerpt from Malcolm X's book gives us some insight into what Obama learned about Malcolm X's life-long goal when he read his writings. George Breitman – *Malcolm X Speaks* page 21:

"I am going to organize and head a new mosque in New York City, known as the Muslim Mosque, Inc. This gives us a religious base, and the spiritual force necessary to rid our

[49] *Dreams from My Father* page 86
[50] *Dreams from My Father* page 87

people of the vices that destroy the moral fiber of our community. The political philosophy of black nationalism means: we must control the politics and the politicians of our community. Our accent will be upon youth: we need new ideas, new methods, new approaches. We will call upon young students of political science throughout the nation to help us. We will encourage these young students to launch their own independent study, and then give us their analysis and their suggestions. We are completely disenchanted with the old, adult, established politicians. We want to see new faces – more militant faces. The Muslim Mosque, Inc., will remain wide open for ideas and financial aid from all quarters."

Does Malcolm X's ideology of going to the youth to control politics of the communities ring a bell? What age group did Obama reach out to and hold captive during his campaign? How many colleges did he take his campaign to? It was the youth! Louis Farrakhan, in one of his speeches, addressed and praised Obama for drawing the youth to his campaign rallies. Malcolm X was a Muslim and he was advocating the use of *politics* and *youth* to gain Muslim prominence in the United States. Let's do a comparison here between Malcolm X's speech and Obama's climb to the presidency. If Obama is, in fact, following Malcolm X's call, we are on our way to becoming a Muslim world. That was Malcolm X's goal.

Obama said he read Malcolm X's book(s), and he appears to be taking the exact steps that Malcolm advocated in his book *Malcolm X Speaks*. Malcolm said, *"I am going to organize and head a new mosque in New York City, known as the Muslim Mosque, Inc. This gives us a religious base."* (Obama found and joined a church that he attended for twenty years.)

Malcolm X said, *"We must control the politics and the politicians of our community."* (Obama became a community organizer rather than take an almost sure Supreme Court clerkship.) Malcolm X said, *"Our accent will be upon youth: we need new ideas, new methods, new approaches."* (Obama went to Dartmouth to draw the youth; he focused on youth during his presidential campaign with a hip-hop-type music.)

In my mind, after reading *Malcolm X Speaks* for research, I could see where President Obama could conceivably be carrying out Malcolm X's plan. Malcolm X has been dead for forty-four years, but Louis Farrakhan, leader of Islam, is very much alive and is encouraging Obama with his speeches. I pulled the following from the website Louis Farrakhan newspaper *FinalCall.com News* dated March 5, 2008. The caption was, *"Farrakhan's addresses world at Saviors' Day —* February 28, 2008":

"Brothers and sisters, Barack Obama to me, is a herald of the Messiah. Barack Obama is like the trumpet that alerts you something new, something better is on the way," the Muslim leader declared. "We have been taught by the Honorable Elijah Muhammad that Master Fard Muhammad had a Black father and a White mother. The man that we call the Savior was born of the two people," Min. Farrakhan said, describing the founder of the nation of Islam in North America and Mr. Muhammad's teacher, who was born in Mecca, Arabia Feb. 26, 1877."

Farrakhan seems to be encouraging Obama to step back and reflect on the history of Islam because the first Muslim savior had a black father and white mother. He is, in a sense, telling Obama that he is the next savior of the Muslim world. Can Obama be influenced by this man who knows that Obama was born of a Muslim father?

One may wonder why Obama turned to a radical like Malcolm X in search of his identity. It was probably because Malcolm X was also born of a mixed couple and hated the fact that he was half white; and, too, Malcolm was a Muslim.[51] Anyone who reads Malcolm X's book(s) will learn very quickly that the only white people Malcolm considered worthy were those who had accepted the Muslim religion. He openly called the United States corrupt and incited hate against America and Christianity.

---

[51] Malcolm X mixed blood - *Dreams from My Father* page 86

There seems to be a parallel between Malcolm X's hate speeches against God and Christianity and Reverend Wright's hate sermons against America? Could that similarity, knowing how Malcolm felt about God and Christians, have held Obama in Wright's church for those twenty years?

With the on-going Muslim movement in our country and a President whose family and friends are Muslim, we need to explore more about the teachings and beliefs of Islam and how they are infiltrating our country.

Does the name Ayatollah Khomeini ring a bell? He is a Muslim and the most wanted terrorist enemy of our country; yet in 2004 Muslims in Irving, Texas were allowed to hold a tribute to this man. Some people believe that the Muslims are a peaceful people because all we see here in the United States are men and women walking through our stores and markets dressed in strange garb. If they are peaceful Muslims, why did the Muslim community allow and promote the tribute to a terrorist enemy that calls on them to kill us!

While the Muslims in Texas approved of the tribute to Khomeini, Americans voiced their objection to the activity. Charles John of the *Dallas Morning News* voiced the Texans' disapproval in an article published in their newspaper on December 21, 2004:

"The Dallas Morning News finally weighs in on the appalling display of support from Muslim groups for an enemy of the United States. Most Americans remember the Ayatollah Khomeini. He was one of the great villains of the 20th century, who bequeathed his patrimony of fanaticism and hatred to the 21st. Khomeini led the 1979 Iranian revolution that overthrew the corrupt shah and replaced the government with a brutal Islamic theocracy that today is locked in battle with reformers seeing to end a quarter century of repression. Khomeini preached worldwide violent Islamic revolution, thundering that 'those who study Islamic Holy War will understand why Islam wants to conquer the whole world.'"

Johnson goes on to quote what Khomeini said in his speech speaking to a crowd of Muslims in Texas:

"Why do you only read the Quranic verses of mercy and do not read the verses of killing?" Khomeini challenged fellow clerics in a 1981 speech. "Qu'ran says: kill, imprison. Why are you only clinging to the part that talks about mercy? Mercy is against God," The tyrant also exhorted his followers to "kill all the unbelievers just as they would kill you all."

Another article on the Khomeini tribute was posted by Art Moore *WorldNetDaily.com* December 15, 2004:

"The leader of Iran's Islamic revolution in 1979, Khomeini famously viewed the U.S. as the "Great Satan" and said "Islam makes it incumbent on all adult males...to prepare themselves for the conquest of countries so that the writ of Islam is obeyed in every country in the world."

Was the Khomeini speech to awaken the Muslims living in Texas and other parts of our country? You bet it was! Let's go to Islamic law quoted word-for-word directly from the Qur'an.

The Holy Qur'an C.51 274 – 274 - *"We now return to the subject of Jihad, which we left at 2:214-216. We are to be under no illusion about it. If we are not prepared to fight for our faith, with our lives and all our resources, both our lives and our resources will be wiped out by our enemies."*

The Qur'an demands that Muslims use *all* of their resources. Let's say that President Obama is a Muslim and decides to use the resources that he has been given as the President of the most powerful nation in the world to fight Islam's enemy (that's us). President Obama has *all* the resources at his fingertips. He is the Commander-In-Chief of the most powerful military in history. He pulls the purse-strings on one of the largest budget on Earth. He appoints Supreme Court Judges, the U.S. Attorney General, U.S. District Attorneys, Federal Judges and the Secretary of State. He sets policy for all federal law enforcement and regulatory agencies as well as the I.R.S. His laws and economic policies impact every state, county, municipality, business, educational system and citizen within these borders.

So, how difficult will it be for Obama to impose his will on America? If his loyalty is stronger for Islam than for America, can we depend on an impartial, objective media to accurately report his activities? Can we depend on anyone within his administration, especially his appointees, to blow the whistle? And once we open our eyes and see that he is in fact injecting the Muslim Shari'a law into our criminal justice system and is in fact flying us into a mountainside by borrowing money from our Islamic enemies, disarming us and generally selling us out, will be have the power, resources and solidarity to stop him?

The Holy Qur'an C51 275 - *"For Allah's cause we must fight."*

ALLAH is the FALSE god of Islam. NOT the GOD of our HOLY BIBLE.

The Holy Qur'an 9:73 - *"O Prophet! Strive hard against the unbelievers and the hypocrites, and be firm against them. Their abode is hell – an evil refuge indeed."* Strive Hard in Arabic is JIHAD, Holy War against infidels.

The Holy Qur'an C 220 47:4 - *"Therefore, when ye meet the unbelievers, smite at their necks."*

The Holy Qur'an C 98 9:23 - *"O ye who believe! Fight the unbelievers who gird you about, and let them find firmness in you."*

The word [gird] translates to [restrain]. In other words if we as a free nation try to stop them in their quest to conquer the world for Islam, they are to fight and kill us if necessary.

What has to take place before Islam can pull the world together as one under Islam without military force? For one thing, Islam needs to find a way to incorporate their Shari'a Law into our government. Second, the United States has to be convinced that we need to pull [all] nations together before we can have peace in the world.

But peace and globalization at what cost? There are many cultures that we should not want to be at peace with. If we do what it takes to get along with the Islamic world, then what will we become? There are many things worth fighting and dying for. It has cost the lives of many good men and women to make this country the bastion of Christianity and freedom that it is, [tenuous and unstable as that bastion has become in recent years]. I for one am not willing to throw all that away just to get along with people who worship a false god and want to murder all of us who will not.

And right now Obama is doing a good job of convincing the United States and the world to do just that. Remember what Obama said in his campaign speech in Germany, *"Tear down the walls."* Shortly after he won the presidential race, and before he took office, he voiced to the world his global outreach plans to *"reboot"* our image to the Muslim world. Aaron Klein posted this on *WorldNetDaily*.com on December 10, 2008:

"JERUSALEM – President-elect Barak Obama declared in an interview he plans to deliver a major address in an Islamic capital as part of his global outreach, which he said would target the Muslim world. "I think we've got a unique opportunity to reboot America's image around the world and also in the Muslim world in particular," Obama said in a free-ranging interview yesterday with the Chicago Tribune, promising an "unrelenting" desire to "create a relationship of mutual respect and partnership in countries and with peoples of good will who want their citizens and ours to prosper together." The Tribune reported Obama spoke of a major address in an Islamic capital, but did not provide specific details."

Less than two weeks after President Obama took office he confirmed that he was dead serious about his plan to reach out and *"reboot"* America's image to the Muslim world. The following was reported by Paul Schemm – *Associated Press* Writer January 27, 2009:

"CAIRO, Egypt – President Barack Obama chose an Arabic-language satellite TV network for his first formal television interview as president, delivering a message Tuesday to the Muslim world that "Americans are not your enemy." The interview taped Monday underscored Obama's commitment to repair relations with the Muslim world that have suffered under the previous administration. "My job to the Muslim world is to

communicate that the Americans are not your enemy," Obama told the Dubai-based Al-Arabiya news channel, which is privately owned by a Saudi businessman. Obama called for a new partnership with the Muslim world "based on mutual respect and mutual interest." He talked about growing up in Indonesia, the Muslim world's most populous nation, and noted that he has Muslim relatives."

I believe that President Obama established the fact that he feels a closeness to the Muslim people when he visited Cairo, Egypt on June 4, 2009 and made it clear to the Muslim world that he is for them and wants to see them succeed in their plight to rise up in America.

The following congratulatory message to Obama was posted by *WorldNetDaily* November 6, 2008:

"If you take steps on the divine path and follow the teachings of divine prophets, god, the Almighty, will help you to make up in part for the heavy damage inflicted [by the U.S.] in the past."

Obama is no longer inhibited about admitting he has Muslim relatives. Isn't President Obama's message above to the Muslim world an answer to President Ahmadinijad of Iran's plea in his congratulatory message? Was President Obama using his *resources* to help the Islamic cause?

Now, it should be said in the interest of fairness, that President Obama is right in the sense that we want peace with the Islamic nations. But are his statements made in the same context as those of the rest of America? Is his definition of peace the same as mine and yours?

None of us want to see our best and brightest march off to war and come home in flag-draped coffins. I believe that every true American sheds a tear when they see the coffins of our dead being unloaded off the cargo planes that transport them home, then see the grief on the faces of spouses, parents and the children of those fallen heroes. We all want peace in the sense that we don't want to be involved in military conflicts around the world. And we want to maintain steady and prosperous trade agreements with other countries, as long as it does not cost Americans their jobs, does not introduce products into our country that are injurious to our health and welfare and does not upset an appropriate balance between exports and imports.

But we also realize that freedom is not free, and someone has to protect our interests from those who would destroy us. That being said, do we want peace if it means subjugating ourselves to Muslim dictators? I think not.

And if President Obama *does not* intend to move us in that direction, then he is entitled to our prayers and this author's sincerest apology. If he does in fact have a plan that can rescue us from this economic collapse that does not involve selling us out to our enemies, then he has my sincerest support. But in light of the evidence, one must be at least a little suspicious.

Our country has been a safe-haven to Americans for over two hundred years. We have the best high-technology security forces in the world to warn us of an impending attack from other nations; an attack that could bring us under a tyrannical dictatorship. But my friends, the kind of threat we are facing is not from outside our borders. A more powerful threat is coming from *within* our borders, and there is no technology or protective force (military of civil) that can protect us against it except our own common sense, our Christian values that allow us to determine right from wrong and the solidarity to courageously stand up and fight for the principles that sustained us through the tough times and made us the great nation that we once were.

People, we need to open our eyes to what is coming next. We are a strong country militarily....but psychologically [because we are a generous nation] we are not prepared to fight a battle with Islam's voiceless movement in the United States. Many Americans do not know the history behind the Islamic religion. Muslims believe that they are commanded by Allah, their false god, to bring the entire world into Islam. That means killing if necessary to cleanse the earth of non-believers. No, I'm not exaggerating. They believe in a *one world* religion and that is Islam. It's a forced religion; it's not like America's *freedom* of religion. And the scary thing about it is these people come in under the radar as just another harmless religious group moving into the United States.

I sincerely believe that they have a motive for being here! And I honestly believe, from researching the Muslim religion, that someday soon the citizens of the United States are going to regret voting someone virtually unknown into the Oval Office. Let's take a look at what happened in Cuba before Castro came to power. The following article was written by a *legal* immigrant citizen of the United States. Unlike natural born United States citizens who have never experienced dictatorship, this man has legitimate reason for being suspicious of Obama. This story has a lot of merit:

This letter to an editor appeared in the Richmond (VA) *Times-Dispatch*, July 7, 2008 entitled *"Beware of charismatic men who preach "Change."*:

"Editor: Each year I get to celebrate Independence Day twice. On June 30 I celebrate my independence day and on July 4, I celebrate America's. This year is special, because it marks the 40th anniversary of my independence. On June 30, 1968, I escaped Communist Cuba and a few months later I was in the United States to stay. That I happened to arrive in Richmond on Thanksgiving Day is just part of the story, but I digress. I've thought a lot about the anniversary this year. The election-year rhetoric has made me think a lot about Cuba and what transpired there. In the late 1950's, most Cubans thought Cuba needed a change, and they were right. So when a young leader came along, every Cuban was at least receptive. When the young leader spoke eloquently and passionately and denounced the old system, the press fell in love with him. They never questioned who his friends were or what he really believed in. When he said he would help the farmers and the poor and bring free medical care and education to all, everyone followed. When he said he would bring justice and equality to all, everyone said "Praise the Lord." And when the young leader said, "I will be for change and I'll bring you change," everyone yelled, "Viva Fidel!" But nobody asked about the change, so by the time the executioner's guns went silent, the people's guns had been taken away. By the time everyone was equal, they

were equally poor, hungry, and oppressed. By the time everyone received their free education, it was worth nothing. By the time the press noticed, it was too late, because they were not working for him. By the time the change was finally implemented, Cuba had been knocked down a couple of notches to Third-World status. By the time the change was over, more than a million people had taken to boats, rafts, and inner tubes. You can call those who made it ashore anywhere else in the world the fortunate Cubans.

And now I'm back to the beginning of my story. Luckily we would never fall in America for a young leader who promised change without asking, what change? How will you carry it out? What will it cost America? — Manuel Alvarez, Jr."

The above quote was from a man who has a legitimate fear that what he saw happen in his homeland Cuba will happen in the United States. An unknown politician, Fidel Castro, came on the scene promising *"change."* Unlike Fidel Castro who came out of the blue, Obama somehow made his way to a Senate seat in preparation for his introduction to the United States. Still, Obama appeared to have kept his personal life low-key, but when he suddenly announced that he was going to run for the presidency, the media immediately scrambled to report to the nation something about a virtually unknown candidate. However, Obama continued to choose not to divulge anything about himself, making the media suspicious and giving them cause to investigate his background. That's when the media found that Obama had been a member of Reverend Wright's radical church for twenty years, a church that preached hate sermons. Still we knew nothing of his background, only that he had worked as a community organizer in Chicago, Ill. It was as if his life had begun in Chicago.

The news media pushed on to give the nation more information about the man who was running for the president of our country. Bits and pieces of Obama's background began to surface. We learned that he had a white mother, African Muslim father and a Muslim stepfather; was raised in the Muslim country of Indonesia and eventually ended up in Hawaii. Our nation was soon captivated by this mysterious man. When it was learned that he had close connections with the Muslim world, our nation was already caught up in euphoria that he was the one who could help our nation over the crisis. So much so that they, in a sense, committed their very lives to Senator Obama, believing in his campaign promises.

Immediately after Obama won the presidential race the promises seem to have been put on hold. Instead he began to focus on the Arab countries. He was sworn in on January 20, 2009 and on January 26, 2009 he chose an Arabic-language satellite TV network to speak to the Muslim world. Why was he in such a hurry to tell the Muslim world that we are not their enemy? What is President Obama's train of thought? These are the enemy who endorsed Obama. These are the people who hijacked planes and crashed them into the Twin Towers in New York, killing over three thousand people in a blazing inferno. These people are the only people in the world who are committing terrorist acts against our country within our own boarders! They are the only immigrants who are brave enough to demonstrate against us. And they are the only religious group who openly tell us, in our own country, that Christianity is wrong. Grant you, we have other religious groups in our country who do not believe in the God of Christianity, but they don't retaliate against us for not believing their way.

Not only did Obama contact the Muslim nation, look closely at what he has put in place in the short time he has been in office. He has signed an order to close Guantanamo Bay and halted all trials. Is he doing an act of kindness for the people of Islam? If not, then what is the purpose of closing a terrorist prison camp and postponing trials to put these Muslim terrorists away for life so they can't act again. It doesn't make sense that an American citizen, especially the President of the United States, would lean in favor of terrorists who were probably responsible for bringing down the Twin Towers in New York and will strike again if they get out of prison.

What *are* the motives behind President Obama's off-the-wall decisions? Read the following article about America's money (yours and mine) that he is sending to a country that is out to kill us!

Just two months into his presidency President Obama sent Secretary of State Hillary Clinton to the Middle East to proudly commit $900 million dollars to the multi-nation relief package for the Palestinians, supposedly to rebuild what Israel has destroyed. Remember the live video of Muslim kids in GAZA being trained as terrorist to kill Americans. President Obama is sending money to those same people! Aaron Klein posted the following article on *WorldNetDaily* March 2, 2009:

"JERUSALEM – Secretary of State Hillary Clinton announced today that a $900 million U.S. aid package for the Palestinians was meant to foster regional peace and would not fall into the hands of the Hamas terrorist organization. But the aid is slated to be received both by a U.N. agency that openly employs Hamas as well as by the Palestinian Authority, which is in talks to create a unity government with Hamas."

The first few weeks in office it appears that Obama has looked to the needs of Muslims more so than the United States. Do we have an argument against the idea that President Obama is trying to isolate our partnership with Israel? One has to wonder if Obama's strategy is to so infuriate and betray Israel that Israel herself actually severs its alliance with the Untied States, rather than Obama having the courage to face the outrage here in America of taking the initiative and severing our alliance with Israel.

And with something resembling 800 billion dollars going out to American banks and automakers in the form of bailouts, isn't there a more dire need for that $900 million right here in America?

Is Obama going to be another Fidel Castro? Is he silently leading us down a road to a dictatorship with his ideas of bringing the Muslim world together with us? Living under a Muslim dictatorship, with their acts of intimidation to force people into their religion or die, will far outweigh the atrocities of Fidel Castro's dictatorship.

Before I go any further with the writing of this book I need to explain that I am not prejudiced. I have been on mission trips to the country of Haiti (Africans), counseled and lived with street people of all colors in inner-city rescue missions. My concern here is the possibility that a man who professes to be a Christian is using Christianity as a cover up for his intent to destroy our country as we know it. I am not concerned about his color. I'm concerned that he is Muslim with a Muslim agenda. And I repeat…. I believe, based on the evidence gathered for the writing of this book, that his agenda is to Islamize the United States for Allah…the Muslim's false god.

Another concern I have about Obama is how he misquoted Holy Scripture in his second book. Some who do not understand the Bible will accept Obama's offensive misquoted rhetoric against the Holy Scripture as truth. The following excerpt was taken from Obama's book, chapter on faith. Barack Obama - *The Audacity of Hope* page 218:

"Whatever we once were, we are no longer just a Christian nation; we are also a Jewish nation, a Muslim nation, a Buddhist nation, a Hindu nation, and a nation of nonbelievers. But let's even assume that we only had Christians within our borders. Whose Christianity would we teach in the schools? James Dobson's or Al Sharpton's? Which passage of Scripture should guide our public policy? Should we go with Leviticus, which suggests that slavery is all right and eating shellfish is an abomination? How about Deuteronomy, which suggests stoning your child if he strays from the faith? Or should we just stick to the Sermon on The Mount – a passage so radical that it's doubtful that our Defense Department would survive its application?"

On Page 222 of the same chapter he quotes the Book of Romans out of context. He said,

"I am not willing to have the state deny American citizens a civil union that confers equivalent rights on such basic matters as hospital visitation or health insurance coverage simply because the people they love are of the same sex – nor am I willing to accept a reading of the Bible that considers an

obscure line in Romans to be more defining of Christianity than the Sermon on the Mount."

It seems that Obama needs to re-read that passage of Romans. President Obama, let me clarify the writing of those passages. The Sermon on the Mount in Matthew was written to Christians. The Book of Romans was written to people whom God had given over to Satan because of their sinful acts. President Obama, please don't just read the Bible....study it! Nothing you ever did in your life ever discredited you and revealed you as a fraud more than when you misquoted the Bible for your own selfish agenda. Those few words revealed to the entire Christian sector of the United States that you are not a Christian, nor do you believe in the same God that we do. To set you straight, Mr. Obama, please read what Scripture really says.

The Holy Bible – Romans 1:24-28 "Therefore God also gave them up to uncleanness, in the lusts of their hearts, to dishonor their bodies among themselves, who exchanged the truth of God for the lie, and worshiped and served the creature rather than the Creator, who is blessed forever Amen. For this reason God gave them over to vile passions. For even their women exchanged the natural use for what is against nature. Likewise also the men, leaving the natural use of the woman, burned in their lust for one another, men with men committing what is shameful, and receiving in themselves the penalty of their error which was due. And even as they did not like to retain God in their knowledge, God gave them over to a debased mind, to do those things which are not fitting." NKJV

Obama needs to go back to Leviticus 18:22 in the Holy Bible – "You shall not lie with a male as with a woman. It is an abomination." NKJV

Leviticus 20:13 "If a man lies with a male as he lies with a woman, both of them have omitted an abomination. They shall surely be put to death. Their blood shall be upon them." NKJV

I don't know how much clearer the Bible has to be for President Obama to see exactly what God meant in the books of Leviticus and Romans. What did God mean when He said in

Romans 1:28 "And even as they did not like to retain God in *their* knowledge.." NKJV

God's Word is knowledge of God and it gives us guidelines that He, Himself, set forth for a clean godly lifestyle — living as one man and one woman.

Dr. James Dobson of Focus on the Family answered sharply to Obama's misquoting Scripture and using his name in the article. This is what Dr. Dobson and Tom Minnery had to say in the July 15, 2008 publication of *The Pathway Newsjournal of the Missouri Baptist Convention*:

"Focus on the Family founder James Dobson used his broadcast June 24 to criticize Barack Obama's usage of Scripture, saying the presumptive Democratic nominee misrepresents biblical passages. 'I think he is deliberately distorting the traditional understanding of the Bible to fit his own worldview – his own confused theology,' Dobson said on the radio program."

"Tom Minnery, president of government and public policy for Focus on the Family, said Obama's interpretation is off the mark. 'Laws that applied to [the Israelites] then – the Levitical code, the dietary laws – no longer apply,' Minnery said. '...[it] seems that he is vastly confused about the details of biblical exposition. I think he is dragging biblical understanding through the gutter. I just don't know whether he's doing it willfully or accidentally.'"

Is Obama a Christian who simply does not understand the Holy Bible? I had my doubts about Obama's salvation before I read his book, but those doubts were confirmed when I read the following excerpt. A true born-again Christian may not understand the Bible entirely, but usually that is only because they are a new Christian. One thing a Christian *does know (even a new Christian)*; however, is where we will go when we die. Barack Obama does not have that understanding. Barack Obama - *The Audacity of Hope* page 226:

"I thought of Sasha asking me once what happened when we die – "I don't want to die, Daddy," she had added matter-of-factly – and I had hugged her and said, "You've got a long, long way before you have to worry about that," which had seemed to satisfy her. I wondered whether I should have told her the truth, that I wasn't sure what happens when we die, any more than I was sure of where the soul resides or what existed before the Big Bang."

Obama didn't intend it, I'm sure, but little did he know that he inadvertently gave to his daughter, and the world, the most accurate and honest testimony that he could give of the uncertainty and total absence of assurance and peace that Islam offers its believers.

Does he sound like a Christian? My understanding as a Christian is [and it is true] that we go directly into Jesus Christ's arms the second we die. As for the Big Bang theory, it is the view of an agnostic (not knowing whether God exists), not a Christian's view. As a Christian with a love for reaching out with the Gospel of Christ, I feel sorry for President Obama because he does not have the peace that he can have through Jesus Christ. However, I still have to understand, even though I feel sorry for him, that President Obama is someone that Americans should be very cautious of.

Obama asked what we would teach in our schools if we only had Christians there. Any dedicated citizen of the United States would tell Obama that we would teach exactly what we started teaching over two-hundred years ago. And that is teaching our children that America is the great nation that it is today because it was founded on the word of God. Our children were taught that we have freedom of speech and freedom of religion because we fought for it under the guidance of God's Holy word, the Bible. It appears that President Obama is doing everything he can to tear those concepts apart.

Has he forgotten, or was he ever taught, that our country *was founded* on the Word of God; that we did much better in the United States when Christianity and American History was taught in our schools. If he were a Christian, or even a sincere American citizen, he would understand that if we allow Muslim,

Buddhist and Hindu religions to dominate our schools, we will be going backward in history. Christians fled from other countries and came to America to escape the tyranny of those false religions. We don't have to *live* other countries' *beliefs* and *values* to understand their history!

As a Christian nation we know that God blessed this country and made it a great nation because we revered Him as the One True God. Did you notice that I used the word [revered] in the past tense? Our country has turned away from everything that God stands for. And by turning away from God's command to have no other gods before him[52] we have opened the door for the radical religious movement to come right into our lives.

These Muslims are practicing their false religion freely and are silently pushing their religious literature into family homes; especially through young children. Islamic books on how to become a Muslim are stacked on the children reading racks of our libraries.

I want to reiterate what Obama said about our being a Jewish nation, a Muslim nation, a Buddhist nation, a Hindu nation, *and* a nation of nonbelievers just to emphasize what Obama may be trying to do. How many of us would know that many of the Buddhists and Hindus in our country practice the Muslim religion? Obama said Muslim, Buddhist and Hindu, leading us to think that the Buddhist and Hindu religions are entirely different from Muslims. If you will look at Islamic history, there are Arab Muslims, Buddhist Muslims and Hindu Muslims. Believers are people who accept Jesus Christ as God's only Son and our Savior. Buddhist, Hindus and Muslims believe in something, but it definitely is not the Holy God of Christianity.

Obama said that we are no longer a Christian nation! What is Obama alleging? Was he silently communicating to Islam in his book that we are on our way to becoming a Muslim Nation? Or was he massaging our complacency about the influx of Muslims?

---

[52] *The Ten Commandments* – Exodus 20:1-6

Obama Finds Comfort in His Father's Native Land

Obama has been in this country [the main land] long enough to knows that our nation has become a nation of complacency and unruffled by the influx of a cultic nation that wants to bury us in their ideology. The Islamic movement has waited years for our country to be unmoved by religious changes in our society. With fear of terrorists in our country, wars in the Middle East, unprecedented tornados and earthquakes in America; with so many unparalleled happenings on our minds, we have become blinded by the fact that a different kind of enemy and war is silently festering among us, the Islamic movement into the United States.

It was time now! The Islamic nation could see that the people in the United States were complacent and ready for any kind of change without question. The next step...They needed to put someone of their own into a political office so their voices could be heard.

Obama seems to have heard, and answered, President Mahmond Ahmadinejad of Iran's plea for him to make up for the damage inflicted by the U.S. in the past. With all the evidence presented so far, is it conceivable that Barack "Hussein" Obama is the person who is going to listen to Islam's voice and will be the one who will fight for their cause? Thus far he has proposed $900 million dollars for the Muslim cause.

Just how does Obama really feel about the United States? He calls American "our country," but what about the close connection Obama has with his Muslim father's homeland Kenya, Africa? He tells us a different story in his first book about where his loyalty lies.

He was at the Kenyatta International Airport in Africa waiting for his sister Auma. Let's examine the feeling he felt as he waited for his sister. Barack Obama - *Dreams from My Father* page 304-305:

"The rush of anticipation had drained away,, and I smiled with the memory of the homecoming[53] *I had once imagined for*

---

[53] Emphasis on "homecoming"

myself. clouds lifting, old demons fleeing, the earth trembling as ancestors rose up in celebration."

"For the first time in my life,[54] I felt the comfort, the firmness of identity that a name might provide, how it could carry an entire history in other people's memories, so that they might nod and say knowingly, "Oh, you are so and so's son." No one here in Kenya would ask how to spell my name, or mangle it with an unfamiliar tongue. My name belonged and so I belonged, drawn into a web of relationships, alliances, and grudges that I did not yet understand."

Obama said, *"...for the first time in my life, I felt the comfort, the firmness of identity that a name might provide."* He also said, *"My* name *belonged* and so *I* belonged...." Obama was stressing the importance of *his name* to the Africans. He said his *name* belonged, so he belonged. In what did Obama find comfort.... the firmness of identity? Was he saying he had found identity in his *Muslim* name, in a *Muslim country* where his Muslim grandmother and siblings live? Would you say that he did not find comfort in being a citizen of the United States?

During his presidential campaign he appeared to avoid any confrontation about his middle name. After he won the presidential seat, however, he decided to use his Muslim name *Hussein* that he was so proud of when he stepped off the plane in Africa, but had kept low-key in the United States until he was elected.

How did his sudden decision to use his middle name affect the Islamic world's thinking? Will this well-known name in the Muslim history have an impact on Islam's endeavor to take over our country for their false god? I suspect that it will! That name, *Hussein,* has been revered by Muslims for centuries and honored throughout Muslim history.

Readers, have you any idea how long Islam is willing to wait for a chance to claim the United States for Dar al-Islam? It took them hundreds of years to conquer most of Europe. They didn't stop at Europe. They have literally moved into most

---

[54] Emphasis on "for the first time in my life"

countries of the world, and they are closing in on the United States. They are above us in Canada and below us in South America.

I keep repeating it because most of us do not comprehend that we have approximately twenty-one million Muslims in the United States. A few have taken the leap and now hold political offices. Muslim organizations in the United States such as Muslim American Society[55] are encouraging Muslims to become involved in the political arena.

Here is another entanglement with Obama's Muslim involvement that we need to address. Obama appointed Hillary Clinton as U.S. Secretary of State, one of the highest offices in the nation. We think we know who she is, but did we know that her husband, former President Bill Clinton, received from $10 million to $25 million from Saudi Arabia for the Clinton Library in Arkansas. The story was picked up by Beth Fouhy and Sharon Theimer – *Associated Press December* 18, 2008:

"Former President Bill Clinton's foundation has raised at least $41 million from Saudi Arabia and other foreign governments that his wife Hillary Rodham Clinton may end up negotiating with as the next secretary of state. The Kingdom of Saudi Arabia gave $10 million to $25 million to the William J. Clinton foundation, a nonprofit created by the former president to finance his library in Little Rock, Ark."

Tell me! Why would a Muslim nation express such an interest in a library in America? Can we surmise that there was a motive behind the gift? I doubt that it was the library that they were interested in. Islam does not let go of $25 million without a reason behind it. And why did they choose, out of millions of good causes in the United States, to donate up to $25 million to the Clintons? You be the judge!

Whether the Clintons were aware of it or not, the logical intent of the Muslims would be to become friends of the influential political Clinton family. Why? Because those countries keep a close eye on what goes on in the United States.

---

[55] MAS – Joseph Abrams – *FOXNews.com* Thursday 08, 2009

They knew that eventually Hillary Clinton would run for the presidential office. Probably in their eyes Obama would pose no threat to them, but if Hillary Clinton got in, they need what they think will be a backup to get to the right people in the White House. To what extent are the Clintons involved in the Islamic movement? No one can tell. However, it makes sense that Obama would know about the large contribution from the Muslim countries. It made the news!

There was opposition to appointing Hillary because of Bill Clinton's ties to the Muslim world, but Obama chose to ignore the warning and appointed her, knowing that she was associated with the Muslim world. The degree to which the Clinton's would be influenced by the Muslim world against our country cannot be determined at this time, but it doesn't change the fact that Saudi Arabia (the location of the sacred city of Mecca that Muslims pray towards five times a day), and other Muslim nations contributed large sums of money to the husband of the newly appointed U.S. Secretary of State.

As it stands now we have a President who has a Muslim family and whose associates are Muslims. We also have a Secretary of State whose husband has powerful Muslim friends. Obama also appointed Eric Holder, Jr. as U.S. Attorney General, a man who pardoned from jail a convicted terrorist who was helping Iran during the time they were holding our people hostage.

What will come next from President Obama? He has already begun to surround himself with a team of people who either have Muslim ties or criminal backgrounds.

Can anyone convince me that our country is not being set up by Islamic extremist? Take a look at how representatives (Muslims) of the Islamic world are speaking out today. Islam was never so outspoken and bold about financial issues in the United States as they have been since Obama was elected. The $787 billion Stimulus Package opened the eyes of the Islamic world to the fact that the United States is in a crisis. I have not seen, in my lifetime, Islam let the news media report anything about their Shari'a law.

Why is Islam suddenly coming into view? They are standing by with their billions of dollars, ready to help us out of this crisis. And we all know that money controls. Watch the news! Obama, his appointees and a liberal Congress and Senate are ready and eager to welcome the Arab world's money. Whether we want to admit it or not, citizens of the United States no longer control what happens in our country. President Obama set the boundaries by appointing radical people who will adhere to his authority.

True, Presidents have always utilized the patronage system, either overtly or secretly, to surround themselves with supporters and reward those who made their election possible. But it's never been so threatening to our culture and the continued survival of our nation.

For those of you who say, "This is a bunch of nonsense, these people appointed to Obama's team are Americans," let me burst your bubble. Let's go to a newspaper article about Ahmed Omar Abu Ali, a Muslim who was born in the United States; the man who plotted to assassinate President George Bush. Matthew Barakat – *Associated Press* – *Published in St. Louis Post Dispatch* June 9, 2008:

"Born in Houston, Abu Ali, 27, grew up in the Washington suburb of Falls Church and was valedictorian of a private Islamic high school. He joined al-Qaida after traveling to Saudi Arabia to attend college in 2002. As a member of a Medina-based al-Qaida cell, Abu Ali discussed potential terrorist attacks, including a plan to assassinate Bush and a plan to establish a sleeper cell in the United States."

Is it unthinkable that America has become so complacent that we are allowing foreign enemy to silently infiltrate with the intentions of killing us? An active al-Qaida terrorist in the United States, schooled in a *private Muslim School in our own country,* was planning to establish a sleeper cell right here in the United States. Let's not try and rationalize by saying, "Well, he was born in the United States, he did not infiltrate into the Country." Did you notice that he attended a *private Islamic high school?* Students generally live with their parents during their high school years, and foreign parents usually send their children to schools that reflect their traditions and values. That makes Abu Ali's parents Muslims living right here in the United States! Can we see the long-term planning in his life? Another Muslim terrorist, Khalid Shaikh Mohammed, the self-described orchestrator of the September 11, 2001 attack on the New York City Twin Towers is in prison for the crime. Will you be surprised to learn that he was educated right here in the United States? This article was published in the *Los Angeles Times* and picked up by the *St. Louis Post Dispatch World News*. Josh Meyer – *Los Angeles Times* - published in the *St. Louis Post Dispatch* May 26, 2008:

"Muhammad, who is believed to be 43 or 44, was once the operations chief and third in command of al-Qaida, a U.S. educated engineer who claimed credit for dozens of terrorist plots and attacks in a preliminary court proceeding last year at Guantanamo. He bragged for instance, about how he had orchestrated Sept. 11 "from A to Z" and how he beheaded Wall Street Journal reporter Daniel Pearl because he was a Jew."

The following excerpt about Daniel Pearl was taken from Hal Lindsey – *The Everlasting Hatred – The Roots of Jihad* page 3:

"The video shows the tortured face of an American news reporter named Daniel Pearl. He is forced to confess, "My father is a Jew, my mother is a Jew and I am a Jew." Then suddenly a hand with a knife appears on the video screen and slashes his throat. Then his head is hacked off and held aloft by a hand in front of the cameras. The video cuts to his murderers repeatedly stabbing his lifeless corpse. The final scene cuts to Pearl's head lying on a pile of newspapers as a message scrolls across the screen: "If our demands are not met, there will be more like this."

That attitude of radical jihadist activity is prescribed by the Muslim's own laws in their Qur'an.

The Holy Qur'an 5:33 - *"The punishment of those who wage war against Allah and His Messenger, and strive with might and main for mischief through the land is: execution, or crucifixion, or the cutting off of hands and feet from opposite side, or exile from the land."*

This kind of mercilessness brutality is not directed only to the Jews, even though the radical Muslims yell, "Kill the Jew and Christians." It is directed to anyone who disagrees with the Muslim religion, even believing Muslims who want to leave the cult and convert to Christianity, like the American Muslim teenagers in Texas who were killed by their own mother and father because they wanted to be "American."

<u>Obama – Another Muslim Connection</u>.

Our society has another problem in Shelbyville, Tennessee with 700 Muslims working at Tyson Food, a nation-wide food chain. Tyson Foods took away Labor Day as a paid holiday and replaced it with the Muslim holiday, Id al Fitr. You have it right! This happened while former Senator Obama was running for the presidency. The unions that represented the Muslims also endorsed Obama for president.

By Michelle Malkin – August 4, 2008 – Story by Brian Mosely – Shelbyville, Tennessee *Times-Gazette*:

"UFCW President Joe Hansen spoke with the RWDSU Executive board at a meeting in Washington, D.C., this morning, discussing the importance of electing Sen. Barack Obama in the presidential election, the upcoming UFCW convention in Montreal, and the issue of immigration reform." [56]

"'The Retail, Wholesale and Department Store Union (RWDSU), a union that endorses Barack Obama in his 2008 Presidential candidacy, has negotiated with Tyson foods recognize a Muslim holiday Eid al-Fitr instead of the traditional American Labor Day holiday.' The union also claimed that in addition to the observance of the Muslim holiday, 'two prayer rooms' have been created to allow Muslim workers to pray twice a day and return to work without leaving the plant.'"

---

[56] Article from *UFCW* website – 6/10/08

Why did this Union fight for the rights of Muslims instead of fighting for the Americans working at the plant! Obama was not in the Oval Office at the time of this incident, but his name carried a lot of weight for the Muslims. The actions of this union who voted for Obama should give credibility to the beliefs of many people that Obama is a Muslim. Unions are a powerful force in our country, and Obama has them on his side. And yes, Shelbyville, Tennessee has an Islamic mosque in her midst.

It seems almost inconceivable to me that Muslims have been allowed to infiltrate virtually every state in our country without Americans rising up to fight this phenomenon of aggressive, militant people moving into the United States. I have to congratulate and thank Michelle Malkin for keeping track of Islamic activity in our country. Mark my words. Jihad [holy war] is at our doorsteps and we aren't listening! Too many voices are saying, "God is in control, so I really don't need to worry about Muslims, whatever happens will happen."

My friends, do you realize that that is not Scriptural? For those of you who may not know Bible history, and I will remind those of you who do, Islam has fought for hundreds of years to pull people away from our Holy God, and God has used His people as instruments to defeat those who appose Him. Do you really believe that God wants anything less now! Yes, God is in absolute control of this world, but I for one do not want to stand before Him when I die and have Him ask me, "Why didn't you try to stop the Muslims from defaming My Holy Name by bringing a false god into your land?"

Do you want that to happen? Whether you are a Christian or non-Christian, you will be asked the same question. And if we, as Christians and a free people of a great country do not rise up with an allegiance to Almighty God to at least try and stop this movement from taking the next generation away from God and the teachings of His Holy Word, we should not expect anything from Him.

CHAPTER SEVEN

Obama Chooses his Muslim Associates in Chicago

As we mentioned earlier, Louis Farrakhan, whose headquarters and mansion are located in Chicago, is a Leader of Islam. In his book, Obama describes Louis Farrakhan's activity with admiration. And then there was also Wally Thompson, a Muslim co-worker in Chicago, who changed his name to Rafiq al Shabazz. Rafiq was the man who voiced to Obama that the tutelage of the Muslims saved his life. Obama's response, *"Progress was within our grasp so long as we didn't betray ourselves."*

Thompson is a common American name. But Wally Thompson chose to change his name after he became a Muslim. Obama questioned his partner about Rafiq when they went to Rafiq's office and she made a comment that she knew him before he changed his name. Barack Obama - *Dreams from My Father* page 181:

"Sounds like you knew him, Shirley," I said once we were out of the building. "Yeah, before he got that fancy name of his, he was plain old Wally Thompson. He can change his name, but he can't hide them ears he's got. He grew up in Altgeld – in fact, I think him and Will used to be in school together. Wally was a big-time gang-banger before he became a Muslim. Once a thug, always a thug," Angela said."[57]

---

[57] Name "Angela" not a typo

Muslims apparently had recruited Wally Thompson from one of Chicago's tough criminal gangs. Angela called him a *gang-banger, a thug.* According to some media stories about young Muslims in the United States, these are the kinds of unsuspecting men that Islam likes to recruit; rough and tough gang members who will be eager to fight for a cause. From Obama's account of his meeting with Rafiq, it seems that he was drawn to Rafiq and his ideology that being under the stewardship of a Muslim leader could solve life's problems.

I thought about other names mentioned in Obama's book. *Malik* (no first or last name) and the name *al Shabazz* appears several times in his book. If you read Malcolm X's book, you will find that Malcolm X received the name Malik El Shabazz after his pilgrimage to the Holy City of Mecca. Did Wally Thompson achieve his name *al Shabazz* as Malcolm X did, or did Obama use Malcolm X's name as fictitious names in his book?

Obama had the privilege of not disclosing the real names of people in his book, but he didn't try to hide Jeremiah Wright's name, or the fact that he had dabbled in Islam and Black Nationalism. Unlike other people in his book, Obama was very open about this man. Why did he mention in his book that his church's pastor, Jeremiah Wright, had *"dabbled"* in Islam?

Was Obama using Reverend Wright's church as a cover up until he accomplished what he set out to do, to keep his Muslim identity low-key? After all, Wright's was not apposed to Muslims attending his church. Anyone who watches the news knows that Reverend Wright, who is a friend of the Nation of Islam leader Louis Farrakhan, actually accompanied Farrakhan to Libya in 1984 to meet with Muammar Quddafi. This article about Wright's travel to Libya with Farrakhan was posted by Aaron Klein on the *WorldNetDaily website* on June 03, 2008:

"Wright, who accompanied Farrakhan to Libya in 1984, has been involved in Farrakhan initiatives and labeled him 'one of the most important voices in the 20th century' during a national address to the media in April at which Nation of Islam officials were invited guests."

What is Farrakhan's initiative for the United States? His proposal is for god (Islam's god) to destroy America. *WorldNetDaily website* on October 9, 2008:

"Before Farrakhan left Iran for Syria in 1996, a Tehran newspaper quoted him saying: 'god will destroy America by the hands of the Muslims...God will not give Japan or Europe the honor of bringing down the United States, this is an honor god will bestow upon Muslims.'"

Why is this man still walking free on the streets of the United States? He was in another country, but he lives in Chicago, Ill. and that was a threat against America! And this radical Muslim is a close associate of Obama's pastor and mentor, Reverend Wright! What other nation would allow this man to threaten their country and live? These are the people who are becoming more aggressive in pushing their agenda in our country. And that agenda is Islam's doctrine, according to their Holy Qur'an, not to associate with Christians, but to smite (slice, cut, slash, chop) them.

The Holy Qur'an 5:51 - *"O ye who believe! Take not the Jews and the Christians for your friends and protectors; they are but friends and protectors to each other. And he amongst you that turns to them (for friendship) is of them. Verily Allah guideth not a people unjust."*

The Holy Qur'an C. 220 47:4 - *"Therefore, when ye meet the unbelievers, smite at their necks."*

According to the above Qur'an quote Islam abhors the ways of the Christian world; so, if Obama is a Christian, as he claims to be, and is going to lead our country against our enemy (that would be Muslim terrorists), why isn't the Islamic law carried out against him? And why are Farrakhan and Iran's President Ahmadinejad befriending him and praising his win for the presidency (something that the above Qur'an warns against, "Take not Jews and the Christians for your friends")?

Is Obama leading a double life? In the following article Thomas Sowell expresses his opinion about how Obama is living his life. Thomas Sowell – *National Review Online* March 18, 2008:

"There is something both poignant and galling about the candidacy of Barack Obama. Many supporters put their money where their mouths were, so that this recently arrived Senator received more millions of dollars in donations than candidates who have been far more visible on the national stage for far more years. That's the good news. The bad news is that Barack Obama has been leading as much of a double life as Eliot Spitzer. While talking about bringing us together and deploring "divisive" actions, Senator Obama has for 20 years been a member of a church whose minister, Jeremiah Wright, has said that "God Bless America" should be replaced by "god damn America" – among many other wild and even obscene denunciations of American society, including blanket racist attacks on whites."

Thomas Sowell is a black man speaking out against Obama. So we understand that he is not a racist simply voicing his opinion against a black person.

Let's take a look how Malcolm X comes in to play with Obama's relationship with Reverend Wright. Stanley Kurtz – *National Review* May 2008 issue wrote this during President Obama's presidential run:

"The full story of the Rev. Jeremiah Wright's theology and church adds considerable urgency to already-pressing questions about Barack Obama's judgment in choosing this man as his mentor and pastor."

Kurtz went on to say, *"James H. Cone, founder and leading light of black-liberation theology, is the Charles A. Briggs Distinguished Professor of Systematic Theology at Union Theological Seminary, New York. Wright acknowledges Cone's work as the basis of Trinity's perspective, and Cone points to Trinity as the church that best exemplifies his message. Cone's 1969 book Black Theology and Black Power is the founding text of black-liberation theology, predating even much of the influential, Marxist-inspired liberation theology that swept*

Latin America in the 1970s. Cone's work is repeatedly echoed in Wright's sermons and statements. While Wright and Cone differ on some minor issues, Cone's theology is the first and best place to look for the intellectual context within which Wright's views took shape. Cone credits Malcolm X – particularly his famous dismissal of Christianity as the white man's religion – with shaking him out of his theological complacency. "Theologically," Cone affirms, "Malcolm X was not far wrong when he called the white man the devil. The false Christianity of the White-devil oppressor must be replaced by an authentic Christianity fully identified with the poor and oppressed. Malcolm's words: *"The white man has brainwashed us black people to fasten our gaze upon a blond-haired, blue-eyed Jesus! We're worshiping a Jesus that doesn't even look like us! Oh, yes!...The blond-haired, blue-eyed white man has taught you and me to worship a white Jesus, and to shout and sing and pray to this God that's his God, the white man's God. The white man has taught us to shout and sing and pray until we die, to wait until death, for some dreamy Heaven-in-the-hereafter...while this white man has his milk and honey in the streets paved with golden dollars here on this earth.""*

Black Theology and Black Power – (Obama was present).

Stanley Kurtz -*National Review* May 2008 issue:

"In 1998, in anticipation of the book's 30th anniversary, the University of Chicago held a three-day conference in honor of Black Theology and Black Power. Martin Marty, the prominent University of Chicago historian of Christianity who once taught, and has lately defended, Wright, was a key sponsor of that conference. C-SPAN taped the event, and students (some of them still in high school), community members, and politicians (including Obama?) attended. Cone himself spoke, saying, "Thirty years later I am still just as angry.""

It was just eleven years ago that Obama chose to attend a conference where he would hear radical rhetoric from a man who was following close in Malcolm X's footsteps. Was Obama still searching for a way to populate the world that

Malcolm X dreamed of? He said himself that just after reading Malcolm's autobiography, *"I looked to see where the people would come from who were willing to work toward this future and populate this new world."* From what Obama wrote in his book about Malcolm X's dream, it certainly didn't sound as if the world would have a place for Christianity. He had read Malcolm X's autobiography. Barack Obama - *Dreams from My Father* page 86-87:

"All the other stuff, the talk of blue–eyed devils and apocalypse, was incidental to that program, I decided, religious baggage that Malcolm himself seemed to have safely abandoned."

The blue-eyed devils are white people. The religious baggage that Obama said Malcolm X had safely abandoned was definitely Christianity. Malcolm did not abandon the Muslim religion or give up on his goals during his lifetime. He was assassinated in New York in February, 1965 shortly after achieving his pilgrimage to Mecca in Saudi Arabia. He died a committed Muslim at the hands of three other shotgun-wielding, committed Muslims.

As we continue to compare one quote to another in Obama's book, we get closer to the realization that his claiming to be a Christian is a façade. I do believe that Obama's speeches during his presidential campaign reflected a lot of Malcolm X's attitude and demeanor. For those who do not remember who Malcolm X was, here is a quote from his book. George Breitman - *Malcolm X Speaks* page 61:

"Each place I have visited, they have insisted that I don't leave. Thus I have been forced to stay longer than I originally intended in each country. In the Muslim world they love me once they learned I was an American Muslim, and here in Africa they love me as soon as they learn that I am Malcolm X of the militant American Muslims. Africans in general and Muslims in particular love militancy."

This Malcolm X, a radical racist Muslim, is the kind of man Obama chose as a young man to fashion his life after. Malcolm

X, the militant American Muslim, was also deeply involved with Muslims in Africa. Where was Obama's Muslim father from? Kenya, Africa. And we know that Obama still has a passion for his Muslim family and Kenya. He indicated that fact in his book when he said he felt at home there.

You may think I am being overly concerned about Obams's dream of searching for people who are willing to help populate a *new world*. As a Christian I have to be. Especially if I believe, and I do, that his idea is to populate the new world with Muslims.

How can Obama find those people who are willing to help populate the new world? By achieving just what he has done. By sitting in the Oval Office of the United States where he can empower Muslims to control our country. You say he can't do it alone. Oh, but he can, through like-minded individuals that he appoints to fill key positions. He can encourage Muslims to run for office as an act of *"rebooting"* our relationship with the Muslims both abroad and here in the United States. Most of our citizens will not realize that they are voting a Muslim into a political office. We need to be cognizant that not all Muslims in the United States, believe it or not, are from foreign countries. And they do not publicize their Islamic affiliation during their campaigns. But if they are indeed Muslim, then by Muslim law, they are commanded to destroy us.

It has been argued that not all Muslims are violent. I guess that could be true in the same sense that not everyone who claims to be Christian truly believes in the Gospel of Jesus Christ, therefore although they claim to be Christian, they really are not. In that context, someone could claim to be Muslim, but not accept the doctrine of violence that is commanded by the Qur'an.

But keep in mind that anyone who does not adhere to the tenants of the Qur'an, ***all of them***, is considered by Islam to be a non-believer, just as we Christians are, and are therefore condemned to death. With Christianity, there is no threat to your neighbors if you refuse to accept Jesus Christ as your savior. But with Islam, you are either a Muslim who hates America, or you are not a Muslim. If a person is a Muslim, they are a threat. If they don't have the determination to carry out violent acts against us personally, then they fund and support those who do.

Do you remember when the World Trade Center was destroyed? Only briefly did the new media mess up and show American Muslims dancing in the street and raising their hands in the air to praise Allah in celebration of the thousands of Americans who died in the 9-11 attacks. After that one time, the concern for the safety of those Muslims prompted the news outlets to not air that video again. I can't speak for everyone, but even if half-baked or fringe Muslims do not actually carry out acts of violence against non-Muslims, I am just as offended and outraged by the ones who fund, endorse or rejoice over such crimes while living here among us in the country that has been so good to them.

Look at Minnesota's Senator Keith Ellison. He was born in Detroit, Michigan and converted to Islam. He does not look like a Muslim. Ellison was actually not news worthy until Obama got into office. Ellison made sure that news media picked up on his pilgrimage to Mecca so the whole Muslim world would think that we are an easy mark for proselyting. He proudly announced that fact in his interview with the media. Ellison will probably be the catalyst for other Muslims to run for office. And with President Obama in the office, these people will be bold in passing the laws they feel necessary to take control. President Obama gave them "heads up" when he went live with a message to the Muslim world telling them we are not their enemy.

Have you ever wondered where Obama's apparent need to be surrounded by Muslims comes from? Was it from his stepfather? Was he raised up for the purpose of occupying the White House to become the forerunner for Islam? As a young man he sought his Muslim stepfather Lolo's counsel and guidance.[58] Obama wrote in his book about the last time he saw Lolo. It was when his mother helped Lolo travel to Los Angles to treat a liver ailment. Obama describes his stepfather with

---

[58] Obama sought Lolo's guidance – *Dreams from My Father* page 38

admiration.[59] He also said his mother continued to travel back and forth to Indonesia for six to twelve months at a time during a twenty year period;[60] and he made three or four trips to Indonesia during his teenage years.[61]

He was at a young and impressionable age during the time he lived with his Muslim stepfather. According to Obama's book, he was four years old when Lolo first came into his life.[62] Obama would have been under Lolo's tutelage in Hawaii until he was ten or eleven years old.

Obama carried Lolo's last name as a youngster, and his stories about Lolo gives the impression that there was a close bond between the two of them. Is it possible that with such a strong bond, that Obama listened to his counsel about the Muslim religion and has carried that concept with him, remembering a man that he admired as a real father?

It's hard to believe that Obama did not continue to seek Lolo's counsel as a teenager during his time in Indonesia because that counsel appeared to be fresh in Obama's mind when he wrote about Lolo in his book.

More About Obama's Connections With Muslims

We need to look closer at terrorist who are slipping into the United States undetected and Obama's connection with them. Should we, as citizens of the United States, be able to trust our appointed officials to keep incarcerated Muslim terrorists behind bars? Who immediately comes to mind when we think of Obama's connections to Muslim terrorists? Bill Ayres of course. But we have a much bigger crisis than Bill Ayres. We'll get to Bill Ayres later.

I was as surprised as anyone when Hannity and Combs on *Fox News* aired the shocker. Obama had appointed Eric H. Holder, Jr. as the next United States Attorney General. Who is Mr. Holder? He was the attorney general who was in charge of

---

[59] Obama's admiration for Lolo – *Dreams from My Father* page 38

[60] Obama's mother's travel to Indonesia – *The Audacity of Hope* page 276

[61] Obama's return to Indonesia as teen – *The Audacity of Hope* page 276

[62] Obama at age four – *Dreams from My Father* page 31

reviewing pardon requests for prisoners while President Clinton was in office. Marc Rich, who was accused of illegally trading oil with Iran during the Iranian hostage crisis, was indicted for his crime against the United States. Eric Holder was the attorney general, under President Clinton's administration, who was instrumental in granting a pardon for Marc Rich during the last twelve hours of Clinton's term.

Sean Hannity - *Fox News.com* Nov. 18, 2008:

"Fox News Alert" *"According to reports former Clinton deputy attorney general Eric Holder is President-elect Obama's top choice to be the United States Attorney General. That's right, another Clintonite lands in the Obama White House, now there's change for you. But that's not all. What is sure to be a contentious issue over the next couple of months is going to be Holder's involvement in the now infamous Clinton pardon of billionaire financier Marc Rich in 2001. Now, Rich, you'll remember was charged in 1983 for $48 million worth of tax evasion. He was indicted on 51 counts of tax fraud and was accused of illegally trading oil with Iran during the Iranian hostage crisis between 1979 and 1981."*

Who was holding the Americans hostage while Marc Rich was supposedly trading oil with Iran? Muslims....Iranian terrorists. I trust Sean Hannity's account of the story about Eric Holder and Marc Rich, so I researched the hostage incident. This is what I found on *Wikipedia, the free encyclopedia website*:

"The Iran hostage crisis was a diplomatic crisis between Iran and the United States where 52 U.S. diplomats were held hostage for 444 days from November 4, 1979 to January 20, 1981, after a group of Islamist students took over the American embassy in support of the Iranian revolution. The ordeal reached a climax when after failed attempts to negotiate a release, the United States military attempted a rescue operation, Operation Eagle Claw, on April 24, 1980, which resulted in an aborted mission, the crash of two aircraft and the deaths of eight American military men and one Iranian civilian. The crisis ended with the signing of the Algiers Accords in

Algeria on January 19, 1981. The hostages were formally released into United States custody the following day, just minutes after the new American president Ronald Reagan was sworn in."

And Eric Holder, the man Obama appointed as the United States Attorney General, pardoned the man who supported our enemy! Is this crazy or what? Certainly our country has the right to question Obama's motives for bringing people into his administration who are sympathizers with our enemy!

Let's go back to the legacy that Reverend Wright wants to carry on. Did Wright mean a legacy of radical movements? Who else in Obama's life is a radical terrorist? Bill Ayres wrote the book *"Fugitive Days"* about his life as a radical against the United States. Ayres is another friend of Obama's. This story about Ayers was published by *Dinitia Smith* on September 11, 2001. The story was rerun by *The New York Times* on Thursday, January 29, 2009:

"In his book Mr. Ayers describes the Weathermen descending into a "whirlpool of violence." "Everything was absolutely ideal on the day I bombed the Pentagon," he writes. But then comes a disclaimer: "Even though I didn't actually bomb the Pentagon – we bombed it, in the sense that Weathermen organized it and claimed it."

Another article about Ayers was written by *Stanley Kurtz* and posted by *Talk Straight.org* on Wednesday, September 24, 2008:

"In 1969, Ayers left the mostly-pacifist SDS to join the newly founded Weather Underground Organization. During the SDS convention of that year, Ayers was one of 11 SDS members to sign on to the foundation of the Weather Underground. This group was founded on the principle of immediate and total revolution against the government of the United States. The Weather Underground, of which Ayers was a vital member, launched their first assault on October 8, 1969, in Ayers' hometown. This event, entitled 'Days of Rage,' was a staged riot organized by Ayers and other Weathermen." "They

destroyed another police station in June 1970. This attack served as a warm-up act for their greatest catastrophe. After two years of planning, the Weathermen (with Ayers heavily involved in the planning details) celebrated **Communist leader Ho Chi Minh's** *birthday by detonating a huge bomb in the ladies' bathroom on the first floor of the pentagon. Following the direct assault on their command center, the United States government placed the Weather Underground Organization on their Top Ten Terrorist Organizations list."*

Dinitia Smith – *New York Times* September 11, 2001 quoted Ayers as saying, *"I don't regret setting bombs. I feel we didn't do enough."*

These people are only a few of Obama's radical friends and associates who hate the United States. How about his friend and his Muslim co-worker, Rafig? Barack Obama - *Dreams from My Father* page 195:

"Rafiq al Shabazz had settled such questions to his own satisfaction. I had begun to see him more regularly, for the morning after DCP met with the Mayor's Office of Employment and Training he had called me up and launched into a rapid– fire monologue about the job center we had asked for from the city. "We gotta talk, Barack," he said. "What y'all are trying to do with job training needs to fit into the overall comprehensive development plan I've been working on. Can't think about this thing in isolation…got to look at the big picture. You don't understand the forces at work out here. Is big, man. All kinds of folks ready to stab you in the back."

What did Rafiq mean by *"the big picture"*?

In Obama's books there were high ranking Muslims; lesser Muslims; terrorists who hate the U.S.; illegal Pakistani immigrants and radical preachers. Where are the true Americans who are honest, upright citizens of the United States? Like the Martin Luther Kings and the Bill Cosbys? Obama didn't seem to want to include good black American citizens into his personal biography. But hate for the white people and our country comes alive throughout his books, especially the first one. He seems to dwell on the history of the oppression of the black people, rather than commending those who were determined to help themselves overcome.

Obama appears to be venting his hatred of white people, his own life and America by exuding a deep anger in his book. Remember when this anger came out, it was not when he was a young man. He was thirty-three years old in 1995 when he penned this anger in his book.[63] Barack Obama - *Dreams from My Father* page 198.

"For a people already stripped of their history, a people often ill equipped to retrieve that history in any form other than what fluttered across the television screen, the testimony of what we saw every day seemed only to confirm our worst suspicions about ourselves. Nationalism provided that history, an unambiguous morality tale that was easily communicated and easily grasped. A steady attack on the white race, the constant recitation of black people's brutal experience in this country, served as the ballast that could prevent the ideas of personal and communal responsibility from tipping into an ocean of despair. Yes, the nationalist would say, whites are responsible for your sorry state, not any inherent flaws in you. In fact, whites are so heartless and devious that we can no longer expect anything from them. The self-loathing you feel, what keeps you drinking or thieving is planted by them. Rid them from your mind and find your true power liberated. Rise up, ye mighty race!"

His friend and co-worker, Rafiq, was not only a black Muslim but a confirmed nationalist. Obama seems to be trying to convince himself that Rafiq's view is correct and Islam is the right answer for the world's problems. Barack Obama:

"In talking to self-professed nationalist like Rafiq [though],[64] I came to see how the blanket indictment of everything white served a central function in their message of uplift; how, psychologically, at least, one depended on the

---

[63] Thirty-three years old – *Dreams from My Father* page xiv
[64] Brackets for emphasis

other." "This process of displacement, this means of engaging in self-criticism while removing ourselves from the object of criticism, helped explain the much-admired success of the Nation of Islam in turning around the lives of drug addicts and criminals."

Did you catch the phrase *"…the much admired success of the Nation of Islam."*

Will Obama go up against Iran, Afghanistan, Pakistan, Saudi Arabia and other Muslim nations if terrorists from those countries attack us? I wouldn't bank on it! They are all Muslim countries! Then there is Elijah Muhammad, Rashid Khalidi and Eric Holder, the United States Attorney General who, while in the Clinton administration, pardoned the Muslim terrorist, Marc Rich. All of the people mentioned above appear to still be in Obama's life.

And not with people like Louis Farrakhan who didn't waste any time speaking out for President Obama, encouraging him that the Nation of Islam's first savior also had a black father and a white mother. John Under - *WorldNetDaily* October 09, 2008:

"Brothers and sisters," Farrakhan said, "Barack Obama to me, is a herald of the Messiah. Barack Obama is like the trumpet that alerts you something new, something better is on the way." Farrakhan points out that the man Nation of Islam followers refer to as "the Savior," Fard Muhammad, had a black father and a white mother, just as Obama did. "A black man with a white mother became a savior to us," he said. "A black man with a white mother could turn out to be one who can lift American from her fall." "Would god allow Barack to be president of a country that has been so racist, so evil in its treatment of Hispanics, native Americans, Blacks?" He asked. "Would God do something like that? Yeah. Of course he would. That's to show you that the stone that the builders rejected has become the headstone of the corner. This is a sign to you. It's the time of our rise. It's the time that we should take our place. The future is all about you."

We can see in the above statement that Farrakhan is masquerading as a Christian for those who do not understand what Islam is all about. It was a statement that could easily pull some unsuspecting individual into Islam. Farrakhan has taken his statement about the *stone* that the builders rejected right from the Psalms of the Old Testament Bible Chapter 118:22 "The stone the builders rejected has become the capstone."

What Farrakhan failed to say is the passage in the Old Testament Bible is referring to Jesus Christ. He also failed to mention that the same Scripture is repeated in the New Testament books of Acts and Matthew and is referring to Jesus Christ, not a mere man:

Holy Bible – Acts 4:10-12 "This is the 'stone which was rejected by you builders, which has become the chief cornerstone." NKJV

Matthew 21:42: Jesus said to them, "Have you never read in the Scriptures: 'The stone which the builders rejected has become the chief cornerstone. This was the LORD's doing, and it is marvelous in our eyes'?" NKJV

Muslims do not recognize the Holy Bible as we do. They use only two books of the Old Testament and the book of Matthew and Revelation in the New Testament to twist the Truth. They use the book of Matthew to keep Jesus' name in their Qur'an to deceive people into thinking that because they acknowledge Jesus that they are a legitimate religion; when in fact, if you read their Qur'an,[65] you will see where they have twisted the truth about Jesus being our Savior.

The Savior which the world rejected will one day be "King of Kings, and Lord of Lords." Jesus Christ is the True cornerstone of His Church, the born again Christians. Barack Obama definitely is not the Savior of the world as Farrakhan would have people believe, not even for the United States. However, from a Muslim's perspective, like Louis Farrakhan, maybe Obama *is* their savior and a hope to claim the United States for Islam.

Isn't that what the Muslim, Dr. Dwidar, said in the CD "*Obsession - Radical Islam's War Against the West*"? He said

---

[65] Twisting the truth of Jesus – *Qur'an* – Surah C.56 page 134-135

in the CD: – *"One cleric said in his sermon, we are going to the White House, so that Islam will be victorious – Allah willing - and the White House will become a Muslim House."* He went on to say: *"No. They say that through the domination of Islam and its ideas the White House will be changed."*[66]

In the above speech Farrakhan puts emphasis on the fact that the Nation of Islam's first savior, Fard Muhammad, and Obama both have a white mother and a black father. How did Obama receive Farrakhan's speeches during his run for the highest office in the United States? How does he feel about the similarity of Islam's savior's parents and his own parents? How did he feel when Farrakhan called our country a racist country, evil in its treatment of Blacks; how did Obama feel when Farrakhan said, in a sense, that God would make him a savior of the Nation of Islam by making him president of the United States? Did Farrakhan's speeches boost his ego that he was from a Muslim background?

And was Farrakhan inciting Muslims in America to rise up when he said in his speech, *"It's the time of our rise. It's the time that we should take our place."?* Remember what Dr. Dwidar, the Muslim on the CD *[Obsession]* told the interviewer. He said that a Muslim cleric suggested that Muslims march from Mosques to the White House. Does that sound familiar? How many people (remember he is a Leader of the Nation of Islam) did Farrakhan influence to follow him in his million-man march on Washington in 1995?

Obama attended that march![67] Was Farrakhan's forceful speech about Obama being a savior meant to be a reminder to Obama who Farrakhan stands for? That he has been chosen to lead the Muslim world and Obama is expected to honor his leadership?

Is it reasonable to conclude, with the information that we have gathered about President Obama, that he is a closet Muslim? If not, then why has he suddenly given so much

---

[66] *Obsession* CD – Circulated by: The Clarion Fund
[67] Million Man March–*Discoverthenetworks.org* A guide to the political left

attention to the Muslim world? How has he reached out to the Muslim world?

First of all, as we mentioned earlier, he proposed $900 million dollars to be given to the Palestinians[68]; he is closing the Guantanamo Bay prison that houses Muslim terrorists; he sent a message via the Arabic network to the Muslim world after Iran's President Almadinejad's plea for him to make up for the past damage inflicted by the United States.

Then we have Farrakhan's statement that he recognizes Obama to be the Muslim's savior; Obama's counseling in Indonesia from a Muslim stepfather; his Muslim schooling in Indonesia; his relationships with other Muslims in the United States. *Is* he a Muslim?

Does the following excerpt taken from Obama's book about Farrakhan give us additional evidence that he shows marked admiration for Farrakhan and his Islamic teaching?

Barack Obama - *Dreams from My Father* page 200-201:

"Among the handful of groups to hoist the nationalist banner, only the Nation of Islam had any significant following: Minister Farrakhan's sharply cadenced sermons generally drew a packed house, and still more listened to his radio broadcasts."

Obama evidently listens to Farrakhan's radio broadcasts. And how did Obama know, unless he sat in on Farrakhan's sermons, that Farrakhan *generally drew a packed house*? The above excerpt came from Obama's book written in 1995. Thirteen years ago Farrakhan's speeches and sermons were making an impact on Obama. What kind of impact do Farrakhan's speeches make on Obama's today? And was Obama drawn to Farrakhan because of Malcolm X?

If you watch Farrakhan while he is speaking to a crowd, you will see that he appears to be very humble and speaks in a subtle tone to draw people to him. Malcolm X, on the other hand, was very boisterous and *demanded* respect that his listeners respond to his call. We still see Farrakhan's subtle ways in Obama, but

---

[68] $900 million - Aaron Klein - *WorldNetDaily* March 2, 2009

now that Obama is *President* Obama we see Malcolm X's style in Obama's demanding demeanor. I fully expect that, eventually, our country will hear Obama copycat Malcolm X's demand that *all* people respond to *his* dreams.

Will there be a revolution in our country? If so, will it be the kind of revolution that Malcolm X called for in his book. Will President Obama be another Malcolm X, but with more power to act on his dream? Malcolm X said the black revolution is already world-wide. George Breitman - *Malcolm X Speaks* page 9:

"The white man knows what a revolution is. He knows that the black revolution is world-wide in scope and in nature. The black revolution is sweeping Asia, is sweeping Africa, is rearing its head in Latin America. The Cuban Revolution – That's a revolution. They overturned the system. Revolution is in Asia, revolution is in Africa, and the white man is screaming because he sees revolution in Latin America. How do you think he'll react to you when you learn what a real revolution is? You don't know what a revolution is. If you did, you wouldn't use that word. Revolution is bloody, revolution is hostile, revolution knows no compromise, revolution overturns and destroys everything that gets in its way. And you, sitting around here like a knot on the wall, saying, "I'm going to love these folks no matter how much they hate me." No, you need a revolution."

Malcolm X's book also has a chapter on *grass roots*. Obama said in his book, *"Change will come from a mobilized grass roots.*[69]*"* Is Obama trying to pattern himself after Malcolm X?

In Obama's presidential campaign speeches, it was always a call for a *change*. Malcolm's speeches called for a *revolution*. Was there a similarity between the speeches of these two men? Look up the word *change* in a thesaurus and you will see that the word also means *revolution*.

Obama understood that people would not listen to radical rhetoric like Malcolm X used in his messages. No, Obama's technique was that of Louis Farrakhan, the way of a Muslims ….soft spoken …not making any sudden moves. One of

---

[69] Grass roots – *Dreams from My Father* page 133

Farrakhan's ex-aides, Dr. Vibert White Jr., made this statement about the similarity between Obama's and Farrakhan's demeanor. Kenneth R. Timmerman - *Maxnews.com* posted on November 1, 2008:

"A former top deputy to Nation of Islam leader Louis Farrakhan tells Newsmax that Barack Obama's ties to the black nationalist movement in Chicago run deep, and that for many years the two men have had "an open line between them" to discuss policy and strategy either directly or through intermediaries." "If you listen to the rhetoric and you take away Obama's political jargon, you hear a religious tenor to it that is very much Nation of Islam-like. I don't know if anyone has ever touched on it, but Obama's speaking style is very Malcolm-like, very Farrakhan-like," White said."

From what Obama wrote in his book about Farrakhan's sermons and speeches, he was obviously closer to the Nation of Islam Leader than he wanted to publicize. *Does* President Obama still have a relationship with Farrakhan?

The more news media scrutinize Obama, the more we are seeing warnings that Obama could be connected to the Islamic movement. Like Louis Farrakhan, Obama seems to be moving about in inconspicuous ways.

The only way our country can stop the movement in this country is to pay attention to what is happening between President Obama and the Arab nations. Hamas [Muslim terrorist] openly endorsed him; Farrakhan openly endorsed him and now calls him the [savior]; President Ahmadinejad of Iran openly endorsed him and later praised him in a congratulatory message; Pakistan (where terrorists are trained) openly endorsed him. All of these endorsements and congratulatory messages came from Muslim nations.

Should we have reservations about President Obama's relationship with these people? The Nation of Islam celebrated President Obama's victory with high aspirations that Obama will lean toward their cause in the world. Barbara Slavin – *The Washington Times.com* Nov. 6, 2008 wrote this article about what Almadinejad, President of Iran had to say to Obama just after he defeated Hillary Clinton in the presidential election:

"I congratulate you on being able to attract the majority of voters of the participants of the election," he wrote. "As you know, the opportunities provide by the Almighty God, which can be used for elevation of nations." He goes on to say, "He also encouraged Obama, "If you take steps on the divine path and follow the teachings of divine prophets, God, the Almighty, will help you to make up in part for the heavy damage inflicted by the U.S. in the past."

This is the time that America needs to stop and reflect on what is happening in our country and ask ourselves, "Are Americans going to be fooled into thinking that Muslims do not know their own?" The faith of these people, even though it's a misplaced faith, is so strong that they definitely know who belongs to the Muslim world and who does not!

Take Almadinejad for instance, he would no more make a statement like that to a dedicated citizen of the United States or to a Christian. He would not be stepping out so boldly with his advice. This is the country that is ignoring the warnings from the United States to stop developing a nuclear weapons system. A system, by the way, that they have publically declared that they will use to wipe Israel from the map.

You can see from the quote of Almadinejad that Muslims expect Obama to lean towards the Arab countries. And why *is* that! Because they believe Obama is a Muslim and that he will obey their god, Allah. Here again, we need to remember that Ahmadinejad was not speaking of prophets of our Holy Bible; nor was he speaking of Almighty God of Christianity. He is speaking of Islam's own prophets, and their god they call almighty. Ahmadinejad believes Obama is a Muslim and he is appealing to Obama to seek their prophets and Allah, their false god for guidance. Is Obama a Muslim? You be the judge.

I have quoted excerpts from Franklin Graham's book *The Name*. Reverend Graham is the son of the renowned evangelist Reverend Billy Graham. Reverend Franklin Graham expresses his belief that Islam's aim is to overtake the world for Islam. Reverend Graham says:

"The number one difference between Islam and Christianity is that the god of Islam is not the God of the Christian faith. In the Christian faith, the God that is worshiped is the Almighty God, who has revealed himself in human form in the person of Jesus Christ, God's Son."

Franklin Graham reminds us as Christians that we are called to love all people, but he also warns us against the false religion of Islam.[70]

Ayatollah Ruhollah Khomeini of Iran, a devout Muslim and enemy of the United States said, *"The governments of the world should know that Islam cannot be defeated. Islam will be victorious in all the countries of the world, and Islam and the teachings of the Koran will prevail all over the world."*[71]

Will Americans allow Khomeini's prediction to come to pass? According to Hal Lindsey's book the challenge to the Judeo-Christian is enormous. Hal Lindsey – *The Everlasting Hatred – The Roots of Jihad* page 6:

*"**Meet the New Enemy** - With the new threat, however, there are entirely new dimensions with enormously greater dangers. We no longer face a political force but a religion that has 1.3 billion followers worldwide. Islam is the fastest growing religion in the world. And the increasingly radical fundamentalist brand represents not only the greatest threat to world peace and stability, but also the greatest challenge to the Judeo-Christian based western civilization."*

It has been said many times in defense of Islam that all Muslims are not violent, as many Muslims will argue. And that may well be true. In that case, I don't think anyone would object to them worshiping their god as our constitution gives them the right to as long as that worship doesn't prompt violence and intimidation toward others. It's also reasonable to

---

[70] Franklin Graham's book *The Name* page 72
[71] The Two Faces of Islam

assume that if Obama ever does admit that he is Muslim, he will undoubtedly deny any endorsement of violence or hatred toward any group of people. But one has to wonder about his secret, well-masked and undefined values and his situational ethics when one considers his close associations with Muslims who do advocate hatred and violence. And like the so-called peaceful American Muslims who cheered and celebrated when we lost several thousand good people on 9-11, do Obama and the millions of self-proclaimed peaceful Muslims in America secretly cheer and rejoice and offer praise to Allah when good Americans are senselessly murdered? That may be a hard question to answer with any degree of reliability, but as I said before in different words, whether you pull the trigger, or stand at the rear shouting encouragement or helping the shooters reload, your actions are equally contemptible in God's eyes.

We have a challenge in our country today fellow Americans. Please, let's wake up and take a closer look at the man we have elected before it's too late; a man arrogant enough to have suggested to students at Dartmouth during his presidential campaign that he is divine, the Messiah returning. Now isn't that what Louis Farrakhan said in his speech? Was Obama under the tutelage of Farrakhan during his campaign? They both infer that Obama is a messiah! Had Farrakhan convinced Obama that he is a savior? Jonah Goldberg – *St. Louis Post Dispatch* June 9, 2008:

> *"Then there was the Gospel according to Obama himself. In January, he told Dartmouth students that they will know to vote for him because "...a light will shine through that window, a beam of light will come down upon you, you will experience an epiphany, and you will suddenly realize that you must go to the polls and vote for Barack."*

> *When asked in an interview what sin is, Obama defined it as "Being out of alignment with my values."*

Can you see that Obama was likening himself to Jesus Christ? He had no scruples about defaming Jesus' Name. In that statement he appeared to have had the idea that all he has to do to change our world is to *speak* the word and his *values* become *our* values. His wife Michelle is not far behind him. This is what Jonah Goldberg said in the same article:

"The change Barack is talking about is hard," she insists, "so don't get too excited, because Barack is going to demand that you, too, be different."[72]

That statement really concerned me. It's understandable that President Obama can't *demand* that we become *black*. Being black and white is the only difference between us as human beings, so in what *way* will *we* become *different* from what we are now? He certainly can't change each of us individually......
unless he demands that we convert to Islam! His statement was as much a puzzle to me as it probably was to anyone who read the article. Now that Obama has become "President" Obama we need to put the pieces of the "President Obama" puzzle together. In trying to put the puzzle together I pulled the following article from the website about his trip to Berlin Germany during his presidential campaign. His rhetoric in his speech to the German people will give us a hint of what his idea of being "different" really means. Johan Goldberg - *National Review Magazine*- August 2008:

"The greatest danger," Obama declared, "is not terrorism or global warning or even nuclear war. No, the greatest danger of all is to allow new walls to divide us from one another. Then he added: "The walls between old allies on either side of the Atlantic cannot stand. The walls between the countries with the most and those with the least cannot stand. The walls between races and tribes, natives and immigrants, Christian and Muslim and Jew cannot stand. These now are the walls we must tear down."

Read closely what he said. This was not in the United States! This was in Berlin Germany, across the Atlantic Ocean, where he appeared to *dictate* what the United States expects people to do, according to *his* agenda. By the way, Germany has

---

[72] Jonah Goldberg,- *St. Louis Post Dispatch* Monday June 9, 2008

a high population of Muslims and is also surrounded by Muslim controlled countries like France[73] and Netherlands.[74]

As a rule, Presidential candidates do not go to a foreign land to campaign! What would foreigners have to do with his getting into the Oval Office? Notice the phrase *"cannot stand"* mentioned three times. And notice that he played down terrorism and nuclear war as not being the danger in our world. I don't know about you, but I wonder what world Obama has been living in the past eight years. Terrorism and the threat of nuclear war are at our doorstep. We can't turn our backs on it by eliminating our weapon system.

From reading his speech his philosophy to gain peace in the world appears to be to throw down all defenses and depend on the brotherly love, spiritual unity and love of fellow man that the Muslim and communist nations have showed us in the past to maintain a lasting world peace. It would be almost funny hearing him make such a ludicrous suggestion had I not researched the religion of Islam. That is exactly what Islam teaches! Only Muslims understand what being united *as one* means. They see the *oneness* as one religion under Islam. Obama may have made his speech in a foreign country, but the entire world heard his idea of bringing peace to the world by becoming united as one.

We need to keep in mind that the United States is virtually the only country now who still has complete freedom of religion and freedom of speech. Such freedom does not hold true with the Islamic Nations. They have already moved into most countries that *had* freedom of speech. Islam fought against their freedom of speech, and now they control a majority of those countries. Tearing down America's wall will give them exactly what they need to bring *our nation* down.

Our nation was founded on Christianity and *that* wall (Christianity) separating us from other countries and false religions is what holds our country together and keeps tyrannical rule from dictating our lives.

---

[73] France Brigitte Bardot – Muslim control – by: *dhimmiwatch/archives/*2008
[74] The Hague, Netherlands Muslim control - Geert Wilders – posted *FOXNEWS.COM* Wednesday 21, 2009

Jonah Goldberg went on to quote something else in that same article that really caught my eye. Obama said, *"We" are the ones "we've" been waiting for."*[75] Goldberg likened that statement to being messianic rhetoric, but could Obama have been speaking to the Islamic world articulating to them that they [he and Michelle] are the Muslims that they have been waiting for to lead the way? Would that strengthen Farrakhan's prediction that he is the messiah of Islam?

My intention for this book is *not* to go political, but I feel that the following *allegation* against President Obama should be kept alive. The allegation questions his United States citizenship. We, as a free country, have the right and privilege to question President Obama about his citizenship. He was supposedly born in Hawaii. While reading his books, and because of his flip-flopping back-and-forth about his life, I began to think that he was actually born in Indonesia. Reports escalated throughout media that he might have been born in Kenya, Africa and legal steps were taken to prove this to be a fact. Philip J. Berg, a former deputy attorney general for Pennsylvania, has opened the door for the investigation. MichaelSavage.com – *WorldNetDaily* website October 23, 2008:

"The Pennsylvania Democrat who has sued Sen. Barack Obama demanding he prove his American citizenship – and therefore qualification to run for president – has confirmed he has a recording of a telephone call from the senator's paternal grandmother confirming his birth in Kenya. The issue of Obama's birthplace, which he states is Honolulu in 1961, has been raised enough times that his campaign website has posted an image purporting to be of his "Certification of Live birth" from Hawaii. But Philip J. Berg, a former deputy attorney general for Pennsylvania, told the Michael Savage talk radio program tonight that the document is forged and that he has a tape recording that he will soon release. He said the telephone call was from Obama's paternal grandmother affirming that

---

[75] Quote "we" & "we've" for emphasis

she "was in the delivery room in Kenya when he was born Aug. 4, 1961."

Not only is Philip Berg concerned about Obama's citizenship, Alan Keyes also petitioned the courts to investigate Obama citizenship. This was posted on *WorldNetDaily* by Bob Unruh on November 20, 2008:

"Former presidential candidate Alan Keyes and others filed a court petition in California asking the secretary of state to refuse to allow the state's 55 Electoral College votes to be cast in the 2008 presidential election until Obama verifies his eligibility to hold the office."

Should we be concerned when prominent United States citizens question Obama's place of birth and his eligibility to be President of the United States? Just the idea that people are questioning Obama's citizenship gives me hope that more people will wake up to the fact that there is something very wrong with President Obama's insistence to maintain his privacy.

He entitled one of his books *The Audacity of Hope*. Would he have the audacity to try and deceive an entire country? You had better believe he would if he had the right backing? If he is not a citizen of the United States what would he have to lose if he is caught? All he will need to do is deny knowing that he was born outside of the United States. What better opportunity could the Islamic nations have; someone who believes in their cause sitting in the Oval Office appointing Judges for life. If this happens, Islam's Shari'a Law can be implemented into our laws just as it was in France and Canada. France and Canada will tell you now that it is too late for them....is it too late for us?

With all of the above in mind let's go to the Muslim laws that will be forced on us if Muslims control the White House as Dr.Dwidar in the CD *Obsession* suggests. The following quotes are taken directly from the Qur'an:

The Holy Qur'an C. 51 274 – 274 - *"We now return to the subject of Jihad, which we left at 2:214-216. We are to be under no illusion about it. If we are not prepared to fight for our faith, with our lives and all our resources, both our lives and our resources will be wiped out by our enemies."*

The Holy Qur'an 5:33 - *"The punishment of those who wage war against Allah and His Messenger, and strive with might and main for mischief through the land is: execution, or crucifixion, or the cutting off of hands and feet from opposite side, or exile from the land."*

Are the above mentioned Muslim laws still carried out today? You bet they are! What about Khalid Shaikh Mohammed, the self-described orchestrator of the September 11, 2001 attack on the New York City Twin Towers? He bragged about how he orchestrated September 11 from "A to Z" and how he beheaded Wall Street Journal reporter Daniel Pearl because he was a Jew.

The Holy Qur'an 5:51 - *"DO NOT TAKE JEWS OR CHRISTIANS AS FRIENDS* – *"O ye who believe! Take not the Jews and the Christians for your friends and protectors; they are but friends and protectors to each other. And he amongst you that turns to them (for friendship) is of them. Verily Allah guideth not a people unjust."*

The Holy Qur'an 2:216 - *"Fighting is prescribed upon you, and ye dislike it. But it is possible that ye dislike a thing which is good for you. And that ye love a thing which is bad for you. But Allah knoweth, and ye know not."*

Below we have a blasphemous quote in the Islamic Qur'an about Jesus Christ. If you believe in the Holy God of the Bible and Jesus Christ as the Son of God and our Savior, you will understand why we, as Christians, can't understand the Muslim concept that to bring peace means to kill.

The Holy Qur'an Surah 3 -395 - *"Jesus was charged by the Jews with blasphemy as claiming to be God or the son of God. Allah clears Jesus of such a charge or claim."*

Christian's Answer: The Holy Bible – John 10:27-30 "My sheep hear My voice, and I know them, and they follow Me. "And I give them eternal life, and they shall never perish; neither shall anyone snatch them out of My hand. "I and My Father are one." NKJV

In the above Scripture Jesus not only claimed to be the Son of God, but He tells us that He and the Father are one. We have God the Father, God the Son and God the Holy Spirit.

The Holy Qur'an C. 51 275 - *"For Allah's cause we must fight."*

The Holy Qur'an 9:73 - "O Prophet! *Strive hard against the unbelievers and the hypocrites, and be firm against them. Their abode is hell – an evil refuge indeed."* (Strive hard in Arabic is Jihad)

The Holy Qur'an C. 220 47:4 - *"Therefore, when ye meet the unbelievers, smite at their necks."*

The Holy Qur'an C. 98 9:23 - *"O ye who believe! Fight the unbelievers who gird you about, and let them find firmness in you."*

The word *gird* translates to *restrain*. In other words if we, as a free nation, try to stop them in their quest to conquer the world for Islam, they are to fight and, if necessary, kill us.

Christian Answer: The Holy Bible – Matthew 5:41-45 "And whoever compels you to go one mile, go with him two. Give to him who asks you and from him who wants to borrow from you do not turn away. You have heard that it was said, "You shall love your neighbor and hate your enemy, but I say to you, 'love your enemy, bless those who curse you, do good to those who hate you, and pray for those who spitefully use you and persecute you." NKJV

POLYGAMY is in the Islamic Law (four wives allowed).

The Holy Qur'an Surah 4: 3-4 - *"If ye fear that ye shall not be able to deal justly with the orphan, marry women of your choice, two or three, or four; but if ye fear that ye shall not be able to deal justly (with them), then only one, or (a captive) that your right hands posses. That will be more suitable to prevent you from doing injustice."*

The Holy Qur'an Surah 509 - *"The unrestricted number of wives of the "Times of Ignorance" – was now strictly limited to a maximum of four, provided you could treat them with equality."*

The Holy Qur'an 4:34 - Women – *The Qur'an indicates that men are to be the protectors and maintainers of women and that women are to be devoutly obedient to their husbands. If wives demonstrate disloyalty and ill conduct, husbands are directed first to admonish them, second not to sleep with them, and third to beat them lightly. If wives become obedient, husbands are to accept them without punishments.*

When the Qur'an talks about men having the right to *beat them lightly* meaning their wives, it is not necessarily punishment for refusing to go to bed with them, or adultery.

Enough said. I think we can all see that if Shari'a is implemented in America, the tenants that permit honor-killing, torture, gender-abuse, intimidation, imprisonment without due process, murder, rape and all the other atrocities that are commonplace in Muslim nations would also legalize the same crimes here in America. And please don't be so gullible as to believe that Shari'a would marry seamlessly into a mirrored parallel of our laws. There will undoubtedly be those frauds who will propagate the notion that Shari's will offer a fresh illumination for American justice that would fall more in line with a globalized ideal that fosters a deeper love and respect for all men, or that Shari'a would simply add a tint of God's righteousness, glory and equality to an already prejudicial and dysfunctional system that long ago victimized the poor, illiterate and disenfranchised, or some such bucket of regurgitation spewed out of the pearly-white smile of some self-deluded, self-proclaimed messiah who thinks the Americans are ignorant and that he is so slick that he can slide uphill. Shari'a militates against American justice. The very tenants and underpinnings of Shari'a that so hypocritically attempts to justify all the atrocities in Islam are actually crimes in America. There can be no compromise. They are both diametrically opposed to one another and one would have to be abolished for the other to succeed. And considering the complacency and humanism of the liberal electorate and the cowardice and self-service greed that is characteristic of the politicians that they elect, you can guess which system would win out.

Muslim women would be terrified of what would happen to them if they became involved with another man. But that punishment is not reserved only for infidelity. The punishment is equally brutal for not preparing the meal correctly, or even glancing at another man. These women end up with broken bones, not a slap on the face where the punishment can be seen visually.

The sad thing about their life is that Muslim women have been brainwashed into thinking that they have no choice. According the Shari'a they must endure the physical abuse from their husbands. Somehow we need to help American Muslim women and children in our country understand that in America they have rights to be protected by *our* laws. That the Shari'a does not apply in our country; that what is happening to them is not a natural thing.

Christian Answer: The Holy Bible – 1 Corinthians 7:12-14 "But to the rest I, not the Lord, say: If any brother has a wife who does not believe, and she is willing to live with him, let him not divorce her. And a woman who has a husband who does not believe, if he is willing to live with her, let her not divorce him. For the unbelieving husband is sanctified by the wife, and the unbelieving wife is sanctified by the husband; otherwise your children would be unclean, but now they are holy." NKJV

I feel sorrow in my heart for the many American Muslim children who want to escape the radical commandments of the Islamic law. If you have children, put your child in the place of the two young girls who were killed because they wanted to be *American*.

After you read the quoted article, think what it will be like if we are forced to institute the Islamic Law (Shari'a) in our country. Your children may suffer the same consequence as the two young American Muslim girls did. This article was posted on the net by Glenna Whitley - *Dallas Observer* on June 18, 2008:

"For a week, Amina, an 18-year-old senior at Lewisville High School, had been living a nightmare. Her father, Yaser Said, had pulled a gun on Christmas Eve and threatened to kill her because of her relationship with Eddie. From the time they were little, Yaser told his daughters they were to have no American boyfriends, ever. Yaser and Islam kept strict watch over the girls to ensure they didn't disobey the command."

The Holy Qur'an Surah 60 - *"Let not believing women be handed over to unbelievers. No marriage tie is lawful between them."*

Glenna Whitley – *Dallas Observer* continued:
"The calls from her mother started early the next morning, but Amina refused to come home. Finally, Tissie drove the few blocks to Eddie's house and pounded on the door. Amina argued while her mother stood unmoving in the doorway, saying her father had forgiven her. A few hours later, the bullet-riddled bodies of Amina and Sarah Said were found in a bloody taxi outside an Irving hotel. Yaser Said has disappeared and now is a fugitive, wanted for their murders."

In our country we have established laws that protect women against a husband's abuse and laws that protect children from the brutality inflicted on them by their parents. While working in rescue missions I counseled with many abused women and children who had no place to go because they were running away from an abusive husband or father; most turning to a rescue mission because they knew they could lose their identity without questions.

Staff working in rescue missions deal mostly with homeless people coming off the streets. The majority do not have drivers license or any form of identification, so people running away from a bad situation can easily hide themselves from society. Perhaps someone who is reading this book, a young Muslim girl or boy or a family, needs a place to go. There are literally hundreds of Christian rescue missions in this country who are ready and willing to help, Christians who do not have a fear or timidity. Don't be ashamed or afraid to go to a local church and ask for help.

Hear my plea America! Islam is a radical religion, pushing to obey the law of a false god, Allah. I cannot emphasize enough that this is not a passing thing! They are here in our country to stay; and because these radicals look to Obama as a Muslim, they are becoming more forceful in their demands.

Will we sit back and allow Muslims to force their laws on us? Will we submit to a radical Muslim takeover of our country, and allow them to incorporate their Shari'a Law into our laws without a fight? If we do submit, what happened to the two American Muslim daughters could happen to our own children or grandchildren. If our children disobey the Muslim teaching…under Islamic Law the person who does the killing will not be considered a fugitive from justice. It will be considered an *honor* killing.

Can you see the difference between our loving God and the false god, Allah who dictates heartlessness? God put forth a Holy Bible to teach us to, first of all, honor Him as our Creator, then to love others.

A man by the name of Ali Muhammad, a warrior, puts forth the Qur'an as a guide for the Muslims to carry out hatred and terrorism to force people to come into their society, and as a means to force their wives into submission. What do the above Qur'an laws reminds us of? The many stories we see in the news about Muslim women and children being beaten or murdered simply because they disobeyed some Islamic Law.

Take the story of another teenager who was shot to death on the street here in the United States because she disobeyed the Islamic law when she married an American. And just recently a Muslim man beheaded his wife because she filed for a divorce. Yes, it was right here in the United States. The following article was posted on the *Carolyn Thompson* – Associated Press February 18, 2009:

"Muzzammil "Mo" Hassan is accused of beheading his wife last week, days after she filed for divorce. Authorities have not discussed the role religion or culture might have played, but the slaying gave rise to speculation that it was the sort of "honor killing" more common in countries half a world away, including the couple's native Pakistan. On Feb. 12, Hassan

went to a police station and told officers his wife was dead at the TV studio." Michelle Malkin also posted the story on her website on February 14, 2009.

Believe me when I say these radical religious people are acting out a command from their false god, Allah when they execute their disobedient.

Let's refresh our memories about the difference in Christianity and the Islam religion; and how Muslims have misinterpreted the Holy Bible and replaced it with their own man-made god.

Christianity was brought about when Jesus Christ came to earth, died on the cross for the sins of the world, was buried and arose from the grave and ascended back into Heaven. Islam, on the other hand, was founded by a mere human being, a warrior by the name of Muhammad who teaches intimidation to force people into Islam. Muslims can't deal with the concept that it was *Christ* who died for all sinners because he is seen in the Qur'an as being a mere man.

Islam takes the view that they are the ones chosen to lead the people to God. That presents a problem right up front since no where in God's Holy Word, the Bible, does it say that Muslims are the chosen race to serve God. In fact, God does not call a callous, evil people to serve Him in His plan to bring all humanity back to Him. Let's take a quick overview of what the Bible has to say about this:

In the Holy Bible, God promised a man by the name of Abraham that his descendents would be numerous in the world and the whole world would be blessed through his son, Isaac, and Isaac's descendants to come. That blessing was Jesus Christ and the plan of salvation coming through Abraham's line of descendants. The blessing is for anyone who will believe that Jesus died on the cross so that *all* who believe in Him will never die, but go to Heaven. That is what God meant when He said the "whole world" would be blessed through Abraham's descendants.

Islam has twisted the Holy Bible's teaching by teaching that Ishmael, another son of Abraham by an Egyptian slave woman, is the rightful son of Abraham to carry that message. One thing that we need to keep in mind as we read the Qur'an quotes is that the false god Islam calls Allah is not the Holy God of our Bible. It was the God of our Holy Bible who made that promise to His chosen people the true Jews. Ishmael was not a true Jew. He was born of an Egyptian woman. God makes it plain in His Word that His promise was to the Jews and not to the Arab nations. Please take time to read the following Scripture to get a better understanding of why the Islamic religion is wrong according to the Holy Bible:

Holy Bible – Genesis 17:19-21 God speaks to Abraham – Then God said, "No, Sarah your wife shall bear you a son, and you shall call his name Isaac; I will establish My covenant with him for an everlasting covenant, and with his descendants after him. And as for Ishmael, I have heard you. Behold, I have blessed him, and will make him fruitful, and will multiply him exceedingly. He shall beget twelve princes, and I will make him a great nation. But My covenant I will establish with Isaac, whom Sarah shall bear to you at this set time next year."" NKJV

The Scripture below is God's answer to Hagar, Sarah's Egyptian maidservant (who Muslims revere as being the mother of [their] chosen one, Ishmael).

Genesis 16:11-12 "And the Angel of the Lord said to her: "Behold, you are with child, and you shall bear a son. You shall call his name Ishmael, because the LORD has heard your affliction. He shall be a wild man; his hand shall be against every man. And every man's hand against him. And he shall dwell in the presence of all his brethren." NKJV

Holy Bible history records that Ishmael was the father of the Ishmaelites, a nomadic nation which lived in northern Arabia. Modern-day Arabs claim descent from Ishmael. Mohammed claimed Ishmael as his ancestor, as do most Arabs.

At this very moment Israel is at war with Hamas on the Gaza Strip, fighting to keep the land that God allotted to them. Until this administration they were confident that we would stand beside them in a major conflict. Today they are fearful of what the United States will do under President Obama's administration.

The Scripture above clearly tells us in no uncertain terms that Israel is the caretaker (because God owns the title) of Israel. Yet, the Muslims are fighting to take Israel's rights from them. I'm grateful to Israel for taking a stand against these ruthless people. Of course we know that God is with Israel in their fight to keep His Mighty Name alive in their country. How sad that the United States, a professed Christian nation, can't do the same! The ruthless Hamas terrorists who are fighting against Israel are the same Hamas who endorsed Obama, and the same people who Obama wants to give $900 million of our money to.

When I see Israel so deeply involved in conflict, and all of the natural disasters over the world, I wonder if this is not the beginning of Almighty God's wrath against the world because of its wickedness. In end times (just as the Left Behind book series depicted) God will deal with a wicked world that has rejected Him for false gods. And false gods have been brought into the United States. Think back to the unprecedented natural disasters that have been occurring throughout the entire world; and the United States in particular.

I am a member of one of the largest Natural Disaster Relief organizations in the United States. When a disaster hits I am prepared to be on my way within hours of a callout. Not one time have I arrived at a disaster without wondering, *"Is this the beginning of the end?"* Of course I know that, according to the Bible, God will zap me up to Heaven before the going gets too rough. Yet, I am concerned about those of you who will be left behind to endure the tremendous onset of disasters that will occur like none other in the history of the world; and the satanic rule that will prevail in the world because Satan will partner with the Antichrist in a powerful alliance to rule the earth until Jesus comes again.

The following Scripture explains why Christians believe that the disasters are God's warnings, and why Christians will not endure God's wrath on earth during a predicted dreadful seven-year period on earth. Let's take a look at some Bible prophecies:

The Holy Bible – 1 Thessalonians 4:16-17 – "For the Lord Himself will descend from Heaven with a shout, with the voice of an archangel, and with the trumpet of God. And the dead in Christ will rise first. Then we who alive and remain shall be caught up together with them in the clouds to meet the Lord in the air. And thus we shall always be with the Lord." NKJV

The above Scripture is talking about the Rapture (take up into the air) that will happen when Jesus comes back to take the believers away from earth. Jesus will not step foot on the earth at this time. He will meet us in the air.

Up until recent years we have enjoyed peace and prosperity in our country and calm in our atmosphere. Why, after two hundred years of peace and prosperity, are we experiencing unprecedented events in our country, and now a major recession? As a side note, yes, I realize that this is not our first recession, and if the economy slides into a depression, it will not be our first. But why do we have to repeat the mistakes of the past when recent historical events are recorded so accurately for us to learn from? The complacency, greed and irresponsible fiscal policies that lead to the earlier depression are so thoroughly chronicled, why must we make the same mistake so soon after seeing how devastating the first depression was?

We, as a Christian nation, once revered God Almighty as the only God and Creator. We were the most powerful nation in the world and a springboard that God uses to reach out to the rest of the world with the Gospel of Jesus Christ; a Christian nation whose missionaries God uses as a light for the entire world to see who Jesus Christ is. Now churches in our country are afraid to speak out against the false Muslim religion intrusion into our Christian nation. Not only that, but God-focused Christianity has been perverted into a Health and Wealth/Prosperity sideshow where man's self-fulfillment is the focus instead of the will of God, and in fact, God is reduced to a level and status equal to a banker or fairy godfather who's job it is to grant our every wish.

Now we are no longer a light for the entire world to see or hear who Jesus Christ is because our country is accepting humanism and a pagan religion into a Christian society. Along with that, we are seeing a blessings because we have become a nation that endorses the murder of unborn babies in the name of women's rights and openly celebrates sexual sin and homosexuality, which is an abomination in God's eyes.

Why should God continue to bless a country that is throwing Him aside? No one knows the day or hour that Jesus will return, *but with the phenomenal happenings that we're seeing on a daily basis and the calloused indifference toward God,* I expect to meet Jesus in the air any minute.

Christians would like to see our country turned back around to God's way of doing things. But the only way we are going to be able to turn things around is to speak out and stand up against liberalism, humanism and this cultic religion, Islam.

Let's take a glimpse of what is going to happen, according to the Bible, *after* all of the believers *[born-again Christians]* are taken out of the earth.

The Holy Bible – Revelation 8:6-13 "So the seven angels who had the seven trumpets prepared themselves to sound. The first angel sounded: And hail and fire followed, mingled with blood, and they were thrown to the earth. And a third of the trees were burned up, and all green grass was burned up. Then the second angel sounded: And something like a great mountain burning with fire was thrown into the sea, and a third of the sea became blood. And a third of the living creatures in the sea died, and a third of the ships were destroyed. Then the third angel sounded: And a great star fell from Heaven, burning like a torch, and it fell on a third of the rivers and on the strings and water. The name of the star is Wormwood. A third of the waters became wormwood, and many men died from the water, because it was made bitter. Then the fourth angel sounded: And a third of the sun was struck, as third of the moon, and a third of the stars, so that a third of them were darkened. A third of the day did not shine, and likewise the night. And I looked, and I heard an angel flying through the midst of Heaven, saying with a loud voice, "Woe, woe, woe to the inhabitants of the earth, because of the remaining blasts of the trumpet of the three angels who are about to sound!" NKJV

Revelation 9:1-10 "Then the fifth angel sounded: And I saw a star fallen from Heaven to the earth. To him was given the key to the bottomless pit.

And he opened the bottomless pit, and smoke arose out of the pit like the smoke of a great furnace. So the sun and the air were darkened because of the smoke of the pit. Then out of the smoke locusts came upon the earth. And to them was given power, as the scorpions of the earth have power. They were commanded not to harm the grass of the earth, or any green thing, or any tree, but only those men who do not have the seal of God on their foreheads. And they were not given authority to kill them, but to torment them for five months. Their torment was like the torment of a scorpion when it strikes a man. In those days men will seek death and will not find it; they will desire to die, and death will flee from them. The shape of the locusts was like horses prepared for battle. On their heads were crowns of something like gold, and their faces were like the faces of men. They had hair like a women's hair, and their teeth were like lions' teeth. And they had breastplates like breast; plates of iron, and the sound of their wings was like the sound of chariots with many horses running into battle. They had tails like scorpions, and there were stings in their tails. Their power was to hurt men five months." NKJV

The Holy Bible – Revelation 16:1-11 Then I heard a loud voice from the temple saying to the seven angels, "Go and pour out the bowls of the wrath of God on the earth. So the first went and poured out his bowl upon the earth, and a foul and loathsome sore came upon the men who had the mark of the beast and those who worshiped his image. Then the second angel poured out his bowl on the sea, and it became blood as of a dead man; and every living creature in the sea died. Then the third angel poured out his bowl on the rivers and springs of water, and they became blood. And I heard the angel of the waters saying: "You are righteous, O Lord," The One who is and who was and who is to be, Because You have judged these things. For they have shed the blood of saints and prophets, and You have given them blood to drink. For it is their just due." And I heard another from the altar saying, "Even so, Lord God Almighty, true and righteous are Your judgments. Then the fourth angel poured out his bowl on the sun, and power was given to him to scorch men with fire. And men were scorched with great heat, and they blasphemed the name of God who has power over these plagues; and they did not repent and give Him glory." NKJV

The Holy Bible – 2 Peter 3:11-12 "Therefore, since all these things will be dissolved, what manner of persons ought you to be in holy conduct and godliness. Looking for and hastening the coming of the day of God, because of which the heavens will be dissolved, being on fire, and the elements will melt with fervent heat?" NKJV

God has made a way for everyone to escape those horrendous sufferings, and that is to put our trust in Jesus Christ as God's only Son and the Savior of the world.

There *is* a consideration that we are the last Christian country to be conquered by a people who want to wipe out Christianity. If we are conquered, then the only "light" to show who Jesus Christ is will be snuffed out. Why should God wait any longer to bring this earth to an end?

I am not trying to predict the date or time when God will carry out what He has said He will do. But I *can* quote His warnings.

With the above in mind let's explore why God does not want the false Muslim religion to conquer the world. God himself says He is concerned about His Holy Name.[76] The following excerpts are taken directly from the Muslim's Holy Qur'an's man-made laws. The Christian's answer is taken from the Holy Bible, God's Word.

The Muslims believe that there is a paradise waiting for those who die in jihad (Holy War). The paradise is not the same paradise that Christians look forward to. The following Qur'an quotes will help you understand why men are not afraid of dying for their false god. They are promised a false paradise that will have virgins waiting for them:

The Holy Qur'an – Sura 55:47-59 - *"For those who reverence their Lord, two gardens. Which of your Lord's marvels can you deny? Full of provisions. Which of your Lord's marvels can you deny? Two things are in them, flowing. Which of your Lord's marvels can you deny? Of every fruit in them, two kinds. Which of your Lord's marvels can you deny? While relaxing on furnishings lined with satin, the fruits are within reach. Which of your Lord's marvels can you deny? Their beautiful mates were never touched by any human or jinn.*

---

[76] God's Holy Name - Ezekiel 36:21 (*The Holy Bible*)

Virgins as fair as corals and rubies. Then which of the favors of your Lord will you deny?"

The Holy Qur'an Sura 37:48 - *"They will sit with bashful, dark-eyed virgins, as chaste as the sheltered eggs of ostriches."*

The Holy Qur'an Sura 52:17-20 - *"They shall recline on couches arranged in rows. To dark-eyed maidens we shall wed them."*

The Holy Qur'an Sura 56:17, 22 - *"Round about them will (serve) youths of perpetual (freshness)…And (there will be) Companions with beautiful, big, and lustrous eyes."*

Christian Answer: The Holy Bible – Matthew 22:29-32 Jesus answered and said to them, "You are mistaken, not knowing the Scriptures nor the power of God. For in the resurrection they neither marry nor are given in marriage, but are like angels of God in Heaven. But concerning the resurrection of the dead, have you not read what was spoken to you by God, saying, 'I am the God of Abraham, the God of Isaac and the God of Jacob'? God is not the God of the dead, but of the living." NKJV **(Note: God does not mention Ishmael here.)**

The Holy Qur'an C. 215) - *"If Christians go back to Jesus, he was but a man and a servant of Allah; He came to still the jarring sects, not to create a new one."*

Christian Answer: The Holy Bible – "Behold, the virgin shall be with child, and bear a Son, and they shall call His name Immanuel." Which is translated, "God with us." **Matthew 1:23** NKJV

Christian Answer: The Holy Bible – John 14:6-7 Jesus said to him, "I am the way, the truth, and the life. No one comes to the Father except through Me. If you had known Me, you would have known My Father also; and from now on you know Him and have seen Him." NKJV

The Holy Qur'an Surah 2.122 - *"The argument now proceeds on another line. Ye People of the Book who go back to Abraham! Not only is your claim to exclusive knowledge of Allah false and derogatory to the Lord of All the Worlds. If you must appeal to Abraham, he was also the progenitor of the Arab race through Ishmael. Indeed Abraham and Ishmael together built the House of Allah in Makkah (long before the Temple of Jerusalem was built)."* [77]

The Holy Qur'an Surah 121 - *"Indeed Abraham and Ishmael together built the House of Allah in Makkah (long before the Temple of Jerusalem was built). They purified it and laid the foundation of the <u>universal</u>[78] religion, which is summed up in the word Islam, or complete submission to the Will of Allah. Abraham and Ishmael were thus true Muslims."*

First of all, God's first temple was built in Jerusalem, not in Makkah. Makkah, also known as Mecca is in Saudi Arabia. The Temple of Jerusalem was known as Solomon's Temple; the first stationary temple to be built for God. Solomon's Temple was completed in 960 B.C. Islam as a religion and civilization made its entry into the world stage with the life and career of the Prophet Muhammad ibn Abd Allah. Muhammad was born in 570 A.D. and died in 632 A.D.

Read the history and figure it out for yourself. Solomon built the Temple in Jerusalem some 1600 hundreds years before the Muslim religion began.

Christian Answer: The Holy Bible – 1 Kings 6:1 "And it came to pass in the four hundred and eightieth year after the children of Israel had come out of the land of Egypt, in the fourth year of Solomon's reign over Israel, in the month of Ziv, which is the second month, that he began to build the house of the LORD." NKJV:

The Holy Qur'an 4659 - *"Jesus was a man, and a prophet to the Children of Israel."*

Christian answer: John 20:30-31 "And truly Jesus did many other signs in the presence of His disciples, which are not written in this book; but these are written that you may believe that Jesus is the Christ, the Son of God, and that believing you may have life in His name." NKJV

The Holy Qur'an C. 48 - *"If the People of the Book rely upon Abraham, let them study his history. His posterity*

---

[77] Makkah aka Mecca
[78] Underscored "universal" for emphasis

included both Israel and Ishmael. Abraham was a righteous man of Allah, a Muslim, and so were his children. Abraham and Ishmael built the Ka'ba as the house of Allah, and purified it, to be a centre of worship for all the world."

(Note that the Qur'an said *"centre of worship for all the world."* And their intent is to claim the world for Islam.) The following excerpt taken from Hal Lindsey's book is a good description of the Kaaba. Hal Lindsey – *The Everlasting Hatred – The Roots of Jihad* page 92:

"It is a 50-foot cubic structure of gray stone and marble. Positioned in Mecca (Saudi Arabia) so that its corners correspond with the four points of the compass, the Muslims claim the Kaaba contained 360 idols – one for each of the lunar calendar days. The cornerstone of the Kaaba is the sacred Black Stone. It is a meteorite of ancient origin. Muslims believe it has the power to absorb sin from the one who kisses it. Arabs believe that the Black Stone is a god who protects their tribes."

Christian Answer: The Holy Bible – Psalms 33:13-15 "The LORD looks from Heaven; He sees all the sons of men. From the place of His dwelling He looks on all the inhabitants of the earth; He fashions their hearts individually; He considers all their works." NKJV

Christian Answer: The Holy Bible – 1 Chronicles 16:27 "Honor and majesty are before Him; Strength and gladness are in His place." NKJV

How wonderful it is to know that we have a heavenly Father who looks down on us from Heaven and is not contained in a cubical of stone with 360 idols.

From the beginning of this book I have said that I am a Christian fighting to uphold our Holy God's Word and to keep Islam from bringing its false doctrine into this country. I forced myself to listen to President Obama's campaign speeches as part of my research to write this book. I will have to admit that, at one point during his speeches, his casual demeanor with promises of change caught me off guard. I had to remind myself, as I do now, that President Obama twisted Holy Scripture apparently building himself up in the eyes of society, and probably helping him win the election. And with everything I have researched about him; his ties with Muslims and his quick actions to reach out to the Muslim world after he took office, I feel a desperate need to rush this book for publication.

Did Obama call Almighty God a *'sky god'*? Jonah Goldberg - *National Review* August 2008 issue wrote this about Obama:

"He explained to San Francisco fat-cats that rural Americans bitterly[79] "cling" to their bizarre rituals, unnecessary weapons, and ancient sky god, all because they've been left out on globalization."

With his speech in San Francisco, was Obama simply trying to put into our society's minds that we are an *angry* nation who *depends* too much on off-the-wall *traditional values*? Was he implying that a *weapons system* to keep us safe is of no value? And was Obama implying that we put too much faith in a God that he apparently believes has no merit?

Is Obama a Christian as he professes to be? Or is he a Muslim who secretly prays towards the Kaaba? Would a Christian or a dedicated American citizen demean the Holy God of Christianity by calling Him a *sky god* as Obama did above? *And* what are the *bizarre rituals* that he was talking about? Was he talking about *American* traditions? And what did he mean by *unnecessary* weapons? Wasn't that the same message he gave in Germany? Maybe someone should suggest that President Obama watch footage of the Twin Towers inferno in New York coming down.

President Obama believes (he said it himself in one of his speeches during his presidential campaign) that we should sit down with our enemy and simply talk through our differences. And he lost no time after his election making contact with the Arab nations via the *Arabic-language satellite TV network*. The Arab nation is a Muslim nation. They have no desire to have peace with a Christian nation. Their Qur'an clearly tells us that. Obama is from a Muslim background, and he probably knows very well what the Islamic law says about associating with

---

[79] "Americans bitterly" italicized for emphasis

Christians. These people are not going to sit down and talk to him without some strong concessions.

Let's revisit his speech in San Francisco, why do you think he emphasized our nation's obstacles right up front in his speech, then at the end of his speech suggested that the reason we have obstacles is because we've been left out of globalization?

If he had simply thrust the idea of globalization first in his speech, his audience probably would not have agreed with what he was trying to do; however, he was using Farrakhan's method of arousing doubt in his listener's minds about the way our country was run *before* presenting his solution. That speech was aired on national television and in media print. How many people do you think, (those who do not understand that globalization of the world would mean becoming a part of a cultic religion) would give a positive consideration to going global if it means peace in the world? My bet is a lot of people will go along with globalization or nationalism without realizing what they are doing.

Something else troubled me about that speech. Obama could have put into the minds of others that God is not relevant because He is an *ancient* "sky" god!

Was this something that the mythical religion taught him while he was in Indonesia? Calling God a *"sky god."*

Just recently he said he has an idea for a new school system. He hasn't pinned it down yet, but he is working on it! Now, that is a scary thing! He just recently visited the country of Turkey on April 6-7 where, coincidentally (?), Turkey was hosting the Alliance of Civilization Conference in Istanbul, a conference with emphasis on promoting the idea of teaching Muslim youth to reach out to the word via internet. Can you imagine what it will be like if he comes back with an idea to reform our entire school system to incorporate other religions into our children's text books? Read what he thinks a well-rounded education means. It incorporates a lot of off-the-wall religions: Barack Obama - *The Audacity of Hope* page 203:

"This isn't to say that she provided me with no religion instruction. In her mind, a working knowledge of the world's great religion was a necessary part of any well-rounded education. In our house hold the Bible, the Koran, and the Bhagavad Gita sat on the shelf alongside books of Greek and Norse and African mythology."

I can't imagine what it would be like for a young boy's mind to be filled with so many mythical religions. And what are the teachings of the above books? They are: Koran or Qur'an (Islam - Muslim), Bhagavad Gita (Hinduism -Muslim), Buddhism (Buddhism – Muslim), Norse (Scandianvian – Muslim country) and African mythology; all of which teach a mythical religion and lifestyle.

When Obama talks about God he appears to be putting Him in the same category of these mythical beings. He can't seem to put life into perspective as a gift received from God; that we are not spirits moving about in the universe. He just can't seem to get it together. In his book *The Audacity of Hope* he lumps Christianity with the religion of the Muslims. But then down a few paragraphs on the same page he talks about the Judeo-Christian tradition to soften what he said earlier.[80] So what does Obama really believe!

As a Christian, it scares me to think that we have someone in the highest office in our nation that sets no standards against demeaning Christianity. I always had my doubts about Obama claiming to be a Christian, but when he made the statement in his book about The *Sermon on The* Mount and asked the question, *"Whose Christianity would we teach,"* I knew without a doubt that he is not a Christian. He asked, *"Whose"* Christianity would we teach?"

How many "Christianity's" does he think there are? President Obama evidently doesn't understand that there is one Christianity and is based on Jesus Christ. Christianity does not come through anyone else.

Is Obama trying to combine Islam and Christianity to get some sense of religion? It won't work!

---

[80] *The Audacity of Hope* page 218

As a Christian I wanted to look at Obama's first book objectively. I tried to convince myself that he had an unfortunate childhood; that he wasn't entirely at fault with the choices he made for his life. However, after a realizing that there are numerous by-racial children in the United States who have moved right into society and are making a life for themselves, I came to the conclusion that Obama had the intelligence to make the right choices in his life.... unfortunately, according to what he wrote in his books, he chose to travel down a road of hate and disappointments. Where will that hate take him (and the United States) from here?

CHAPTER EIGHT

Islam's Eyes Are on Our Children
Dr. Franklin Graham

Obama's first book reflects the life of a hoodlum taking his vengeance out on society because of his mixed blood. The book is full of hate, resentment and low self-esteem. The book is not the kind of book one would expect a person of President Obama's intelligent to write. His second book, however, is more polished, giving the impression, with comparing the two books, that someone either wrote the first book for him, or someone helped him write the second book.

After reading President Obama's two books I have a problem believing that Obama made a decision to run for the presidential office because he is patriotic. There must have been some kind of driving force behind his determination to rise to the level of the most powerful man in the world. If you read his first book, you will find that Obama didn't appear to have confidence enough in himself to get through life, much less rise to the presidency. Who, or what, is the driving force behind Obama's unprecedented rise to the White House? We have seen no evidence of Obama having wealthy friends, other then Muslims, who could finance his phenomenal presidential campaign.

President Obama is already in the Oval Office, and we can't change that. However, we can be alert to the fact that more Muslims will be on the voting ballot. And with an understanding of what we are up against, we can be more cognizant of who we vote into political offices during the next four years. It's the only way we can stand up against this radical religious movement.

As I mentioned earlier, we already have a Muslim congressman who is advocating Muslim involvement in politics. Keith Ellison, a Minnesota congressman, is the first Muslim congressman in the United States and, like Malcolm X, has just completed the hajj pilgrimage to Mecca. This is happening in our country today. Below are two articles about Keith Ellison and his relationship with Muslim radical organization. The articles spell out plainly what Ellison's feelings are about the Muslim movement in the United States and what he expects other Muslims to do. The first article was written just after Ellison first won his seat to congress in 2006. Ted Sampley - *The U.S. Veteran Dispatch* January 1, 2006:

"You can't back down. You can't chicken out. You can't be afraid. You've got to have faith in Allah, and you've got to stand up and be a real Muslim," Keith Ellison, the first Muslim elected to the United States Congress, instructed a cheering crowd of Muslims last month in Dearborn. He urged the group to remain steadfast in their faith and push for justice. The crowd roared in return, Allah akbar, Allah akbar," – God is great.

"Allha akbar were the last words heard on the cockpit voice recorder of Flight 93, just before Muslims murdered all its passengers by crashing the jetliner into the ground."

You got it! The Muslims in the United States are becoming more confident and aren't the least bit afraid to shout out the last words heard on Flight 93 before it went down. Ellison, two years later, is bragging about his pilgrimage to Mecca and how the United States is accepting the Muslims in the country. And yes, he also mentions Obama's presidential win and what he hopes will happen during Obama's administration. The following is a second article picked up on Ellison. Joseph Abrams *FOXNews.com* January 08, 2009:

"Minnesota rep. Keith Ellison's groundbreaking pilgrimage to Mecca last month was paid for by an American Muslim

organization that has ties to Islamic radicals and is "the Muslim equivalent of the neo-Nazi party," his critics say. Ellison, a Democrat, became the first U.S. congressman ever to make the hajj pilgrimage when he visited Islam's holy city in December. The trip was funded by the Muslim American Society of Minnesota, a non-profit interfaith group that is one of 55 branches of the MAS nationwide. The pilgrimage was hailed by Muslim activists in the U.S. "A U.S. congressman going on hajj sends a very positive message to the Muslim world about America and the religious diversity in America," said Ibrahim Hooper, communications director for the Council on American-Islamic Relations, a Muslim advocacy group."

"People were encouraged about the role the U.S. will play under President-elect Barack Obama," Ellison said. The fact that Obama's middle name is Hussein and he had a Muslim father came up in conversation, "People think that the (incoming) president might have a higher level of sensitivity," Ellison said."

Here we have a Muslim congressman who encouraged other Muslims to stand up and be a *real Muslim* in the United States. What is a *real* Muslim? Are the *real* Muslims the ones who belong to the *Muslim American Society of Minnesota*, a *neo-Nazi* party type organization who is not bashful about boasting their power within our country? This Muslim organization paid for Ellison's hajj pilgrimage to Mecca! Was there a motive behind their financing his trip? You be the judge!

The Muslim American Society of Minnesota knew that Ellison's trip would make headlines….and it did in a big way! It was a well-timed strategy to get the word out that the United States has no problem with Muslims occupying political offices. Not only that, but in his interview Ellison told the reporter that his trip was sending a *"very positive message to the Muslim world about America and the religious diversity in America,"*

Would you say that Ellison made it clear that now is the time to move ahead? Obama said, **"We** are the ones *we've* been waiting for."[81] Farrakhan said *"It's the time of our rise. It's the*

---

[81] *National Review* page 20

time that we should take our place."[82] Remember what Obama said in his book, "*Rise up, ye mighty race!*"[83] Aren't all of these motivational speeches to the Muslim world?

All of these events have happened since Obama came on the scene. Ellison was the first Muslim to step out and openly profess his religion. That was two years ago. Obama came on the scene with the middle name "Hussein" and Ellison made it public about his pilgrimage to Mecca (Saudi Arabia).

What was Ellison's reaction to the question about Obama's middle name? He believes that, because of Obama's historical middle name, this president will have a higher level of sensitivity. Ellison didn't say that Obama would be more sensitive to the Muslim movement because he is Muslim. These people are not going to say anything that will prevent what they believe will eventually become a victory for the Muslim movement in this country.

<u>Muslim's Response Before President Obama's Inauguration</u>

If you think *Ellison* is a true supporter of Obama, read the *following article* picked up by Bob Unruh. Bob Unruh – *WorldNetDaily* January 9, 2009:

"*Chavis Muhammad writes that 'with some 1.25 billion Muslims across the globe, the Islamic world couldn't be more excited and anticipatory about the possibility of increased dialogue, understanding and unity that Obama's presidency will undoubted bring. As an African American Muslim, I can say my prayers were answered when Obama was elected,' Chavis Muhammad writes.'" "Also cited by Chavis Muhammad is Imam El-Hagg Talib Abdur-rashid of the Mosque of Islamic Brotherhood in New York, who says, "Obama has a job ahead of him of immense proportions. But so do we as Muslims in America."*

I don't know about you, the reader, but the statement above bothers me. The Muslims are not interested in material things,

---

[82] *WorldNetDaily* October 09, 2008
[83] Barack Obama - *Dreams from My Father* page 198

they are a wealthy society. Wasn't *Chavis Muhammad* saying that it was time for Muslims to proselyte us when he said, *"But so do we as Muslims in America."* Who exactly is the Brotherhood? Let me quote what Noreen S. Ahmed-Ullah, Sam Roe and Laurie Cohen – Tribune staff reporters wrote on September 19, 2004, "Over the last 40 years, small groups of devout Muslim men have gathered in homes in U.S. cities to pray, memorize the Koran and discuss events of the day. But they also addressed their ultimate goal, one so controversial that it is a key reason they have operated in secrecy: to create Muslim states overseas and, they hope, someday in America as well. These men are part of an underground U.S. chapter of the international Muslim Brotherhood, the world's most influential Islamic fundamentalist group and an organization with a violent part in the Middle East. But fearing persecution, they rarely identify themselves as Brotherhood members and have operated largely behind the scenes, unbeknown even to many Muslims. Still, the U.S. Brotherhood has had a significant and ongoing impact on Islam in America, helping establish mosques, Islamic schools, summer youth camps and prominent Muslim organizations. It is a major factor, Islamic scholars say, in why many Muslim institutions in the nation have become more conservative in recent decades."

These men want to create Muslim states in the United States and they are here hiding in our own country planning their strategy. Will anyone stand up to these radical people!!

How much of Malcolm X's vision or Farrakhan's vision will our country tolerate before we admit that Islam has dramatically touched Obama's life? All of us should have a fear of the *Council on American-Islamic Relations organization;* a fear that they will become more forceful in advancing in the political arena of the United States. They are *the* organization that will push to get laws changed.

I apologize for being redundant, but it can't be stressed enough that Obama is not the norm for a president of the United States. And we need to think back to how Obama's book reflects admiration for Malcolm X and Louis Farrakhan and the mannerism similarity between these three men, as Dr. Vibrate, Farrakhan's aide suggested.

Farrakhan makes no bones about how he feels about Obama. But how does Obama feel about Farrakhan? This article was also taken from Kenneth R. Timmerman -*Newsmax.com* on November 1, 2008:

"Farrakhan has called Jews "bloodsuckers," "santanic" and accused them of running the slave trade. He has labeled gays as "degenerates." In a 2006 speech, the ADL again condemned Farrakhan when he said: "These false Jews promote the filth of Hollywood that is seeding the American people and the people of the world and bringing you down in moral strength...It's the wicked Jews the false Jews that are promoting lesbianism, homosexuality. It's wicked Jews, false Jews that make it a crime for you to preach the word of God, then they call you homophobic!"

Obama was careful to "denounce" Farrakhan's comments – but not the man[84] – during the Democratic primary season earlier this year, but only after Hillary Clinton called him out for benefiting from Farrakhan's support."

Farrakhan was accusing the Jews of causing the moral failure of the world. Obama did not *reprove* Farrakhan until he was forced to do so. Farrakhan eliminated the Americans and Jews, so he must have been speaking to his own Muslim people when he said *"..... false Jews that make it a crime for you to preach the word of God."* The god the Jews make it a crime to worship would be the false god, Allah. A true Messianic Jew reveres the Holy God to their very depths. Obama did not reprove Farrakhan for blasting the Jewish people. This takes us back to Obama's middle name and a Hussein in recent history who hated the Jews.

History Behind Obama's Name - "Hussein"

Islamic history reveals to us why Hamas and other Muslims are excited about Barack *Hussein* Obama becoming the President of the United States; and what significance the name

---

[84] Underscore for emphasis

Hussein has for Muslims throughout the world. Let's take a short walk through some history.

Obama claims he can bring peace between the United States and the Middle East (Muslim nations) by simply sitting down and talking with the enemy. How many times have representatives from the United States traveled to the Middle East for such talks? Most of those proposals for peace were rejected.

Bin Laden's 'letter to America' should make it clear that those people do not want us in their land. The *guardian.co.uk Sunday 24 November 2002* posted the full text of bin Laden's letter, but I will quote only one excerpt from his letter given the length of it:

"We also advise you to pack your luggage and get out of our lands. We desire for your goodness, guidance, and righteousness, so do not force us to send you back as cargo in coffins."

I realize that bin Laden does not represent the entire Muslim world; however, *he is* the enemy and it's the enemy who will not come to terms with letting the United States interfere with their goal to rule the world. That means a *continuous war* until they have won. These people are not engaging in war against us to occupy our land....they don't need it. It's a religious thing!

Christians fight against evils of the world to bring people peace, and to the saving Grace of Almighty God. We send missionaries to the ends of the earth to tell people about Jesus Christ. We strive to push on regardless of the consequences because we know it is a cause for Christ.

We know that Jesus' last words before he ascended back into Heaven were, "Therefore go and make disciples of all nations,...."[85]

The Muslims, likewise, have a command from their false man-made god, Allah, to bring all people into Dar-al-Islam, the land of those who have submitted to Allah. Their command, however, is contradictory to the way Christians lead people to our God. We do it with loving kindness and give others a choice

---

[85] Matthew 28:19 - *The Holy Bible*

to either accept or to refuse God's grace of salvation. God has given us freedom of choice and we, as Christians, acknowledge that freedom.

The Muslims, on the other hand, believe that their command has no restraints to bring people into Dar-al-Islam. They are taught that Islam is the religion of the world and they are to proselyte everyone on earth into Islam, by intimidation if necessary, and the infidels who refuse to accept their religion are to be removed.....they have no place on earth.

You might be surprised to know that Obama's middle name *Hussein* has a sacred meaning in Islam's culture. It also plays a definite roll in the Muslim's allegiance to fight for the sake of that name. Saddam *Hussein,* for instance, was revered by Islam as a martyr, not a dictator. He became powerful because he carried the name *Hussein. Was* Saddam a dictator? We need to go back into history to find out a little more about Saddam.

Saddam Hussein likened himself to another king in history, King Nebuchadnezzar. Nebuchadnezzar was the King of Babylon (modern-day Iraq) who, during Old Testament Bible days, ruthlessly captured Jerusalem, destroyed God's Temple and carried the people of Judah (modern-day Israel) into Babylonian captivity.

Saddam used a unique strategy somewhat like Nebuchadnezzar to force the Iraqi people into submission and recognition of his power. He had statues of himself erected in strategic places and his picture posted throughout the country and on money reminding the people that he was another savior *Hussein.* He evidently was raised from a child with the idea that his name was going to be significant in the Muslim world. History has it that Saddam was raised by his uncle Kharirallah Talfah who filled Saddam with dreams that he would follow the pathway of King Neuchadnezzar.

I found this interesting story about Saddam Hussein on the *Voice of America website – by Margaret Besheer – Irbil, Iraq* Dec. 29, 2006:

"Doctor Jerrold Post, a professor of psychiatry at George Washington University, wrote a psychological profile of Saddam for the U.S. Central Intelligence Agency. He says

Saddam's uncle was a significant influence in his life. His uncle filled him with dreams of glory and told him some day he would have a heroic role to play in the history of the Iraqi people, that he would follow in the pathway of Nebuchadnezzar and Saladin and liberate Jerusalem," said Jerrod Post."

When we see the word *liberate* we think of setting people free. That probably was not what Saddam's uncle was proposing. He more than likely helped Saddam to almost achieve what he saw as Saddam's future...to liberate Jerusalem. The kind of liberation Saddam's uncle saw was not freedom for Jerusalem, but to bring it back to a Muslim nation as it was in the time of Nebuchadnezzar and Saladin. From news media sources we could see that the Jews were a central focus in Saddam's regime. (Saladin was an Arab Sultan who in 1187 also took Jerusalem.)

Farrakhan is encouraging Obama to look to the future of leading the nation (the United States) that he, Farrakhan, wants to see become a Muslim nation. Saddam's uncle encouraged Saddam to become a leader because of something *he* wanted to see happen. What a similarity between the ambitions of the two men who were mentors to young people.

Could Saddam's quest to eliminate the *practice* of the Jews (which is worshiping the true God of our Bible) have been carried over into the United States through Louis Farrakhan, Leader of the Nation of Islam? How well did Farrakhan, a hater of the Jews, know Saddam Hussein?

There are probably hundreds of Muslims with the name "Hussein," but how many with that name have made history? Farrakhan evidently visited one of the history-making Hussein's in 1997. The story was picked up on *World News* website posted December 11, 1997:

"In 1997 Farrakhan made a trip to Iraq defying a U.S. ban on travel by its citizens to Iraq. Though the travel ban carries a penalty of up to 12 years in prison, it is rarely enforced. Farrakhan said he does not expect to be charged because he did not use his American passport to enter Iraq. He did not say what document he used to enter the country. "I am here as a

Muslim, as a servant of god and as a human being concerned with human suffering," he said. "If we must pay a price for being that, then so be it."

How well does Farrakhan know Saddam Hussein? He traveled to that country against a U.S.'s ban on travel to that area. And somehow he managed to get into the country because he was a Muslim.

We, here in America, have almost forgotten about Saddam Hussein, but the Muslim world is bringing that name *Hussein* alive in America again. We are being educated that there is a Hussein who was considered in the Muslim world to be a martyr; whose death is celebrated each year by Muslims flagellating their bodies. Just how important is that name! Picture the following image in your mind:

Muslim men lying prostrate on the ground with deep cuts on their faces and body, one holding his head with one hand and the other spread across the ground. This was a picture of how Muslims celebrate the name "Hussein." The 4 X 6 inch picture published in the *Post Dispatch* newspaper was a definite encouragement and reminder to Muslims here in the United States that *Hussein* gave his life for his religious beliefs. This is the bizarre behavior of Muslims flagellating (scourging) themselves as penitence for not being with the martyr *Hussein* when he died in battle. Again, picture the man who flagellated his face lying prostrate on the ground. This was a close-up of just one of hundreds who attended this ritual. *St. Louis Post-Dispatch* January 7, 2009 - AFP/Getty images:

"Shiite Muslims take part in ritual ceremonies Tuesday outside the shrine of Imam Abbas in the city of Karbala, about 68 miles south of Baghdad. More than 50,000 foreigners from around the Middle East have converged on the Shiite city, and more were expected, as the 10-day mourning period of the death of Imam Hussein in the year 680 ends today."

I can't remember a time when an American newspaper published a story of this nature, especially on a third page with such a significant photo. This looks to be the first outpouring of Islam's religious beliefs to be shown in a Christian nation.

Islam is well aware that the United States does not condone this kind of practice.

Since President Obama came on the scene we have seen a Muslim congressman exploit his pilgrimage to Mecca, two American Muslim teenagers girls killed in an *honor killing*, another *Muslim girl killed* on the street because she married an American, and a *Muslim woman beheaded* by her Muslim husband because she filed for a divorce!

This is happening in *our* country! Please! Don't anyone tell me that this phenomenon is a passing thing. The Muslims are becoming much more forward with their practices because they see that we have become complacent with their behavior, and they see a President of the United States with a Muslim background.

These reprehensible people are the kinds of people who more than likely look to Barack *Hussein* Obama as another *Hussein* who has become their leader. Why else do we have such an outpouring of Muslim activity in our country today? And why else would the Islamic world allow pictures of such a meaningful ceremony to be published in an American newspaper?

I searched the net for other stories about this religious holiday and found that the stories were on Islamic websites with a warning not to reproduce the photos; yet, this particular picture was allowed to be published in an American newspaper.

Under the Protection of President Bush

Under President Bush's administration Israel had assurance that the United States would be their ally. They understood that President Bush had Christian principles, and they trusted him when he warned Iran and other Arab countries that we would stand beside Israel in any conflict. Today Israel is very cognizant of President Obama's movements because of his Muslims ties, and his sudden interest in the Arab nations. The Arab nations want exactly what King Nebuchadnezzar and Saddam Hussein wanted....Israel. *Should* Israel be concerned about Obama being President of the United States? They definitely should be, especially after his commitment to their security was betrayed by the proposal of a $900 million dollar infusion into the financial veins of the very enemy that was lobbing rockets into Israel. President Obama's life has been, *and still is*, surrounded by Muslims.

To get a bigger picture of why Muslims revere the name Hussein, let's go to the history of the Muslim people and to where the name *Hussein* actually comes from.

This is Hussein's history - by: Ziauddin Sardar *What Do the Muslims Believe* page 60:

"The hereditary leadership is known as the Imamate (the region or country ruled over by an Imam). The Imam (prayer leader of a Muslim mosque) posses extraordinary grace, miraculous power and special (secret) knowledge. Ali was the first Imam and is even mentioned in the Shia call (azan) – much to the dismay of the Sunnis. The central event of Shia theology is the battle of Karbala.

We have seen that Caliph Ali's accession was contested by Mauwiya, the founder of the Umyyad dynasty. Ma'awiya was succeeded by his son, Yazid. The Muslim community split between Muslims who supported Ali and Muslims who supported Yazid. After Ali, his supporters gathered around his son, Hussain, the prophet's grandson. Hussain decided to fight for the leadership of the Muslim community. On 10 October 680 Hussain, and his devout followers faced Yazid's army. A hereditary monarchy was challenged by spiritual heredity. The battle was fought on the west banks of the Euphrates at Karbala (in Iraq). Hussain, who had only six hundred followers, didn't have a chance, but refused to surrender and was defeated by Yazid. Because of the slaughter of Hussain and his men, Islam became divided permanently. Each year the events of Karbala are re-enacted on the tenth day of the Islamic month of Muharram. It is a day of mourning because of the plight of Hussain. Ta'iziyyah, Shia martyrdom plays, are performed. Processions are led through the streets. Men and women alike bear their chests, and wound themselves with knives and chains; it is an expression of a guilty conscience for having abandoned Hussain in his hour of need. The Shia also go to Karbala on pilgrimages. The reason behind prostrating their heads on round tablets of Karbala clay when they pray is for a constant reminder of the events at Karbala." [86]

Each year Christians celebrate a Man who gave His life on the cross for our cause. But we don't beat ourselves, cut ourselves, flagate ourselves in guilt because of Jesus Christ's death. We celebrate His death and His resurrection at Easter time with praises of joy in song, reflecting back on why He died on that cross. And that was to save us from our sins so that we can be with Him in Heaven when we die. What a difference between the religion of Christianity and the religion of Islam.

Do we, as a Christian nation, want to be forced to celebrate religious days the way these cultic people celebrate?

This Muslim movement has already forced their way into unwilling countries by violence and jihad, taking over churches and worship centers and converting them into Islamic Mosques. Most of those countries were coerced into the Muslim religion by persecution or by a death threats.

Without direct coercion the same thing is happening in the U.S. The Muslims understand that they can't force the United States by open violence, so they are silently moving about building their mosques, spreading their propaganda through our public schools and public libraries. And just like in other countries, they are taking *our* churches and converting them into Islamic Mosques. Unchurched and biblically uninformed people who are looking for a church could conceivably attend one of these mosques thinking it is a Christian church.

The census for Muslims living in the United States was estimated to be nine million-five-hundred-thousand; however, that count was for adults. With approximately twenty-one million Muslims already in our country and with Muslim politicians like Ellison broadcasting to the Muslim world that America is a country of religious diversity, that count is going to rise quickly. We might still have restrictions on how many Muslims from the Arab nations are allowed to come into our

---

[86] Words enclosed in parentheses for clarification

country, but there are literally thousands of Muslims who are not from Arab nations.

The Nation of Islam has already been busy organizing councils to rise up and fight for their equal rights and representation in the United States. That would entail incorporating their Shari'a Law into our legal system. The following excerpt was taken from The Oxford History of Islam:

John L. Esposito - *The Oxford History of Islam* – page 631:

"The scramble to identify the next threat to Western democracies that ensued after the fall of communism has not yet abated. Islam and Muslim culture have been depicted by certain interests in the United States as the next challenge, if not the enemy challenging the West."

We must remember that freedom of religion in the United States was founded on the Word of God, and not Allah's word. God, of the Holy Bible, warns us not to embrace false gods. If we yield to Obama's idea to bring all peoples together as one, for he said we must pull down all walls, we will pay the consequences. Let's revisit what the difference is between the God of Christianity and the god of the Muslim's Allah. There is a vast difference between the Holy Bible of God Almighty and the The Holy Qur'an of a fanatical religious group.

Remember that the Holy Bible was authored by God, Himself, and is a Book of peace. The Qur'an, on the other hand, was written by a human being named Muhammad who came up with a false god who commands that all peoples of the world be brought into Islam – by intimidation if necessary. The God of Christianity gives us a choice. We can either accept God of the Holy Bible as the only true God and accept His Son Jesus as our Savior and go to Heaven when we die; or pay the consequences for worshiping a false god and go to fiery hell. God makes that clear in the Scripture below:

The Holy Bible – Exodus 20:3 – "You shall have no other gods before Me. You shall not make for yourself a carved image – any likeness of anything that is in Heaven above, or that is in the earth beneath, or that is in the water under the earth; you shall not bow down to them nor serve them.

For I, the LORD your God, am a jealous God, visiting the iniquity of the fathers upon the children to the third and fourth generations of those who hate Me, but showing mercy to thousands, to those who love Me and keep my commandments." NKJV

Please notice in the Scripture above that God does not say He will punish *all* children for the sin of the fathers to the third and fourth generation, *only those who hate Him*, but showing love to a thousand generations of those who love Him.

Those who love Him are Christians, born-again believers through the blood of Jesus Christ. So, let's ask ourselves, are we going to succumb to a president who may one day force us into the wrong direction, to false gods by allowing Muslims to control our country? Or, are we going to continue what the United States has done for over two hundred years…that is stand up and fight for our country and the religious right to worship the true God of the Holy Bible? When I say "stand up and fight," I am not saying to *physically* stand up and fight as in an uprising, although someday it might come to that. What I am saying is that we need to speak out, vote the right people into office during the next four years, then vote into the presidential office someone whose history we know.

Every American can do something to help deter this movement in our country. Write a book as I am doing. Speak out in your churches about the Muslims. And don't be intimidated by some members of the congregations who have a fear to be open about what is happening.

The Bible tells us in 2 Timothy 1:7 "For God has not given us a spirit of fear, but of power and or love and of a sound mind." NKJV

Whatever you do, please don't just sit back and allow our country to turn into a pagan nation. God has given us power to fight against these people!

<u>Farrakhan's Warning to America</u>

I have given details about Malcolm X's position on the United States and Islam; now let me quote for you what Farrakhan sees in store for the United States:

"There is one God, Allah. The Qur'an and the truth of the Bible are to be believed, though the present Bible is corrupt and must reinterpreted. Allah's prophets and their scriptures must be accepted. The judgment of Allah will take place first in America."[87]

Do we understand what Farrakhan is saying? His focus now is to take America for Islam. He could conceivably mean that the Islamic terrorists will rise up and start jihad (their holy war) against us. Remember in 1995 he led a million Muslims in the streets of Washington. The twenty-one million Muslims already here in our country could very well be instrumental in an uprising. And my friend, we are not talking about an ethnic group who is afraid to die. On the contrary, read what their Holy Qur'an commands the Muslims to do. Paul Marshall, Roberta Green, Lela Gilbert - *Islam at the Crossroads* page 25:

"Islamic thought divides humankind into two lands: (1) Dar al-Islam, the land of those who have submitted to Allah, the Muslim community (umma), and (2) Dar al-barb, the land of war or conflict, in which non-Muslims (barbis) dwell. Jihad is intended to bring the people of Dar al-barb under the authority of Allah and Islamic law. From this point of view, the house of Islam and the house of the infidel are always at war, and the property of the infidel legally belongs to the umma. Jihad seeks to reclaim all property and bring it into the Dar al-Islam. This is seen as the only way to harmony among peoples. Muslims who die as martyrs in jihad are believed to be guaranteed a place in paradise. This, along with a zeal for conquest, is the motivation behind suicidal attacks. Several Qur'anic passages describe paradise: "For those who reverence the majesty of their Lord, two gardens. Which of your Lord's marvels can you deny? Their beautiful mates were never touched by any human or jinn. Virgins as fair as corals and rubies. Then which of the favors of your Lord will you deny? (Sura 55:47-59) They will sit with bashful, dark-eyed virgins, as chaste as the sheltered eggs of ostriches (Sura 37-48) "They shall recline on couches

---

[87] Quote from: *What You Need to Know About Islam & Muslims* page 67

arranged in rows. To dark-eyed maidens we shall wed them (Sura 52:17-20) "Round about them will (serve) youths of perpetual (freshness)...And (there will be) Companions with beautiful, big, and lustrous eyes (Sura 56:17, 22)."

Farrakhan said, *"The judgment of Allah will take place first in America."* Where are the Muslims who may be preparing to inflict the judgment of Allah on America? I could point out many locations in America, but I will direct your attention to New Mexico. You read above that Dar al-Islam is a land for those who have submitted to Allah. Well, it is right here under our noses. John L. Esposito - *The Oxford History of Islam* page 618:

"The Dar al-Islam Foundation Islamic Center Village was built in Abiquiu, New Mexico, in 1980-1981. Designed by the renowned Egyptian architect Hassan Fathy, the mosque is the centerpiece of a complex that includes a school, clinic, a shopping center, and other public buildings."

You got it! And they have been there for twenty-seven years. They are claiming land in the United States as *their own land*. The above excerpt said *"The property of the infidel* (unbeliever)[88] *legally belongs to the umma."*

I challenge you to go to your telephone yellow pages and look up *Temple or Mosques*. I will guarantee that if you live in a city of any size you will find at least six Temples listed. In my city alone there are seven Mosques scattered throughout the city.

There is one thing we need to be aware of, and that is that the Islam mimics Christianity just enough to fool people who are not knowledgeable enough of the Bible to resist being pulled into their cult.

The book I am writing is intended to make our society aware that there is a vast difference between Islam and Christianity. The Muslims teach that Jesus Christ was a mere man. There were literally thousands of rumors going around that President Obama is the Messiah. Did Obama refute that

---

[88] Unbeliever added for clarity

claim? Not with a compelling answer. That rumor stirred the minds of a lot of people who are biblically uninformed. Let me quote what the Muslim Qur'an teaches about the *real* Savior, Jesus Christ:

The Holy Qur'an Surah 139 page 747 - *"Next comes the story of Jesus and his Mother, Mary. She gave birth, as a virgin, to Jesus. But her people slandered and abused her as a disgrace to her lineage. Her son did defend her and was kind to her. He was a servant of Allah, a true Prophet, blessed in the gifts of Prayer and Charity, but no more than a man: to call him the son of Allah is to derogate from Allah's majesty, for Allah is High above all his creatures, the judge of the Last Day."*

As you can see Islam mimics Christianity by bringing Jesus' name into the Qur'an. If the author of the Qur'an had not included Jesus' name in their Book, he would have risked people denying the Qur'an because Jesus' name is recognized in most of the world. By calling Jesus a prophet, but a mere man, the Qur'an explains away His deity and replaces Him with the false prophet Muhammad.

Unfortunately, millions have fallen for this deception and have been drawn into a false security instead of the eternal security that God promises us through Jesus Christ. However, if our society becomes more knowledgeable about the teachings of Islam, we will avoid being pulled into their cultic, or mythical-type, religion.

Most people have seen movies like Sindbad the Sailor in the Arabian Nights' Entertainments, and we were amused when Sindbad called jenns or *genies* in the bottle to come out and carry out his commands. Let me enlighten you. These jenns are real in the eyes of Muslims. The *Webster's New Collegiate Dictionary* defines the jinns this way:

"One of a class of spirits that according to Muslim demonology inhabit the earth, assume various forms, and exercise supernatural power. A supernatural spirit that often takes human form and serves his summoner."

This following excerpt taken from The Holy Qur'an will support the Webster's Dictionary's definition:

The Holy Qur'an 229 page 323 - *"Both the Qur'an and the Hadith describe the Jinn as a definite species of living beings. They are created out of fire and are like man, may believe or disbelieve, accept or reject guidance. The authoritative Islamic text shows that they are not merely a hidden force, or a spirit. They are personalized beings who enjoy a certain amount of free will and thus will be called to account."*

Let's also go to another source to find the bizarre teachings of the Muslims. Hal Lindsey's *The Everlasting Hatred The Roots of Jihad* page 91:

"Arabs believed (and noted in the Koran and Hadith) that jinns were a category of spirit creatures halfway between angels and men. They believed they can be good or bad, though most are considered to be malicious. They can possess animals and inanimate things such as rocks, trees, wells, etc. Jinns were adopted into Muslim theology and the Koran. Legends about jinns or genies are resplendent of Arab legends – such as the genie in the bottle, etc."

The Muslims have incorporated into their religious beliefs everything that is contradictory to the Holy Bible. The Bible does not speak of jinns. Nor does the Bible speak of God appearing in the person of Fard Muhammad as the messiah.

Farrakhan teaches the concept of Fard Muhammad being the messiah, yet he is voicing a different position sense Obama came onto the scene. What could be a better way, though, to draw people to Obama than to conjure up a story that he is the long-awaited-for Savior! That's an untruth, of course. But the Bible does warn us about a false Christ coming to deceive the world, and there have been many false Christs throughout history. I doubt very seriously that Obama is _**the**_ false Christ, the Antichrist, but he certainly displays some of the traits that the Antichrist will have.

Grant you, the Bible does say the Antichrist will come from out of nowhere. But the false Christ to come will be Satan himself indwelled in a man. God gives us this warning:

The Holy Bible – Matthew 24:23-27 "Then if anyone says to you, 'Look, here is the Christ!' or 'There!' do not believe it. For false christs and false prophets will rise and show great signs and wonders to deceive, if possible, even the elect. "See I have told you beforehand. Therefore if they say to you, 'Look, He is in the desert!' do not go out; or 'Look, He is in the inner rooms!' do not believe it. "For as the lightning comes from the east and flashes to the west, so also will the coming of the Son of Man be." NKJV

Why do some people believe that President Obama could be the Antichrist? Because the United States has never experienced such a political phenomenon as we have seen in the rising up of President Barack Hussein Obama. The entire country has been overwhelmed with his charisma; yet, many Americans can't pinpoint exactly what got President Obama to the top! The only thing we knew about him when he was running for the presidential office was that he has a white mother and a black African father; he was raised in the Muslim country of Indonesia by his mother and a black Muslim stepfather and later moved to Hawaii to live with his white grandparents.

Although news media pounced on the idea that he was a Muslim, still people rallied to him. Although he denied it vehemently, he was accused of being associated with powerful people in Islam, yet people rallied to him. His picture was on the cover page of Reverend Wright's radical magazine *Trumpet* with the title *"The Legacy Lives On,"* yet people ignored it. Farrakhan, Hamas and the president of Iran indorsed him, yet people ignored it. His picture was just recently on the front cover page of the Muslim magazine *élan*, yet people are still ignoring all of the warning signs. That is the way it will be with the Antichrist. He will be a master deceiver.

The following are just a few stories of Muslims who are praising Obama. Bob Unruh of *WorldNetDaily January 09, 2009* also brought to light that Obama's picture was featured on the front page of the Muslim magazine **elan**:

"A magazine that proudly promotes itself as Muslim has announced a special edition for Barack Obama's inauguration as president, with Editor Nida Kahn claiming, "It's our time." The publication, Elan magazine, also includes endorsements of Obama's familiarity with Islam from the daughter of Malcolm X and Benjamin F. Chavis Muhammad, the chief of the Hip-Hop Summit Action Network. The magazine, which calls itself the "guide to global Muslim culture," is distributed in the U.S., Pakistan, Indonesia, Canada, Qtar, the United Kingdom and the United Arab Emirates, as well as online. Its cover story for the edition, "Muslim World Embraces Obama," "explores the hopes and aspirations of Muslims regarding America's new president."

This is another Front Cover Page article in *élan posted on January 8, 2009.* The front cover page displayed a waist-up picture of Obama standing with his arms folded across his waist and a big grin on his face. Next to Obama's picture was the phrase *"Muslim World Embraces Obama."*

The article below should be very disturbing to anyone who has an interest in keeping our country free of a Muslim regime. The following article is in a Muslim magazine. The youth are eager to make their voices heard. How will they make their voices heard as Muslims? They will need Muslim representation. Obama has said we need to *"reboot"* our relationship with the Muslim world, so I suspect that he will give them the opportunity to run for political offices, and their voices will be heard. We need to absorb what this article is articulating to the Muslim world.

"elan magazine, the premiere voice for young Muslim professionals, has announced a special edition commemorating the inauguration of Barack Obama as the 44th President. The Inauguration Edition explores the "hopes and aspirations" of Muslims in regards to the new President including a look at the diversity the man brings to the position. The edition includes various commentary, as well as "exclusive features written by Ilyasah Shabazz, a daughter of Malcolm X, and by Dr. Benjamin F. Chavis Muhammad, a civil rights leader." "Young

Muslims today are eager to make their voices heard and to promote a better understanding of Muslim contributions to contemporary culture," affirmed Moniza Khokhar, publisher of **elan.***"*

Is Obama the leader of the United States citizens, or is he a leader of the Muslim world? You tell me! Obama has posed for a Muslim magazine and one of the feature writers for the special edition on Obama will be written by Malcolm X's daughter. This should give us a hint that Obama has not forgotten Malcolm X. Malcolm X's daughter had this to say in the same magazine **élan**:

"Ilyasah Shabazz, the daughter of Al Hajj Malik Shabazz, aka Malcolm X, says were her father alive today, he would "share everyone's joy about the prospect of returning the United States to a position of credibility, respect and leadership. Forty-four years after his martyrdom, he remains the most famous and recognized Muslim American as well as a role model for men and women alike advocating for social justice," she said."

Our country might be fooled by Obama sending U.S. troops to Afghanistan, a Muslim nation. If he is a Muslim, you might ask, then why is he sending 17,000 more U.S. troops to Afghanistan to fight against Muslim terrorists. Wait a minute….he is also pulling U.S. troops *out* of Iraq. All he is doing is giving the terrorists more leeway in Iraq. What we need to understand is that there are Sunnis Muslims and Shiite Muslims and they have been fighting against each other since Hussein was killed and beheaded at Karbala. The Sunnis and Shiite still share the same religious beliefs, but they war against each other. So even though Obama sends troops against Muslims, it doesn't necessarily mean that he is not a Muslim.

Islam's Eyes Are on Our Children

We have covered numerous aspects of Obama's life; now let's go to something near-and-dear to the hearts of Americans…..our children. The Oxford History of Islam book lists the location of one Saudi Academy in the United States —

North Virginia. Let's just have a look at who came out of a Saudi Academy in our own country. John L. Esposito - *The Oxford History of Islam* page 623:

"The most famous high school is the Saudi Academy in northern Virginia; 95 percent of its graduating class goes to college."

Where did the terrorist, Ahmed Amar Abu Ali, who planned to assassinate President Bush then plant an al-Qaida cell in the United States, attend school? At a private Islamic high school in Fairfax, Virginia.

Public Schools and Libraries Targeted by Islam

Some Islamic schools in the United States are becoming targets for investigation into allegations that they are training Islamic students for jihad. The investigations also bring to light that kids in some of our public school are being introduced to the Islamic religion. This is happening all over our country. I want to quote an article from Michelle Malkin, a dedicated American who is fighting to protect our kids and to keep our country free from the radical Islamic takeover. *Michelle Malkin, Syndicated Columnist and a Fox News contributor* June 13, 2008:

"I wrote about the incendiary textbooks used in the Fairfax, VA Islamic Saudi Academy. After "revisions" the texts still advocated rule under an Islamic caliphate and the death of apostates and adulterers." Malkin goes on to say, *"Tarek ibn Ziyad Academy – "Katharine Kersten's excellent investigative work on the Minnesota taxpayer-funded Islamic school, TIZA, has led to a state probe of the institution. It has also shed light again on the spread of Shari'a in U.S. secondary public schools."*

We can find, by reading the Muslim's Qur'an, what *death of apostates* and *adulterers* mean to Muslims. The word adulterers sounds innocent enough, but an adulterer to Muslims is *anyone*, man or woman, who denies Allah as the only god. For either offense the sentence, without remorse, is death. I quote directly from Islam's The Holy Qur'an:

The Holy Qur'an 9:73I - "*O Prophet! Strive hard against the unbelievers and the hypocrites, and be firm against them. Their abode is hell – an evil refuge indeed.*"

The Holy Qur'an 5:33 - "*The punishment of those who wage war against Allah and His Messenger, and strive with might and main for mischief through the land is: execution, or crucifixion, or the cutting off of hands and feet from opposite side, or exile from the land.*"

I admire Michelle Malkin for being straightforward about what is happening to our kids. Michelle Malkin's quote continued:

"*These militants and their supporters have set their eyes on our children, and attempting to brainwash them by supplying free textbooks which whitewash the truth regarding Muslim extremism, while promoting Arab and Palestinian political goals. These "teaching materials" also impugn and devalue America, Western nations, Israel, Judaism, and Christianity. The article, 'Textbooks for Jihad,' found here is a good analysis of these developments. The Council on American-Islamic Relations, some of whose members have been "outed" as terror supporters, has an active program to supply these this type of propaganda to libraries across the nation. Naturally, like schools, the librarians are more than happy to accept inexpensive, or free, material to fill their shelves. Yet these same books and audio-visual material are filling our children's minds with lies that are tantamount to propaganda that teach hate. Efforts should be made by local activists and PTA or PTO members to scrutinize the reading lists at our "educational" institutions.*"

You may think that Muslims can't do any harm teaching in our public schools. We have no idea what is taught in Muslim schools here in the United States, or in our public schools that are run by Muslims; they won't let anyone on the inside to monitor their curriculum.

What comes to mind when you think of Muslim children. Do you think of only Muslim children here in the United States? What about the children of Iran, Saudi Arabia or Iraq and Indonesia. Are American children, who have Muslim teachers and principles, being taught the same curriculum as Muslim children in Palestine?

We learn from media sources coming from across the world that Muslim male children are taught to embrace the idea that to kill the infidel, Americans and Jews, for Allah's sake will guarantee them a place in paradise. This teaching isn't confined to Palestinians, or to the Middle East. Our children, and anyone who wants to, can look on the internet and see how young Muslim boys are taught to hate the Jew and Christians. I will revisit a previous chapter where I wrote about the Haaretz video about kids being taught marshal arts for Hamas.

We need to realize that these kids, when they are adults, can come to the United States on a visa any time they choose. These practices not only go on in the Gaza Strip, but every Muslim country teaches their kids the same tactics. The video mentioned above can very easily be used by extremists in the United States to train kids here to hate us. These are the kind of things we need to be alert to. Suicide bombers come from these camps. Kids are being pounded daily with the idea that Jews are the enemy and the United States is the devil and should be annihilated for the sake of Allah.

Many of us have seen news specials showing Muslim children, wearing booby-traps around their waists, sent out against the enemy for the sake of Allah.

Let's return to American students in the United States and look at a strategy that Islam is using to induct American students into their culture. And I might add…with the help of an American.

We can scrutinize the educational material here in the United States, but what about U.S. universities in a foreign country? Say for instance Abu Dhabi, which is in the Persian Gulf. You got it! Arab country! Read the following article about the President of a major New York university who wants to send our college students to the Middle East. Lyric Wallwork Winik - *St. Louis Post – Parade Magazine on June 7, 2008*:

"New York University will soon open NYU Abu Dhabi, a liberal-arts college campus in the United Arab Emirates. We spoke with NYU President John Sexton about why he believes American universities must become a key U.S. export."

The article went on to say in bold letters, **"Why is there a need for "global universities"?** *The world is getting smaller. Our students must encounter other religions, nationalities, and ideas...."*

Did anyone investigate the benefactor for the university in Abu Dhabi? Omar Saif Ghobash, a Muslim, approached Mr. Sexton first! MONEY TALKS. This article was in The New York Times and was posted on a website by Tamar Lewin February 10, 2008:

"When John Sexton, the president of <u>New York University</u>, first met Omar Saif Ghobash, an investor trying to entice him to open a branch campus in the United Arab Emirates, Mr. Sexton was not sure what to make of the proposal – so he asked for a $50 million gift." "It's like earnest money: if you're a $50 million donor, I'll take you seriously," Mr. Sexton said. "It's a way to test their bona fides." In the end, the money materialized from the government of Abu Dhabi, one of the seven emirates."

Does this man, Mr. Sexton, have any idea what he has done? He has virtually *opened* the gates wide for Islam to proselyte American kids into their religion. Even though it will be considered an American university, their Shari'a laws will dictate how the university is run. We need more Michelle Malkin's to monitor our New York University's educational curriculum in Abu Dhabi. Even if the curricula are based on a United States educational system, these young university students living in that culture, some without knowledge of the Holy Bible could be influenced into the Islamic religion.....and eventually into jihad.

Taking Michelle Malkin's advice, I browsed through the children's section of one of our many libraries. She is absolutely right. I was alarmed at what I found. Beautifully bright color illustrated books lined lower shelves; definitely an attention getter for children. The books have bright colored pictures to attract kids, and are written with large print. The following are titles and excerpts from some of the books:

What Makes Me A Muslim - KIDHAVEN PRESS - Content: Beginning of Islam; Muslims belief; how they practice their faith; their religious holidays and challenges facing their religion.

The excerpt below was voiced by a picture of a smiling bright-faced boy of seven or eight years of age:

"Fourteen hundred years ago, an angel visited a man named Muhammad. The angel, Gabriel, appeared to him many times. He told Muhammad that God, or Allah, was unhappy with the way people were living their lives and practicing religion. He gave Muhammad instructions for teaching people a different way."

This is only one short excerpt of what the Muslim child in the book is conveying to our children. First - The child said, *"God or Allah,"* indicating that our God is the same as their false god, Allah. Second – the child is telling our children that Christianity is wrong. The book is short, but quickly tells the story of Islam in a way that an innocent child would enjoy enough to go to another book on Islam, especially if our child thinks God is unhappy with his/her life. Would young children listen to what that happy Muslim child is saying? Absolutely!

"I Am Muslim - PowerKids Press New York." This is the most powerful pictorial book I found. It was brightly illustrated with the picture of a six to eight year old Muslim boy on the cover:

*"My name is Ahmet. I live in Detroit. I am Muslim. That means that I practice the religion of Islam. We believe that a man named Muhammad was one of Allah's **prophets** (PRAH-fits). Muslims call him the Great Prophet and the Chosen Messenger. The book about how Allah wants us to live our lives was **revealed** (re-VEEID) to Muhammad in Arabic. This book is*

*called the **Qur'an** (kor-ON). It was written in Arabid. Muhammad taught us that there is only one Allah."*

The bold print is the actual print in the book. There are other disturbing books entitled *"Places of Worship"* and *"Muslim Mosques,"* and picturesque book for all ages. *"American Islam"* is a very disturbing book and is on the junior high and above level. Another book promotes Holy War (jihad).

These full-color books cover every aspect of Islam, and explain to a young person why they should become Muslim. Can you see how Islam is silently moving about in our country without constraints? Islam is proselyting our children right here in our own country by placing Islamic materials in our libraries and schools. I encourage parents to visit their libraries, scrutinize the shelves and ask the head librarian to remove those books or put them on shelves where small children can't get to them.

Please don't dismiss this concern by thinking some children are too young to read the books, or that the ones who *can* read them cannot understand what they are reading.

The Islamic book publishers know exactly what they are doing! I have been in libraries and have watched a child grab a book from a shelf and beg mom, "Take *this one.*" The mom gives in and the book goes home and the mom reads the book to the child! Now, an adult is reading a book on Islam's belief that is made very simple. It's understandable that if the adult does not have a good knowledge of the Bible, that adult is likely to explore the Islamic religion.

Some of the books explain what the Muslim's call to prayer is and why they call Muslims to prayer five times a day. I have a friend who lived in the country of Turkey for a year. She tells stories about the eerie sounds of the Muslim's Muezzin cries during their call-out to prayer. It's a cry that we have yet to hear in our country. The cry to start their prayers is mandated in every Muslim country in the world. The book *Islam at the Crossroads* gives a good description of that call to prayer. Paul Marshall, Roberta Green and Lela Gilbert - *Islam at the Crossroads* page 19:

"The first trace of dawn dims the stars and, as the morning light gradually spreads from one time zone to the next, the sound begins. It is a wailing – disharmonious, even eerie, to many Westerners. The summons "AllabuAkbar...AllabuAkbar" awakens the cities of Asia, the Middle East, and beyond with a call to the mosque and to fajr, the morning prayer, the first salaat of the day. From tapes and loudspeakers surrounding a neighborhood mosque in Istanbul, or from the urgent summons cried out by a live muezzin atop a minaret in the heart of Casablanca, Baghdad, Tehran, or Jakarta, the call rings out."

These are the kind of fond memories Obama wrote about in his book. He said,

"When I think of that island, and all of Indonesia, I'm haunted by memories – the feel of packed mud under bare feet as I wander through paddy fields; the sight of day breaking behind volcanic peaks; the muezzins's call at night."[89]

It boggles my mind to think that Obama would want to return to Indonesia with his wife and children to share that part of his life knowing that a poll showed Indonesia has a higher opinion of Osama bin Laden than President Bush, and are killing Christians. If he is a Christian and the Muslim in Indonesians are killing Christians[90] why would he want to expose his family to such danger?

We need to be very aware of a strategy that President Obama may be using to represent himself as being a President for everyone in the United States. In his book *Dreams from My Father* he appears to be trying to instill into the hearts and minds of his readers that his ancestors were an important part of American history.

He is part of everything so that everyone can identify with him. For history buffs his great-great-grandfather supposedly was Christopher Columbus Clark, a decorated Union soldier.

Clark's wife's mother was rumored to have been second cousin of Jefferson Davis, president of the Confederacy. Obama

---

[89] Muezzin's call - *The Audacity of Hope* pages 278-279
[90] Killing Christians – *The Everlasting Hatred - The Roots of Jihad* page 142

is also an Irishman[91] for the New York vote, and he is part Cherokee Indian for the American Indian vote. [92] Although he appeared to be boasting about his ancestry, he described very vividly how his family was ashamed of being a part of the beginning of American history....the American Indians!

Barack Obama - *Dreams from My Father* page 12-13:

".......although another distant ancestor had indeed been a full-blooded Cherokee, such lineage was a source of considerable shame to Toot's mother, who blanched whenever someone mentioned the subject and hoped to carry the secret to her grave."

<u>Mosques and Private Islamic Schools in the United States</u>

We shouldn't dismiss what I said earlier in the book about the Muslim's goal to reclaim all property and bring it into the Dar al-Islam? Guess what!...... It's already on its way!

It was brought to the attention of the reader earlier in the book about the Dar al-Islam Foundation Islamic Center Village in Abiquiu, New Mexico, but what about the Islamic Center in New York located on 96th Street on Manhattan's Upper East Side; and other mosques in Evansville, IN; St. Louis, MO; San Francisco, CA; Denver, CO; Quincy, MA; Dearborn, MI; Houston, TX; the Muslim Student Association (helped establish several hundred mosques on U.S. and Canadian campuses); Muslim World League (New York City); Saudi Arabia Islamic Headquarter (New York); Islamic Circle of North America; Muslim American Society of Minnesota; Council on American-Islamic Relations; Saudi Arabia Academy in North Virginia and private Islamic schools in Minnesota? ......and the list goes on!

Is the U.S Department of State keeping an eye on the influx of Muslims into the United States? The following article about the influx of Muslims and what our administration is trying to do about it was pulled from *The Oxford History of Islam* page 611:

---

[91] Irishman – *Dreams from My Father* page 279
[92] Ancestors – *Dreams from My Father* pages 12, 13

"In the United States several measures have been taken to restrict Muslim immigration. The quota system has recently been revised to favor white European immigrants, especially from Ireland and eastern Europe. There are reports that the U.S. Department of State has given instructions to its consular offices overseas not to accept people with an Arab background."

The above article says the U.S. Department of State was instructed not to accept immigrants with an *Arab* background. But what about the non-Arab Muslims, people in other countries who have converted to Islam? And with Obama in office, how long will this scrutiny continue?

According to *The Oxford History of Islam* page 604, these are the statistics of Muslims living in non-Arab countries. Keep in mind that this book was published in 1999, so these statistics have changed:

France 3,000,000; Germany 2,500,000; United Kingdom 2,000,000; Canada 250,000 (above us); Latin America 2,500,000 (just below us). Are these non-Arab immigrants allowed to come into the United States?

Are *WE* there yet?

Have we opened the gates for the Muslims to come in as the Europeans did? John L. Esposito - *The Oxford History on Islam* page 629:

"During 1985 and 1986 several bombs exploded in Paris. The headlines in the press were no longer about events far away but about the wounded and the dead downtown. Europeans began to fear what the Muslims next door could do to them. The Muslims were depicted as the obscurantist sinister enemy, ruthless followers of a religion that promotes violence and blind adherence to tradition."

The Webster's New Collegiate Dictionary defines the word *Obscurantist* this way: "a policy of withholding knowledge from the general public; a style characterized by deliberate vagueness; one who or that which obscures, especially by opposing or hindering free thought; hard to understand; inconspicuous."

"Obscurantist sinister enemy!" That's what the Europeans called the Muslims when they realized they had been silently planning for years to take their country. Is President Obama the obscurantist enemy of the United States? I wish I knew! He makes it very difficult to understand what his motivation is for putting our country in peril with this $787 billion Stimulus Package; and why he sent Hillary Clinton to the Palestinians (includes Gaza) with a message that we are going to give them $900 million dollars to help rebuild the areas hit by Israel's missiles, a war that they, GAZA themselves, caused by firing missiles first at Israel.

Not only has President Obama proposed $900 million to the Palestinians (a Muslim country); he just returned from a trip to the country of Turkey where the Muslim population is 99.6%. Hillary Clinton gave us the good news. *CNN's* politicalticker website March 7, 2009:

".... To emphasize the work the United States and Turkey must do together on behalf of peace, prosperity and progress," she said."

Telegraph.co.uk by Tim Shipman in Washington 07 Mar 2009:

"Mr. Obama's visit to Turkey will be an opening step in his long-standing promise to improve relations with the Muslim world. The visit, which will follow the G20 summit in London on April, is expected to coincide with the Second Forum of the United Nations Alliance of Civilization, due to be held in Istanbul on April 6 and 7. The forum seeks to 'address some of the ongoing tensions and divides across cultures and religions.'"

The news media at the time didn't say that President Obama would attend this conference; however, according to the *TUSIAD-US Web site Turkey News*: January 19-25-2009 President Obama was invited to the Conference:

"Turkey's Prime Minister stressed the preservation of relations and the strategic U.S.-Turkey partnership in his message of congratulations to President Barack Obama, the Anatolian Agency (AA) reported over the weekend. 'The preservation of the relations and the strategic partnership between Turkey and the United States is of great importance not only for the national interests of our countries but also for regional and global peace and stability,' Erdogan said in his message to the White House. Erdogan <u>re-affirmed his invitation to the U.S. president for a forum meeting of the Alliance of Civilizations</u>[93] which is scheduled for April."

Obama did attend the Conference and it's surprising that our president would attend such a conference since it is the United States that most countries have patterned themselves after. The last sentence in the quote above, *"...address some of the ongoing tensions and divides across cultures and religions"* caught my eye. And I was curious about The Second Forum of the United Nations Alliance of Civilization and wanted to find out more about the event; so I browsed the net and found answers. A website opened up to a powerful image of what this Islamic Conference was all about. A large, very impressive, brilliant colored globe depicting the world popped up on the screen. The globe is made up of puzzle pieces, and written directly under it in all caps are the words "ALLIANCE OF CIVILIZATION." The colorful puzzle pieces are flags of other countries. A large Turkish flag puzzle piece with the Islamic symbol on it centers the globe with all the other pieces connecting directly to it.

Most of the countries shown on the large globe have a *low* Muslim population; United States 3.5%; India 13.4%; China 1.5%; Russia 10.2%; Brazil 1.1%; Spain 1.2%; South Africa 2.0% as apposed to Egypt's 90% and Turkey's 99.6%. Even though the percentage rate appears to be low for some countries, please keep in mind that these countries have a high population. China has 1,321,851,888 population; and India has 1,166,079, 219. So we can suspect that to the Islamic world they have

---

[93] Underlined for emphasis

millions yet to convert in the country puzzle pieces on the globe. Keep in mind, too, that this census was taken years ago. The Muslim religion is soaring to phenomenal heights with their outreach strategy. And that is what this Conference in Turkey is all about.....to Islamize the world. The United States percentage shows only 3.5%, but according to experts there are approximately twenty-one million Muslims in the United States right now. Would the average American understand why only countries with a low Muslim population are on the visible part of the globe? Or would the average American even see the globe? I doubt it! But maybe those who attended the Islamic classes at Kennesaw State University in Atlanta, GA saw the Globe; but did *they* understand that the Globe could have significance for the United States? Could we assume, based on the evidence given in this book about the Muslim movement, that the countries with low Muslim population on the globe represent (to the Muslim world) countries yet to be conquered by Islam. Isn't it interesting that the United State's puzzle piece is connected to the very top of the Islam puzzle piece? Please read between the lines when you are dealing with what the Islamic people do and say. They are not so foolish as to tell us specifics about their plans.

This conference was Islam's outreach to other parts of the world, and while leaders of various countries and some universities received the invitation to attend these incentive conferences, most people are not aware that such conferences exist. And the majority of the world probably will not understand that Islam was more than likely using this strategy of calling leaders of the world together to further their agenda to gain entrance into their countries.

The UNAOC was a conference to express distinct ideas to bring civilization together. This Turkish article actually came from a website with a heading *ALLIANCE OF CIVILIZATIONS www.unaoc.org*. The article is quite lengthy, so let me quote two paragraphs. As you read these articles remember that you are reading articles from a Turkish world pulled up by an American:

"The UNAOC Forum seeks to address some of the ongoing tensions and divides across <u>cultures and religious,</u> and to examine some of the broader challenges of good governance of cultural diversity in an age of <u>rapidly accelerating globalization.</u> It will convene a powerful network of <u>global leaders,</u> heads of <u>international organizations,</u> corporations, the media, civil society and <u>youth groups,</u> to forge partnerships aimed at building substantive interaction between diverse communities and strengthening trust and <u>reconciliation across cultures.</u>" [94]

We can clearly see from the excerpt above that the intent of Islam's Conference was to address tensions across cultures and religions, and address challenges of *governance* (power, supremacy, authority) over cultural diversity. Was there any particular schedule that was geared to politics? The Conference agenda had a definite religious slant.

When I read the Conference's schedule of events, Obama's speech in Germany immediately came to mind when he said, "The walls between races and tribes, natives and immigrants, Christian and Muslim and Jew cannot stand."

Now let's look at the avenues Islam intends to use to "bridge" this gap. The next paragraph is from the same article:

"A unique '<u>Marketplace of Ideas</u>' will showcase some of the most innovative and successful <u>grassroots</u>[95] projects aimed at transcending <u>cultural divides</u> and building peace."[96]

The next article came from the Turkish website, *"The Istanbul Forum"*:

"YOUTH – Youth has been identified as one of the key priorities for the work of the Alliance of Civilizations. The AoC Secretarial is actively trying to involve youth directly in its work by collaborating with broad networks of youth organizations. Our goal is to have a youth perspective in the media debate, on cross-cultural and interreligious issues and in all AoC

---

[94] Underscores for emphasis
[95] Grassroots underscored for emphasis
[96] Underscore for emphasis

projects" "The alliance of civilizations seeks to develop a series of <u>online clearinghouses</u>[97] focusing on the AoC's main areas of implementation: youth, education, media and <u>migration</u>. These web-based clearinghouses will feature best practices, <u>materials</u>, and <u>resources</u> on cross-cultural dialogue and cooperation."[98]

Please keep in mind the word "clearinghouses" in the excerpt above and the fact that our libraries here in the U.S. are shelving books on Islam. Online clearinghouses will give young people who like to browse the web an insight to what Islam is all about. This conference was all about globalization!

Going back through this entire book, how many times did President Obama express his ideas about bringing the world together? His speech in Germany was geared to tearing down all walls in the world to bring peace. In San Francisco it was *globalization*. Just to refresh our memories let's re-visit what he said in San Francisco:

"He explained to San Francisco fat-cats that rural Americans bitterly[99] "cling" to their bizarre rituals, unnecessary weapons, and ancient sky god, all because they've been <u>left out on globalization</u>."

Talk about globalization! The *UNAOC* in Turkey is going to use the *youth* as an internet tool to reach out to the world to solve interreligious issues. And what did Malcolm X and Farrakhan say about using the *youth* to further their cause? Farrakhan has put a lot of emphasis on Obama's ability to reach the youth. And did you notice that the writer of the above article also used President Obama's famous phrase "grassroots."

The First Alliance of Civilization Forum was launched by a Turkish and Spanish prime ministers in 2005, so it is not something new to the world, especially the Muslim world. Just a few minutes of research revealed that *UNAOC* scheduled a conference right here in our own country. That's right. The

---

[97] Underscore for emphasis
[98] Underscore for emphasis
[99] "Americans bitterly" italicized for emphasis

event was held at Kennesaw State University in Atlanta, GA on January 29-32, 2009.

Let's get back to a close examination of the fact that President Obama's background indicates that every facet of his life is filled with Muslim influence. Considering all of his quick decisions to connect with Muslim people, Muslim countries; his travel to Turkey during the Alliance of Civilizations International Conference whose focus was to bridge the gap between cultures and religions, could we reason that President Obama was going to Turkey for support in a plan to bring our country into compliance with the Islamic laws?

His travel to Turkey, supposedly, was in keeping with a campaign promise pledge to travel to a Muslim country during his first 100 days in office; but how many people understood what he meant by that statement? Most of us probably thought he was going to Iran. The article posted on *Telegraph.co.uk* said Obama opted for a less challenging political environment:

"Although by choosing Turkey, which is generally regarded a bastion of moderate Islam, he will opting for a less challenging political environment than if he were to travel to the heart of the Arab world."

Excuse me! I thought our problem in the world *was* political. If my memory serves me correct, during his presidential campaign Obama implied that if he were president he would simply go to the Arab nation, sit down and talk. So why did he go to Turkey? Could it be because the Conference in Turkey was about *bringing the world together as one*?

Let's go to his trip to Cairo, Egypt (90% Muslim) on June 4, 2009 to see how he enlightened the Muslim world through his speech about [*his*] plans for [*our*] country. These excerpts are taken from a "word-for-word" dialogue of his speech coming from the Council on Foreign Relations posted www.cfr.org/publication/19564/ Published June 4, 2009.

Did he come away from the Alliance of Civilization Conference with ideas of how to restructure the United States? Just a few short weeks after leaving the Conference he traveled to Cairo Egypt where in his speech to the Muslim country he reiterated the Alliance of Civilization agenda for the world. Did he go to the Conference in Turkey to gain more knowledge about how to bring us into the Islamic world culture and religion? You be the judge after reading excerpts taken from his speech while in Egypt, "In fact, faith should bring us together. And that's why we're forging service projects in America to bring together Christians, Muslims, and Jews. That's why we welcome efforts like Saudi Arabian King Abdullah's interfaith dialogue and Turkey's leadership in the Alliance of Civilizations. Around the world, we can turn dialogue into interfaith service so bridges between peoples lead to action - " I, as a citizen of the United States, was not, and am not, aware of any "forging service projects" that he has introduced to bring Christians, Muslims and Jews together. Is he informing the Muslim world that he does, in fact, have a plan to help them further their agenda to move into a country that has, for over two-hundred years, revered a Sovereign God who has lead our Country into peace and prosperity because we have acknowledged Him as the One and only Creator? Is President Obama pulling our religious and freedom of speech and decision-making right out from under us without a fight from a people who have long enjoyed a peaceful existence under a democracy? His plans to try and bring us into *interfaith* with a cultic, radical religious group will destroy us as a Christian nation. The Alliance of Civilization Conference outlined an agenda to use *online networking* for Muslim youth to reach out to the world to other youth. President Obama used the same concept in his Cairo, Egypt speech, "Our education, we will expand exchange programs, and increase scholarships, like the one that brought my father to America. At the same time, we will encourage more Americans to study in Muslim communities. And we will match promising Muslim students with internships in America; invest *in online* learning for teachers and children around the world; and create a new online network, so a young person in Kansas can communicate instantly with a young person in Cairo."

Let me say this my fellow Americans. If that above excerpt didn't scare you, then you are way out in the left field when it comes to protecting the United States from a tyrannical rule under Islam. This plan of Obama's will take your children and grandchildren (and mine) right out of a freedom that you and I have enjoyed during our lifetime. Islam is not freedom, it is tyrannical; a religion that is commanded to kill anyone who is against Islam. Will the Muslims take an oath on our Holy Bible as all elected officials have done? Not according to Obama's speech printed by the Council on Foreign Relations, "And when the first Muslim American was recently elected to Congress, he took the oath to defend our Constitution using the same *Holy Koran* (not Holy Bible)[100] that one of our Founding Fathers – Thomas Jefferson – kept in his personal library."

I have a copy of their Holy Qur'an, but only for research to refute Islam's teachings against Jesus Christ and our Holy God; but that doesn't make me a Muslim. In that statement Obama didn't explain that Jefferson *was not* a Muslim. He left it for the audience to interpret, giving an impression that Jefferson agreed with the Muslim religion! Jefferson *did not take an oath* on the Holy Qur'an. He took an oath on the Holy Bible as all prior presidents have. Not until Ellison was allowed to do so, has anyone been allowed to take the oath on anything other than the Holy Bible. That was not constitutional! Did the American's allow Ellison to deviate from our law? You had better believe they did, and Obama's speech to the Muslim world just became the catalyst to encourage more Muslims to run for political office by insinuating that they will not be forced to take an oath on the Holy Bible. Did the people who elected him into office know what the Qur'an is all about? I doubt it! Did *we* know, or look into, what Obama actually knows about America's history? It appears that Obama believes that Islam had a big part in bringing knowledge to our country. From his Cairo speech to the Muslim world printed by Council on Foreign Relations June 4, 2009, "As a student of history, I also know civilization's debt to Islam. It was Islam – at places like Al-Azhar – that carried

---

[100] Added (Not Holy Bible) for emphasis

the light of learning through so many centuries, paving the way for Europe's Renaissance and Enlightenment. It was innovation in Muslim communities – (applause) – it was innovation in Muslim communities that developed the order of algebra; our magnetic compass and tools of navigation; our mastery of pens and printing; our understanding of how disease spreads and how it can be healed. Islamic culture has given us majestic arches and soaring spires; timeless poetry and cherished music; elegant calligraphy and places of peaceful contemplation. And throughout history, Islam has demonstrated through words and deeds the possibilities of religious tolerance and racial equality."

How many of Americans know the history of Islam? Islam history, in legitimate American history books, portray an evil religion that is bent on conquering the earth in the name of their false god, Allah. In the following excerpt, from Council on Foreign Relations report of Obama's speech in Cairo, Obama quotes the Qur'an. Tell me, what did President Obama mean when he said, *"We* have the power to make the world *we* seek,......"*? Keep in mind that he was speaking to a Muslim world in a Muslim country. Look back to what he said after he read Malcolm X's autobiography. He said, *"I looked to see where the people would come from who were willing to work toward this future and populate this new world."*[101]

From Council on Foreign Relations June 4, 2009, *"**We** have the power to make the world **we** seek, but only if we have the courage to make a new beginning, keeping in mind what has been written. The Holy Koran tells **us,** "O mankind! We have created you male and a female; and we have made you into nations and tribes so that you may know one another."*[102]

Now let's see what the Muslim's Qur'an really says about loving one-another. What Obama quoted applies only to Muslims according to the Qur'an. This excerpt is taken directly word-for-word from the Muslim Holy Qur'an, "The Holy

---

[101] Dreams from My Father page 85-86
[102] Bold and underlined for emphasis

Qur'an 5:33 - *"The punishment of those who wage war against Allah and His Messenger, and strive with might and main for mischief through the land is: execution, or crucifixion, or the cutting off of hands and feet from opposite side, or exile from the land."*

The Holy Qur'an C. 51 274 – 274 - *"We now return to the subject of Jihad, which we left at 2:214-216. We are to be under no illusion about it. If we are not prepared to fight for our faith, with our lives and all our resources, both our lives and our resources will be wiped out by our enemies."*

Was President Obama's trip to Egypt beneficial to our country, or was it beneficial to the Muslim world? You decide!

The following article is from *The Oxford History of Islam.* The writer asks a very justifiable question that we, as Americans, should be asking: John L. Esposito - *The Oxford History on Islam* page 641:

"What kind of society will Europe and America become as a consequence of the introduction of the new mix of peoples and cultures who affirm a vibrant religion that they insist transcends borders and supersedes all other claims to truth?"

The Muslims were right next door to the Europeans. Knowing what kind of people they were, did the Europeans fight? Evidently not! Read below what happened to those countries because they waited until it was too late. They caved in under the fear of the tyrannical Muslims' quest to conquer the world. I picked this story up about the film actress being fined for speaking out against Islam for destroying her country: Robert Spencer – *Dhimmi Watch* June 3, 2008:

"Bardot fined again for complaining that Muslims are imposing their ways on France. A French court has fined former film star Brigitte Bardot 15,000 euros for inciting a racial hatred. She was prosecuted over a letter published on her website that complained Muslims were 'destroying our country by imposing their ways.'"

Has the freedom of speech been removed from France? What do *you* think? Does what happened in France give us a clue of how powerful the Islam's Shari'a law can be? It should! Let's go on to see what happened to our neighbor Canada. Sunny Dhillon for *Globe and Mail News* – Canada June 6, 2008:

"Shari'a implementation in a Canadian court. "Maclean's counsel not allowed to question conduct of Islamic congress.

VANCOUVER – *"Attempts by Maclean's counsel Julian Porter to question the B.C.director of the Canadian Islamic Congress about the organization's conduct were deemed inappropriate by tribunal judges on Thursday, undercutting the lawyer's line of questioning. B.C.'s Human Rights Tribunal is meeting this week because of a complaint filed by the providence's CIC director, Naiyer Habib, as well as the organization's national president, Mohamed Elmasry. The complaint came in response to an article written by Mark Steyn that appeared in Maclean's in October 2006. Titled The Future Belongs to Islam, the piece has been blasted by Muslim critics for spreading 'Islamophobia.'"*

Did you get that! The *Shari'a implementation* is Islam's law incorporated into Canada's laws. Think what you may. Islam managed to get their Shari'a Law implemented into Canada's laws and France's laws. They are above us in Canada, and according their "globe puzzle" they are after Brazil in South America, a country across the Atlantic Ocean from them. Make no mistake about it; these people are a powerful, determined force.

Again, I urge the reader to research the history of the Islamic movement in the world and its method of taking control of Dar al-barb (non-Muslim) nations. By researching their religion you can be prepared to act accordingly to keep this radical religion from taking control of our children and of our country.

When the American people decide to stand up and fight this radical movement into our country, we can expect warfare. But looking back to how the citizens of the United States rallied together when the terrorists attacked our country and took down the Twin Towers in New York, I know that we can stand together as a nation fighting for what we believe in. We won't give in to intimidation here in our own country.

The stories below will open your eyes to what *can* happen *when* we decide to fight Islam for our right of freedom and freedom of religion. It won't be easy for anyone who dares to speak out against this radical people, but if we don't stand up, we will end up just like France, Canada, the Netherlands and other countries who have succumbed to Islam's intimidation. *Guardian.co.uk* - Tuesday 12 August 2008:

"Random House accursed of cowardice after withdrawing The Jewel of Median amid fears of Muslim controversy. "The lawyer who was threatened by terrorists whilst acting for Salman Rushdie has said that Random House US should pay "substantial compensation" to Sherry Jones, whose novel about Muhammad's child bride Aisha was dropped by the publisher over fears it could provoke terrorist attacks. Jones's The Jewel of Medina was described as potentially more controversial than both Rushdie's novel The Satanic Verses and the Danish newspaper cartoons of Muhammad. The Jewel of Medina was due to be published by Random House US on August 12, but the publisher dropped the book after consultations with academics and security experts suggested that it "might be offensive to some in the Muslim community, but also that it could incite acts of violence by small, radical segment". The move has provoked a storm of controversy across the internet, with some bloggers calling on readers to boycott Random House, and others criticizing Jones for "insulting the Prophet".

In a statement, Random House said: "We stand firm by our responsibility to support our authors and the free discussion of ideas, even those that may be construed as offensive by some. However, a publisher must weigh that responsibility against others that it also bears, and in this instance we decided, after much deliberation, to postpone publication for the safety of the author, employees of Random House Inc, booksellers and anyone else who would be involved in distribution and sale of the book." When Rushdie's The Satanic Verses was published in 1988, attempts were made on the lives of his Norwegian and Italian publishers, and the Japanese translator of the novel was killed.

Publisher Andrew Franklin, director of Profile Books, said that Random House should not have been deterred from publishing by imagined threats of Islamic extremism. "It's absolutely shocking. They are such cowards," he said. Franklin pointed to Penguin's publication of The Satanic Verses in 1988. "I think Penguin acted with great integrity," said Franklin, who was working for Penguin at the time. "They behaved as any publisher in the west should do, and upheld freedom of publication and freedom of speech. They stuck by their guns at no inconsiderable risk to their senior executives. These are the principles we should live and die by."

The Rushdie incident happened twenty-one years ago, but the Jewel of Medina incident happened just a few months ago. Islam is persistent, and their movement isn't just across the oceans now, it is in the heartland of the United States.

The point I am trying to make with the above statements is that Islam is becoming more aggressive with their intimidation and presumption that Americans will tolerate these acts of terrorism. You know what..... It seems to be working! Why should they stop!

I could say it over a thousand times and never feel that enough has been said about Islam's hushed method of maneuvering their way into our country. They *are* the *obscurantist enemy.* As Americans we should understand that our doors have been opened wide for the Middle East to march right into this country because Obama was elected President of the United States. Didn't he tell the Muslim world in his outreach to them that we are not their enemy!

IS THIS REALLY HAPPENING IN AMERICA!!

Dr. Franklin Graham's View on Islam

Having said all of the above in this book, I want to quote what Franklin Graham, son of Reverend Billy Graham, had to say in his book *The Name* about Islam. Reverend Graham quotes the Qur'an (Koran) to back up what his is writing.

Franklin Graham - *The Name* page 65-77: Page 65:

"As I have illustrated through my experiences after the Columbine school shootings and the 2001 inauguration, in America we seem to be embracing the idea that one religion is as legitimate as another. Tolerance of the sincerity of others has become our creed. Sadly, though, we can be both sincere and wrong. When we are, the consequences can be catastrophic."

<u>Page 70</u> – *"Although on the surface there may appear to be similarities between Christianity and Islam, these two are as different as lightness and darkness. Whole books have been written on this topic, but briefly stated, some of the critical differences include the following: Christianity came into being when Jesus Christ – the sinless Son of God and Himself God – died to redeem a lost world back to God by giving Himself on the cross as a sacrifice for our sins. Islam, on the other hand, was founded by a mere human being, a warrior by the name of Muhammad, in whose teachings we see the tactic of "conversion by conquest," through violence if necessary.[15] Clearly, it appears that the ultimate objective of Islam is world domination. Christianity has the Bible as its source of written truth; Islam has the Koran as its source."[103]*

<u>Page 72</u> – *"The number one difference between Islam and Christianity is that the god of Islam is not the God of the Christian faith. In the Christian faith, the God that is worshiped is the Almighty God, who has revealed himself in human form in the person of Jesus Christ, God's Son. The god of Islam is not a father and does not have a son, and to a Muslim, that very thought is blasphemous.[17] The Bible teaches that individuals have a free will in making decisions about God; Islam often relies on force, intimidation, or conquering of entire nations to recruit converts."* [104]

---

[103] Mr. Graham's Footnote [15] *Al Jaami-Al Saheeh* by Imam Al Bukhari, *Oral Collections known as the Hadith,* Section 4:506

[104] Mr. Graham's Footnote s[17] *Sura* 2:116; 5:72-76; 6:101; 9:30; 10:68-69; 35:91

Page 73 – "*For those outside the Jewish and Christian faiths, such as Hindus, the Koran is even less tolerant, and idolaters are candidates for persecution and death. It says, "But when the forbidden months are past, then fight and slay the idolaters wherever ye find them, and take them, and prepare them each ambush[18]." [105]*

Page 77 – *The Name – by: Franklin Graham_– "So why have I presented all this information? Because we need to know the truth about other religions: We are not worshiping the same God. Many people believe that there are many roads to God. Hindus believe that they have a road to God. Muslims believe that they have a road to God. But Jesus said, "I am the way, the truth, and the life. No one comes to the Father except through Me[33]." [106]*

---

[105] Mr. Graham's Footnote [18] *Sura* 9:5
[106] Mr. Graham's Footnote [33] John 14:6 NKJV